10/
86

JESSE OWENS

JESSE OWENS

An American Life

William J. Baker

THE FREE PRESS
A Division of Macmillan, Inc.
NEW YORK

Collier Macmillan Publishers
LONDON

The Free Press
A Division of Macmillan, Inc.
866 Third Avenue, New York, N. Y. 10022

Collier Macmillan Canada, Inc.

Printed in the United States of America

printing number

2 3 4 5 6 7 8 9 10

Library of Congress Cataloging-in-Publication Data

Baker, William J. (William Joseph)
    Jesse Owens: an American life.

    Bibliography: p.
    Includes index.
    1. Owens, Jesse, 1913—1980.   2. Track and field
athletes—United States—Biography.   I. Title.
GV697.09B35 1986   796.4′2′0924 [B]   86–4671
ISBN 0–02–901780–7

For
my mother,
Ethel Baker Hughes

Contents

Preface

LIKE MOST PEOPLE OF MY GENERATION, I grew up admiring Jesse Owens, the legendary champion of the 1936 Berlin Olympics. Five years ago, as I attempted to summarize the Berlin games for a survey text on the history of sport, I became interested in the man behind the legend. What brought him to his moment of glory? What happened to him afterwards? Why did he become so visible, so important for my generation, long after his athletic career was finished? Seeking answers to those questions, I found only repetitive newspaper clippings and Owens's reminiscences. No biography was available, so I set out on a journey that has taken me several years and thousands of miles, examining archives and interviewing Owens's relatives, friends, and acquaintances.

To all appearances, I was an unlikely candidate for the task. Jesse Owens and I seemed to have little in common. He was black; I was white. He was urban and Midwestern, living most of his adult life in Cleveland, Detroit, and Chicago. My own setting, on the other hand, for more than a decade had been rural, small-town New England. His world was one of public appearances and public relations; mine was academic, with an occasional foray into local politics.

Yet we had more in common than met the eye. For a start, our roots were Southern. My mother, like Jesse, was born in northern Alabama. My birthplace was Chattanooga, Tennessee, and I grew up in nearby Rossville, Georgia, within view of both the Alabama and Tennessee borders. A common Southern heritage caused both Jesse and me to undergo name changes. His original name, James Cleveland, was shelved when a Northern schoolteacher mistook his drawled "J. C." for "Jesse." My uniquely Southern name, Billy Joe (spelled "Billie" on the birth certificate), was made more formal to avoid prejudice outside the South.

The South of my youth, like Jesse's, was dirt poor. Our ancestors tended the same sandy, tired soil. His parents escaped to the North to find employment, schooling, and more tolerant attitudes. Mine left the land for local textile mills. For both of us, sport was a way out of the ghetto. In my case, football provided both the impetus and the means for me to become the first college graduate in my family. I quickly learned that an "athletic scholarship" was a contradiction in terms, but like Owens I scraped by in the classroom and strove most to excel athletically before being cast upon the world to cope with life after the cheering ceased.

Our levels of achievement, of course, were altogether different. I captained the Rossville Bulldogs to a state championship in 1955 and in 1957 briefly led the nation in forward passing for Furman University—small potatoes next to Jesse's innumerable records in Big Ten and Olympic competition. Despite our varying degrees of success, sport left an indelible mark on both of us. In the grand tradition of athletes growing old, we retained a mania for sport tinged with nostalgia for spent youth. Vocationally and politically we went different ways, but a competitive ethic colored our paths into adulthood just as surely as did our common Southern roots and impoverished childhoods.

For all our connections, however, our difference in color was fundamental. Like all blacks of his generation, Jesse Owens suffered unspeakable indignities. Black Americans might instinctively recognize his racial and psychological barriers to success, but only by empathy and analogy can I appreciate his difficulties at the hand of Jim Crow. With the help of his friends, I have attempted to understand his unique circumstance, his character, and his struggles on his own terms, in the context of his time.

I have avoided the temptation to treat Jesse Owens as a mere victim of circumstance. Guardian angels as well as devilish tempters met him on the road, and more often than not he discriminated between the two. Like all of us, he devised strategies of survival in the face of obstacles. Within the racial and economic limitations imposed on him, he had options. He made the most of the few choices he had. This book is about those options and choices, and their results.

Numerous individuals have helped me set the record straight. For personal interviews about Jesse's Alabama roots, I am grateful to Oakville residents Elsie Fitzgerald, Marvin Fitzgerald, Ernestine Griffin, Snora Griffin, Spencer Griffin, and John Wiley. On Jesse's relation to his earliest and most important mentor, Charles Riley, Harriet Mae Bottorff (Riley's daughter) provided old newspaper clippings, anecdotes, letters, and photographs. Several members of the 1936 United States Olympics team graciously granted interviews and attended to follow-up queries: Marty Glickman, Francis Johnson, Annette Rogers Kelly, Donald Lash, Mack Robinson, Helen Stephens, Forrest "Spec" Towns, and John Woodruff. Charles Beetham, William Heintz, Eulace Peacock, and Mel Walker, who were also intimately involved with Owens's athletic career, freely shared their memories.

On Jesse's life after athletics, Russell Brown, Harrison Dillard, Herbert Douglas, Al Gardiner, Bud Leavitt, Wayland Moore, Stuart Rankin, Stan Saplin, William G. Stratton, LeRoy Walker, and Ted West came forth with much helpful information, as did Jesse's three daughters, Gloria Hemphill, Beverly Prather, and Marlene Rankin. For miscellaneous information, clippings, and references, I am grateful to John DiMeglio, David Dore, Harry Edwards, Harold Gast, Alice Grab, Jon Hendershott, Roscoe Hildreth, Charles Korr, Arnd Krüger, Barbara Moro, Jerome Nadelhaft, Benjamin Rader, David Wiggins, and Rusty Wilson.

To Ed Bell of Atlantic Richfield Company I am especially indebted for the use of interviews, films, and a diary in ARCO's holdings. Archivists kindly provided copies of pertinent letters and documents from the Eisenhower Presidential Library in Abilene, Kansas; the Federal Bureau of Investigation in Washington, D.C.; the Illinois State Historical Library in Springfield; the University of Illinois Library in Urbana; and the Ohio State University Archives in Columbus.

Maire MacLachlin, my research assistant at the University of Maine, painstakingly located and xeroxed every single reference to Owens in the *Chicago Defender* from 1935 to 1980, providing a steady year-by-year report on his activities. Maire's contribution to this book is inestimable. The University of Maine also generously supported me with a summer research grant, a superb interlibrary loan office, interested colleagues, and sympathetic administrators. Jean Day typed the first half of the manuscript, and my daughter Cynthia typed the second half.

My younger daughters, Clara and Catherine, patiently indulged my preoccupation with this task. My eldest, Christina, sensitively put her pen to some rough spots, allowing me to finish the manuscript while on sabbatical leave in England as a Visiting Fellow at the Institute for the Study of Social History at the University of Warwick. To the director of the Institute, Tony Mason, I am grateful for encouragement and support.

Jules Tygiel, Randy Roberts, and Ruth Nadelhaft carefully read a penultimate draft of the manuscript. In tandem with my exacting editor, Joyce Seltzer, and copy-editor Norman Sloan, they saved me from more factual, stylistic, and interpretive boners than I would like to admit. Most of all, I am beholden as always to my best friend and toughest critic, Tina. She stands tall behind whatever intelligence and sensitivity might be found herein.

W. J. B.
Bangor, Maine

JESSE OWENS

Prologue

As Jackie Robinson began the 1951 baseball season in grand style, one sportswriter observed that he was "off the mark like Jesse Owens getting away from the starting blocks."[1] The allusion needed no explanation, for mere mention of the name Jesse Owens called up images of athletic grace and dominance—pictures of a mellow-brown-skinned young American who carried 165 pounds on a compact but slender 5'10" frame, on legs beautifully chiseled by nature for the breaking of barriers to speed and airborne flight. The name of Jesse Owens meant athletic excellence, Olympian excellence. The images were firmly rooted in a distant time and place, on a stage uniquely prepared for the performance of memorable deeds.

The time was 1936. The place was Berlin, Germany, the site of Olympiad XI. More than any previous Olympics, the Berlin Games bobbed on the surface of political currents. Adolph Hitler stood proudly at the head of the Third Reich. Having earlier marched his army into the Rhineland while setting his anti-Semitic policies in place, he was poised to make his move against weak neighbors. Well before the opening of the Berlin Olympics, he had aroused opposition to his regime.

Discriminatory laws against German Jews provoked an international crusade to boycott the Games, and in the United States the movement almost succeeded. Although it barely failed, it put Hitler on good behavior for the duration of the Olympics.[2]

He diplomatically ordered the temporary removal of all nasty signs and newspaper references to Jews and welcomed the world's attention to a Germany wonderfully recovered from war and economic depression. At great expense he provided the finest facilities and organizational precision ever seen by Olympic athletes. He eagerly put Nazi efficiency on display in the form of unrelenting pageantry to the glory of the Third Reich. Confidently he anticipated a stirring exhibition of Aryan athletic supremacy. He reckoned without the speed and stamina of a large contingent of black American athletes, who simply stole the show from their Aryan opponents during the first week of track-and-field competition.

Jesse Owens led that coup, smashing records and claiming four gold medals in the premier events. First he tied the world record of 10.3 seconds in the 100-meter dash. Then he set new Olympic records of 26 feet, $5\frac{1}{4}$ inches in the long jump, and 20.7 seconds in the 200-meter sprint. Finally, he contributed a strong opening leg in the finals of the 400-meter relay, propelling his team toward a new world and Olympic mark of 39.8 seconds.

Two unforeseen developments added to the drama of the occasion. In the long-jump preliminaries, Owens scratched on his first two jumps, placing himself on the brink of defeat. With one qualifying jump to go, he collected his nerves and calmly soared the required distance to make the finals. His difficulty in qualifying for the long-jump finals was no more dramatic than his late entry on the American relay team at the end of the week, an unexpected move that made his record-breaking four gold medals possible.

All four records remained unbroken until the 1950s; the long-jump mark lasted twenty-four years, to 1960. Impressive by any standard, Owens's achievements were all the more remarkable because of the equipment and track conditions with which he coped in 1936. No starting blocks provided leverage for a fast getaway on the sprints. Each runner had to use a trowel to dig his own starting holes in the cinder track. Unlike modern synthetic surfaces, the crushed cinders at Berlin Stadium soaked up the rain that fell intermittently throughout the week. By the second day, both the track and the path leading to the long-jump pit were churned up, messy, and uneven despite the work of German groundskeepers. Leather shoes, heavy to begin with compared to today's feather-light footwear, became heavier still as they absorbed water. Jesse Owens's Berlin records were simply phenomenal.

His style, too, was extraordinary. Without any hint of strain, he exhibited incomparable smoothness of effort as well as consistency and versatility. Aside from his temporary faltering in the long-jump preliminaries, the pressure of competition seemed scarcely to bother him. Better still, frequent victories failed to turn his head. He exuded a charming combination of confidence and humility. In awe of his skills, opponents warmed to his cheerful personality. One of the enduring memories of the Berlin Olympics was a respectful, affectionate friendship that Owens formed with a blond German long-jumper, Lutz Long.

German spectators also responded warmly to the young Owens. Unlike American fans, the Germans keenly appreciated track athletes. In sharp contrast to the empty spaces at the Los Angeles Coliseum for the Olympics four years earlier, Berlin Stadium bulged with avid spectators. Neither rain nor cold kept the crowd below 100,000 for the afternoon finals. They watched and applauded Jesse's every move. Unaccustomed to seeing black athletes, they were quickly won over by his dominant athleticism and friendly demeanor. In the Olympic Village, at the stadium, and on the streets of Berlin, they clamored to touch him, to get his autograph, to snap his picture.

Hitler, of course, refused to join the throng of hero-worshipers. Blacks, like Jews, revulsed him, triggering all those irrational fears and hostilities that went into the making of a fascist mentality. So great was the divergence between Hitler's ideology and Jesse Owens's achievements that a tall tale attached itself to the scene: Hitler supposedly "snubbed" Owens, refusing to shake his hand after his gold medal awards. The yarn, created by American sportswriters, was repeated so often that people finally took it as fact. It satisfied a fundamental need to believe in a moral order: the evil Hitler insulting the innocent Owens, but innocence and virtue winning in the end.

Like George Washington's cherry tree and Abe Lincoln's log cabin, rail-splitting youth, Owens's snub at the hands of Hitler is the imaginative stuff of hero worship.

Heroes embody a society's faith, hopes, and dreams. At Berlin Jesse Owens became an American hero, for he helped Americans to believe something important about themselves. "In what other country would this saga of Jesse Owens come true?" asked one American journalist. "An American Negro youth ventures onto the stage occupied prominently by a Nazi dictator and steals the spotlight from him for a little while. The bright glow of romance hovers over such a feat."[3]

As the sweating Owens stood on the victory stand at Berlin, his eyes fixed on the raising of the Stars and Stripes, his ears alert to the playing of the "Star Spangled Banner," a thoughtful onlooker might well have grown curious about the young man himself. What set of circumstances had formed his character and brought him to Berlin? What did the future hold beyond the athletic arena? Would "the bright glow of romance" hover always over his head?

CHAPTER 1

Southern Grit

TODAY LITTLE OAKVILLE, ALABAMA, is far removed from the mainstream of American life. Nestled on the Cumberland Plateau in the northern central section of the state, Oakville is a rural community that stretches for a mile or so along a narrow road, surrounded by gently rolling farmland and tree-covered hills. Decatur, 8 miles to the northeast, is a thriving commercial center that first tasted affluence with the coming of the Tennessee Valley Authority half a century ago. With no such benefactor, Oakville languishes. Its road is now of asphalt, which replaced sand. Today its small frame houses and cheap mobile homes sprout television antennae from each roof. Secondhand cars stand in every driveway. But the changes for the better are more apparent than real. The land is petered out, exhausted for anything more than small vegetable gardens. Serious farming is a thing of the past. Some Oakville citizens travel to Decatur or to Moulton, the Lawrence County seat, for menial labor and factory employment. Most, however, are unemployed and discouraged. Most are also black. Despite some slight changes in appearance, Oakville's poverty, geographical isolation, and quiet desperation are still much the same as in 1913, when Jesse Owens was born there.

Had he been born white, Owens could have claimed a solid Alabama heritage. From early in the nineteenth century, white Owens families stood tall in local affairs, especially in the history of Lawrence County. One, Isaac N. Owens, was elected a state senator in 1834. Prior to the Civil War, most owned slaves. According to Jesse Owens's family lore, his ancestors came as slaves from Africa in the 1830s. Their Welsh name came from a slave owner.[1]

After Emancipation, blacks throughout the South became sharecroppers. Legally free but effectively bound by the invisible chains of economic necessity, they accepted the use of the white man's land, farm animals, tools, and a house in exchange for their labor and a fifty-fifty split of the crop at harvest. By 1900 a few ambitious, fortunate blacks accumulated enough capital to rent land outright, making what Roy Wilkins called "the move upward from cropper to tenant farmer." But Henry Cleveland Owens, Jesse's father, never reached such heights. Born of former slaves in 1878, at eighteen he married Mary Emma Fitzgerald, a lively little woman two years older than himself. To the marriage Henry Owens brought only a mule inherited from his father, a sharecropper's shanty, and an agreement with his white landlord, Albert C. Owens, to till several acres each year.[2]

Cotton was the money crop, but by no means was it the only crop. Oakville's hilly terrain and forestation simply did not lend itself to vast expanses of cotton on the order of plantations in southern Alabama and Mississippi. Corn fed hungry children in summer and animals through the winter. Moreover, every sharecropper raised some sort of vegetable garden for his family. Sorghum cane, cut and taken to one of the two mills in Oakville, produced molasses, which was served with everything, at virtually every meal. One of the two "sugary cane" mills stood beside a pond just across the road from the weather-beaten little house that Henry and Emma Owens began calling home in 1895.[3]

The walls of that shanty soon began to bulge with children. As one contemporary later said of his own parents, Henry and Emma Owens were "given to the exasperating and mysterious habit of having babies." By 1912 no fewer than twelve pregnancies produced nine little Owenses, two males and one female having died at birth. The survivors, in order of birth, were three daughters—Ida, Josephine, and Lillie—and six sons—Prentice, Johnson, Henry, Ernest, Quincy, and Sylvester. Apparently Henry and Emma Owens decided not to have any more children, only to be shocked with yet another pregnancy and birth of their last baby on September 12, 1913, who was christened James Cleveland. The mother often referred to him fondly as her "gift child" because, she said, "he was made when he couldn't have been made by us."[4]

He was not a healthy child. Chronic bronchial congestion, aggravated by a poor diet and inadequate heat in the winter, resulted in several bouts with "powerful bad fever," pneumonia. Mysterious growths on his chest and legs had to be crudely and painfully removed with a knife by his mother's hand. He also suffered his fair share of boyish accidents. Once he stepped in a steel hunting trap prepared by his father. On another occasion he barely escaped serious injury when he was run over by a cotton drag.[5]

Yet physical maladies and mishaps scarcely compared to the psychological scars incurred in growing up black and poor in northern Alabama around the era of World War I. Within the week of Jesse Owens's birth, police reports in the *Decatur Daily* tellingly reflected the racist tone of that time and place. On minimal evidence and with no legal assistance, two black men were arrested for burglary, and several others for transporting liquor. Yet another was thrown in jail simply because he was "said to be crazy." On September 12, the day Jesse Owens's weak lungs first gasped for breath in Oakville, a black by the name of John Alexander in nearby South Decatur was arrested and fined $100 for having "offered an insult" to a white woman. While making his round as an iceman, Alexander reportedly "loitered" too long at the home of his accuser. His employer, the Decatur Ice and Coal Company, denied that he was on its payroll.[6]

In rural Oakville the lines were not so sharply drawn between white employers and black laborers. White landowners did, of course, keep as firm a grip as possible on the life and labor of their sharecroppers. But far more white than black sharecroppers lived in Oakville. Owens and Paul Neimark later would evoke a scene where hordes of poor blacks worked an almost boundless stretch of cotton fields for a few white masters, but according to the census of 1910 only about one-sixth of all the 1,138 inhabitants of Oakville were nonwhite. Only 53 blacks and 128 mulattoes lived alongside 957 white sharecroppers, tenant farmers, and a few resident land-owners.[7]

Most Oakville families, whites as well as blacks, had been rooted for several generations in familiar soil. Of those 1,138 residents in 1910, seventeen had migrated from Mississippi, twelve from Tennessee, eleven from Georgia, and six from vari-ous other Southern states, and two were "hired" men from abroad. No fewer than 1,090—97 percent—were born in Ala-bama. Local roots meant traditional attitudes, and tradition in this case meant assumptions of racial inequality, of white superiority and black deference.

The presence of so many poor whites in Oakville increased the likelihood of racial bigotry. In material wealth, education, and social standing, white sharecroppers could show little to distinguish them from their black neighbors. Racial attitudes served a compensatory function. The Owenses were "niggers" to their white Oakville neighbors precisely because color was the only distinguishing mark of status. Years later Jesse Owens told about getting into a fight with his landowner's twelve-year-old son, who had made a crude remark about Owens's mother. In Jesse's account, the white boy called his brothers, who wrestled the young Owens to the ground and threatened to carve their initials on his face—until Jesse's own brothers intervened. The story is dramatic and possibly true. But scraps of that kind were more likely to have occurred be-tween the Owens brothers and similarly poor, disadvantaged white sharecroppers' sons.[8]

Physical confrontation was not a feasible tactic for out-numbered, relatively powerless blacks in Oakville. They found more subtle ways of dealing with potentially dangerous situa-tions. As James Baldwin discovered in a remote Swiss village in the 1950s, the way to cope with a sea of menacing white faces was to be nice, pleasant, and accommodating, "it being a great part of the American Negro's education (long before he goes to school) that he must make people 'like' him." The young Bald-win learned a "smile-and-the-world-smiles-with-you routine." So did young James Cleveland Owens. Years later an admirer noted that he "always smiled after he won and always agreed with what the newspaper said he said." As an adult, Owens always had a ready smile and open hand for everyone he met. "I try awfully hard for people to like me," he once told an interviewer. Born of necessity in rural Oakville, his sunny disposition never failed to disarm his foes.[9]

Childhood poverty did something else. It made Owens keenly sensitive to material symbols of adult success. In Oakville only a few landowners, all white and rich, owned cars. Once Jesse Owens made money after his Olympic triumph, he purchased a new car every year for the rest of his life. Raised in a cramped sharecropper's shanty, he bought both himself and his parents huge new houses the first chance he got. Of all the symbols of material success, however, clothes mattered most. Jesse's memories of Oakville were dominated by ragged clothes and embarrassment. "I remember there was no money to buy clothing. . . . I didn't have enough clothing at that time to cover my entire body. . . . The only time I can remember being embarrassed was when I saw the neighbor girls and I didn't have enough clothing to cover my body. . . . I would run and hide." Little wonder that the adult Owens was a fastidious dresser, always immaculately attired in the best clothes money could buy. They covered his painful memories of childhood.[10]

☆ ☆ ☆

Despite its poverty and racial bigotry, Oakville was no harsh little Harlem, cramped and crime-ridden. Years later Owens, attempting to identify with angry young ghetto blacks, recalled his "bittersweet beginnings," with the emphasis on the bitter. He had paid his dues, he insisted, as he repeatedly described the destitution and racism his family suffered in Alabama. In a moment of private candor, however, he once confided to a friend that his Oakville youth seemed bad only in retrospect. At the time, life seemed anything but intolerable, because he knew of nothing better. Yes, Oakville was a poor, isolated farm community, but everyone was poor, and no distant allurements beckoned, so the young Owens had no standards of comparison. "We used to have a lot of fun," he told his friend. "We never had any problems. We always ate. The fact that we didn't have steak? Who had steak?" In Jesse's own words, he was "the happiest kid in the world."[11]

It was a country boy's happiness. The adult Owens recalled "busting the furrows" behind a mule, taking the hoe to cotton and corn, and picking a hundred pounds of cotton a day for a week or so each year. All that hard work brought little money but lots of food. Heaps of fresh beans, squash, onions, tomatoes, and corn, all from the family garden, filled the table in summer. At summer's end Jesse and his siblings picked berries from the fields and pears, peaches, and apples from nearby orchards for canning or storing through the winter. Each autumn they killed a hog and smoked the meat. They had no steak; they did have ham, ribs, and gravy.[12]

They also had fun. With his brothers, and even with neighboring white boys, Jesse swam and fished in a community pond that is now stagnant from disuse. On summer evenings he went 'possum hunting with his older brothers; with their dogs they often stayed out beside a campfire until early morning. "This all added up to a great experience and a lot of fun," Owens recalled years later. His friends and neighbors remember loosely organized baseball games in which the two oldest Owens boys, Prentice and Johnson, played. Regularly on Saturday and Sunday summer afternoons, an Oakville team competed against nearby communities such as Danville. Prentice, star pitcher for the Oakville nine, was nicknamed "Big Leg" because he kicked so high in his windup. A Danville contemporary, David Albritton, remembers him pitching in a style that Hall-of-Famer Juan Marichal would later make famous.[13]

Too young to compete on the baseball team, young James Cleveland Owens romped and played with children his own age. His family was one of three black sharecropper families who lived behind the landowner's huge white house, separated from "the man" by a little bridge. About ten young children played regularly together, imaginatively devising their own games of tag, keepaway, and hide-and-seek. Almost half a century later, Owens clearly recalled "living and playing with these people behind this bridge where you cross the creek." His older first cousin, Mattie Taylor, still remembers Jesse participating in those childhood frolics "just like the rest of us."[14]

Not surprisingly, games that involved running especially

appealed to the young Owens. "He'd run and play like every-body else," remembers his cousin, "but you never could catch him." Running meant physical freedom, individual expression, a sense of power. "I always loved running," the mature Owens once noted. "I wasn't very good at it, but I loved it because it was something you could do all by yourself, and under your own power. You could go in any direction, fast or slow as you wanted, fighting the wind if you felt like it, seeking out new sights just on the strength of your feet and the courage of your lungs." Most of all, running required no equipment, no rules, no organization. Like most of Oakville, it was simple.[15]

So was religion. Owens later reminisced that his family walked 9 miles to church each Sunday, and on the return walk home aired their dreams for the future. Perhaps church did, in fact, stir hopes of a better life, but not on a romantic dusty road. The Owenses regularly attended the Oakville Missionary Baptist Church just up the road from their home. Henry Owens was a deacon there. The family's religious enthusiast, how-ever, was the mother, who prayed frequently and fervently. She required her children to memorize a different Bible verse each week and often tossed in a homily such as, "If you look hard enough for the devil, the devil'll find you."[16]

Perhaps their Baptist faith provided for the Owens what it did for Roy Wilkins's indigent father in St. Louis: "answers to all his quandaries and comfort in his woe." Henry Owens's fav-orite paraphrase of a Bible verse, "It don't profit a man none if he gits the whole world but loses what's inside himself," osten-sibly had to do with inner character; it also meant consolation for a man doomed never to obtain minimal material comfort, much less "the whole world."[17]

Whatever its psychological benefits, that folk ritual of emotional hymns and fiery sermons shored up in the impres-sionable young Owens a rhetorical cadence, an imaginative turn of phrase and metaphorical language. The adult Jesse himself became a spellbinding public speaker, "an inspira-tional orator of the Martin Luther King and Jesse Jackson ilk," according to Will Grimsley, with "the ringing, inspirational de-livery of an evangelist," Frank Litsky of the *New York Times* wrote. Jesse learned that style early, in his Oakville church.[18]

He learned very little in school. Years later he romanti-cized his "log cabin school," but in fact it was the same old shabby, unpainted building that served as the Baptist church for blacks in the community. Alabama education was racially separate and decidedly unequal. For Oakville the state provided no trained teacher until after World War I. Blacks depended on "a volunteer teacher, anything you could pick up at the time," according to an oldtimer. In the rural fashion of the day, the school calendar was irregular. School doors always closed for the harvest season and again for planting in the spring. "We could only go to school," Jesse recalled years later, "when there wasn't anything [else] going on." He barely learned to read and write.[19]

☆   ☆   ☆

Eulace Peacock, another outstanding black athlete whose family also moved north from Alabama in the 1920s, is all too familiar with racial prejudice and discrimination. "When I look back over my lifetime I can get so bitter about things that happened to me," says Peacock. "And actually I should hate white people, but fortunately my family didn't bring me up that way."[20] Eulace Peacock and Jesse Owens shared much more than sterling athletic careers. Owens's parents didn't bring him up to hate white people either.

Quite the reverse. Only a single generation removed from slavery, Henry Cleveland Owens was a quiet, timid man, resigned to his fate. Dominated by economic and political forces beyond his control, he was a beaten soul, a subservient, obedient sharecropper. He could look no white man in the eye. Soon after the birth of his last child, he moved his family from the property of Albert Owens to the larger farm of James Cannon a mile or so away, to work a spread of 50 acres. But even that exchange of masters probably resulted from no autonomous decision on the part of Henry Owens. It is more likely that Cannon paid off a debt Henry Owens owed his former master, thus effectively purchasing extra manpower for his own farm.[21]

Still a legendary figure in Oakville, Big Jim Cannon was an Irishman, a hard-driving, wealthy landowner who owned several fine horses and regularly organized fox hunts for his white neighbors on his large estate. Reputedly fair but stern with his sharecroppers, his authoritarian governance merely confirmed the elder Owens's inner conviction that he deserved no better. Henry Owens's only form of protest was a painfully slow if steady pace in the fields. One of his Oakville neighbors remembers him moving around "so slow you couldn't see him go."[22]

Jesse remembered his father as a man like many blacks of that generation, immobilized by nameless fears. Unable to read or write, Henry Owens superstitiously believed that if he even touched any book other than the Bible, someone in the family would fall ill. Realistically he feared crop failures, hunger, and economic insolvency. Most of all, he feared the white man's disfavor. He knew his place and thought it safest to remain there. "J. C.," he once told his youngest son, "it don't do a colored man no good to get himself too high. 'Cause it's a helluva drop back to the bottom." With that kind of message from that kind of paternal role model, the achievement of Jesse Owens was little short of miraculous.[23]

The miracle worker was Mary Emma Owens, his mother. A Fitzgerald, she came of a stock remarkably more aggressive than the Owens family into which she married. For a time one of her brothers owned 40 acres of land in Oakville, before finally losing it to a Hartsville grain merchant in a loan foreclosure during the Great Depression. Similarly ambitious, Emma was an active, talkative little woman whose exuberant optimism offset her husband's stoic resignation. For her children she dreamed of better things than the sharecropper's lot. In her folksy wisdom, she drilled into them a kind of work ethic: "What you puts in is exactly what you get out." The despairing Henry Owens put in plenty of hard work, to be sure, but never expected much more than mere survival. Emma Owens seasoned her laborious efforts with buoyant optimism. The difference was profound.[24]

Those contradictory attitudes once emerged clearly in a family conversation about "kolledge." In Jesse's imaginative reconstruction of the event, he had heard from one of his white playmates about a special school far away "where you could become anything in the world that you wanted to become." Informing his parents of his interest in going to such a place, he received a playful tug on the ear and a bear hug from his mother. "James Cleveland Owens," she exclaimed, "where in the world do you get your ideas? You are the one!" "The crazy one," added the father, as the whole family laughed.[25]

An inveterate creator of yarns from his youth pointing to his successful adulthood, Jesse Owens might well have concocted that dialogue. But whether or not the conversation literally occurred is beside the point. For Owens, his youthful dreams were, to his father, so utterly unrealistic as to be dismissed as crazy. For his mother, on the other hand, they were hopes worthy of amazement, to be nursed to fruition. In his maturity, Jesse recognized within himself "a kind of inborn ability to see the gold-medal lining in every cloud even with the story of poverty or oppression all around." In that respect he was his mother's child. In 1936 a Cleveland city councilman said more than he knew when he praised Emma Owens as "the soul and heart of Jesse Owens."[26]

Largely at Emma's insistence, the Owens family packed up its few belongings and boarded a train for Cleveland shortly after World War I. The exact date of the move is unclear. Estimates range from 1919 to 1924. Of the four different dates that Jesse gave for the event, the year 1922 appears most frequently in his reminiscences. Fortunately, the precise year of the move is unimportant.[27]

Even the immediate cause of the move is blurred in contradictions and unlikely tales. In one of Jesse's versions, his family was jolted when a neighbor, Betsy Steppart, died in childbirth, and her husband—whom Henry Owens "had always kind of treated like a little brother"—hanged himself. Another of Jesse's stories had both Stepparts hanging themselves. Both versions insist that shortly after the Stepparts' deaths, Jim Cannon announced to Henry Owens that the terms of their sharecropping agreement would be changed from fifty-fifty to sixty-forty in Cannon's favor. The end of this colorful story has the fearful but exasperated Henry Owens, prodded by his wife, finally summoning the courage to leave Oakville for Cleveland.[28]

The story does not stand up under scrutiny. Although Jesse insisted that Joe and Betsy Steppart began sharecropping about the same time Henry Owens did, no Stepparts are listed in the Oakville census of 1910. As for Jim Cannon (whom Jesse repeatedly referred to as "John Clannon"), both black and white oldtimers in Oakville swear that he was "tough as nails" but impeccably fair and honest. Apparently this oral tradition in the Owens family is more imaginative than factual. Whatever the kernel of truth, the yarn served Jesse well in dramatizing the difficulties of his youth.[29]

No single dramatic event was even necessary to propel the Owenses out of Oakville. Between 1910 and 1920 more than half a million blacks left the South for Northern cities; three-quarters of a million more did the same in the 1920s. Just as King Cotton was being dethroned by the boll weevil, black farm laborers were being replaced by machinery. Urban industrial centers to the North offered jobs formerly filled by European immigrants, whose passage to the United States was severely restricted during the war, then legally monitored on a quota system embedded in federal legislation of 1921. Although the revival of the Ku Klux Klan and clandestine lynchings occurred in the North as well as the South during the postwar era, Southern blacks without political rights, legal protection, or educational opportunities for their children migrated North in overwhelming numbers.[30]

The largest number by far left Alabama, especially from the southern part of the state, where floods in 1916 destroyed whatever cotton crops remained from the ravages of the boll weevil. By 1920 more than 65,000 native Alabama blacks lived in the North. Few moved to New England; most migrated to the central industrial urban belt of New York, Pennsylvania, Ohio, Illinois, and Michigan. Almost one-third of them set their sights on Ohio, where the industrial cities of Akron, Dayton, Springfield, Youngstown, Cincinnati, and Cleveland promised employment.[31]

Black migrants from northern Alabama favored Cleveland, a city with a laudable history of antislavery sentiment prior to the Civil War and of racial integration and civil rights in the early years of the Reconstruction era. By World War I those enlightened policies were largely shelved, though Cleveland officials actively encouraged private agencies to deal with the housing and welfare problems of its new black citizens. But little did Cleveland's reputation, past or present, matter from the perspective of Oakville, Alabama. In a pattern common to the times, one of the Owens girls, Lillie, moved to Cleveland to live with some of her kin who had migrated earlier. She found a husband and a job, making more money than she ever thought possible in Oakville. In turn she wrote home in fractured prose, urging her parents and siblings to join her. Life was better in Cleveland, she insisted.[32]

Still, the decision to leave Oakville was not easy. Not for Henry Owens, for whom known difficulties were better than unknown terrors. Rural poverty—now annually exacerbated by the ravages of the boll weevil—was awful, but at least it was familiar. In Oakville Henry Owens's father and his father's father had lived out their lives. Not well and not long, but in the company of family, friends, and familiar landmarks. No corn or sorghum cane grew in Cleveland. "We'd never make it, Emma," he protested. "We'd starve."[33]

Years later Jesse Owens fancifully recalled his mother, the "queen bee" in the family, nudging his father toward a decision to move north. The parents discussed, argued, and compromised secretly, away from the children, but Jesse claims he once eavesdropped behind a large boulder in the field. "We're nearly starving here," he reportedly heard his mother exclaim. Why not move to Cleveland? Other Oakville folks had done it. "It's crazy to go on like this, Henry!" By Jesse's account, when his parents returned to the house, the decision was sealed. The father would take his two oldest sons with him to Cleveland to make enough money for the family to join them shortly.

"But where're we gonna go, Momma?" asked the young J. C.

"We're goin' on a train," she answered.

"And where's the train gonna take us, Momma?"

"It's gonna take us to a better life."[34]

Henry Owens was still not so sure of that. To one of his white sharecropping neighbors he explained that he was leaving because of the "better opportunities" available for his children in Cleveland. Today that neighbor, a comfortably successful octogenarian, says that the elder Owens went north "because he thought there was a golden apple up there."[35]

He misread Henry Owens, whose experience taught him that most apples have worms. Golden apples were for fairy tale characters, not for black Alabama sharecroppers. Years later Jesse remembered that as he scampered around helping his father pack for the train, they bumped into each other. Henry put both his hands on his youngest son's shoulders, but removed them quickly. His hands were shaking with fright.[36]

CHAPTER 2

Friends, Mentors, and Heroes

FOR SOUTHERN BLACK MIGRANTS, Cleveland was no golden apple. During the war the city's earlier tradition of racial tolerance and integration collapsed under a deluge of poor blacks, all seeking employment and housing. By 1920 just over 34,000 blacks represented 4.2 percent of Cleveland's 800,000 inhabitants; by 1930 the total population increased only to 900,000 while the number of blacks more than doubled. An enlarged black presence evoked white prejudice. Churches, schools, public transport, and the ballot box remained nominally open, but during the 1920s a color line descended on the city's theaters, hotels, restaurants, and recreational facilities.[1]

A sign of the times—of native whites feeling beleaguered by both foreign immigrants and black Americans—was the revival of the Ku Klux Klan in Cleveland. By 1921 the local Klan claimed several thousand members. Throughout the following decade they regularly paraded and burned crosses in front of prominent blacks' homes in the white districts of the city. Never once in all his reminiscences did Owens ever mention the Klan. His silence says more about where the Owens family lived in Cleveland than it did about the Klan itself, for the

Owenses took up residence in the East side, a ghetto that even Klansmen avoided.[2]

By no means was it merely a black ghetto. Enclaves of immigrant Italians, Poles, Hungarians, Slovaks, Rumanians, Greeks, and Syrians, as well as migrant blacks, made up the East Side. The largest groups by far were the Italians and Poles. The Owens family first settled in an area that was predominantly Polish, and there Jesse learned to play kickball in the streets, to slip into the local cinema, and to steal apples from the corner grocer. He got on very well with the Poles. They ignored his strange color; he ignored their strange accents. They were "peasants and strangers" all, newcomers to an alien environment.[3]

Adaptation was immeasurably more difficult for the normally outgoing Emma Owens. She kept her shades drawn for the first six months, fearful of inquisitive strangers. Immobilized, she refused to go out shopping for food unless her eldest daughter accompanied her. Had she been acquainted with the urban facts of life for blacks, she would have been all the more uneasy. In 1920 the percentage of blacks dying of pneumonia about tripled the pneumonia death rate of whites in Cleveland. No less frightening were the dangers of crime, violence, and heavy-handed police action. According to Cleveland police records, in 1922 one-third of all the persons arrested were black. Seediness as well as crime flourished in the ghetto. In 1928 the Cleveland *Gazette*, a black weekly, observed that "dope dealing and peddling, boot-leggers and speakeasies galore, prostitutes and their male 'consorts'" all operated freely in the East Side.[4]

Local branches of the National Association for the Advancement of Colored People (NAACP) and the National Urban League attempted to deal with those problems by finding decent housing and jobs for Cleveland's new black citizens. Unfortunately, both groups languished in the 1920s. Virtually bankrupt, the Urban League still managed to make friendly, moderate appeals to white employers, and with some success. As Cleveland's economy expanded in the mid-1920s, the Urban League placed about three-fourths of its job applicants. Henry Owens and all three of his working-age sons landed jobs in a steel mill. Cleveland seemed, at first, like "a horn of plenty," Jesse recalled years afterward. Characteristically, he best remembered the new shoes and new clothes that "the steel mill money" bought. Shortly after arriving in Cleveland, Jesse himself got a job in a shoe repair shop, sweeping floors, washing windows, cleaning machinery, and shining shoes in the evenings and on weekends.[5]

But first he enrolled in Bolton Elementary School, just three blocks from his home. According to popular lore, an interchange on his first day at Bolton gave him the name "Jesse." In response to his teacher's asking him his name, he reportedly replied "J.C. Owens" in a thick Southern drawl. The teacher understood him to say "Jesse," and asked if that was correct. "J.C., ma'am," he timidly mumbled. Once more she misunderstood, and again asked him if he had said "Jesse." Eager to please, he gave up: "Yes, ma'am, Jesse Owens."[6]

That was his first exposure to a racially integrated school, accounting, at least in part, for his timidity. Yet Bolton was not unlike Oakville in the sense that blacks were in a distinct numerical minority. Southern and East European immigrants made up the bulk of the student body. Bolton's principal, assuming that a black child from Alabama could neither read nor write, put Jesse in the first grade. Two or three years older than most of his classmates, he towered over them and could scarcely fit at the small desk to which he was assigned. Fortunately he proved the principal wrong and was immediately moved into the second grade. Still, throughout his schooling he would always be a couple of years older than his classmates.[7]

After Bolton he attended Fairmount Junior High School, another ethnically diverse situation. In good American ghetto fashion, teachers dealt lightly with academic subjects but came down hard on matters of citizenship, discipline, and manners. They sought to "Americanize" foreigners and to "civilize" migrants such as Owens. "They'd give you certain little responsibilities, and this is what you were supposed to do," Jesse remembered years later. "I didn't know what they meant, but I knew that they asked me to do it, I knew it had to be done, and so I did it."[8]

At Fairmount he established the two most enduring relationships of his life. One was with Minnie Ruth Solomon, a pretty girl popular with all the boys. She impressed Jesse because "she was always dressed nicely." He passed her notes in class and soon began carrying her books to and from school.

He was fifteen, she thirteen. Both were newcomers to Cleveland. Her parents reportedly owned land in Griffinville, Georgia, before their move north. Decades later Jesse recalled that she was "a giggly youngster with a sensitivity far beyond her years" when first they met. He was too. Their spontaneous puppy love would grow.[9]

At Fairmount Jesse also met David Albritton, who fast became his closest friend. They had much in common. Both were black Alabama natives, Dave having been born only five months earlier than Jesse in Danville, a mere 6 miles from Oakville. Although they could not recall ever having met before their move north, their older brothers and sisters remembered each other from the baseball games between Oakville and Danville. In addition to their common roots, mutual interest in food, girls, and sports bound Jesse and Dave together. They often shared a snack for lunch, finishing off with a cupcake furnished by Albritton. One of Ruth Solomon's close friends was Dave's sweetheart for a while; later, Albritton dated Ruth's sister. More than anything else, though, a growing love of sport cemented the friendship. Dave, the taller, heavier, more pugnacious of the two, played basketball, boxed, and competed on the track team. Jesse dabbled in basketball but mostly devoted himself to track-and-field competition.[10]

Jesse Owens's athletic skills first blossomed in junior high school. For there, in addition to new friends, he found a mentor for life.

☆   ☆   ☆

In the transition from adolescence to young adulthood, mentors are supremely important. Several years ago a Yale University research team studied the life cycle of "successful" middle-aged American males and concluded that every one of them had an early mentor who nourished their lively but inarticulate childhood dreams of the kind of life they wanted to live as adults. According to that study, a mentor can be a teacher, patron, adviser, or exemplar; most probably he is all those things. He helps to define and to direct youthful dreams by attentively treating the youth as a novice, an apprentice in need of both psychological support and fatherly guidance. Usually older than his protégé, the mentor combines the roles of surrogate parent and mature friend. He does what a father cannot do for his son because of the father's prior involvement in pre-adolescent development. He evokes in his charge feelings of admiration, respect, gratitude, and love.[11]

Males are especially susceptible to mentors, and all the more so if the father is weak (as was Henry Owens) or tyrannical. Harry Edwards's experience in an East St. Louis ghetto school in the early 1950s—where teachers took promising young athletes under their wings, providing them with food, attention, and advice in order to keep them in school—illustrates the unique attraction of mentors for a schoolboy athlete. If a teacher does not lay hold on him, a coach will. When the roles of teacher and coach are combined, the influence can be altogether life-changing—for better or worse. In Jesse Owens's case, it was for the better. Ever afterward he gratefully referred to a coach and physical education teacher at Fairmount Junior High School, Charles Riley, as the man who made all the difference in his life.[12]

Jesse's various accounts of their initial encounter are muddled in contradictions. Whenever and however they first met, he found Riley physically unprepossessing. He was a gaunt, short man, about 5 feet, 8 inches tall; he had a shock of unruly gray hair, wore glasses, and was hard of hearing. But there was more to him than met the eye. He possessed a sharp Irish tongue and a wry sense of humor. Although he was precisely the same age as Jesse's own father, he seemed boundlessly enthusiastic and energetic. "I grew to admire and respect his words and his actions and everything else," the still-mesmerized Owens recalled thirty years later. "I wanted to be like him because he was a wonderful person, well-liked by everybody, no problems with anybody, and he preferred working over there with those Negro kids rather than going into another area that was perhaps a white area."[13]

Riley was white. A native Pennsylvanian, he grew up in little Mauch Chunk working in a slate mine and ribbon mill. He never finished high school but for a time attended Temple University as a special student. At Fairmount he was poorly paid, requiring him to spend each summer managing a Cleveland playground in order to pay the bills for his family of five. Both of his own sons were athletic disappointments. One was simply not interested, and the other was crippled from birth. If Jesse Owens found in Riley an attentive father figure, Riley in turn found a surrogate athletic son, the difference in color not-withstanding.[14]

He certainly latched onto the young Owens, recognizing his natural athletic talent as a rough gem worth polishing. Thinking Jesse undernourished, he often brought him breakfast. Frequently on Sunday afternoons he drove from his home in West Cleveland in his old Model T Ford to take his young pupil home with him for lunch. Riley's daughter still remembers those scenes, with Jesse "just a part of the family" but having to be taught proper table manners. He sometimes addressed Riley as "Coach"; more frequently he called him "Pop." In fact, the relationship was warm and respectful, not intimate. Riley "never played with me, never kidded me," Jesse recalled, but to the end of his life he lauded his white "Pop" as "a rare man, as much a father to me as Henry Owens was."[15]

Their relationship hinged on Jesse's athletic promise. Riley challenged him "to do more than we do in our gym class" in order to develop his natural speed. Upon hearing that he had to work after school, Riley agreed to meet him each morning for track practice an hour before school. By the eighth grade he had Jesse competing in junior high meets, but without much success at first. Jesse tended to give up when he was behind down the stretch, provoking a gentle but firm tongue-lashing from his mentor. More often, though, Riley taught by asking questions or by telling simple little parables with obvious points. Once, after Jesse lost a race because he grimaced and strained rather than running relaxed, Riley took him to a race track east of Cleveland to watch the horses run. He quietly instructed Jesse to observe how the better horses never changed expression of face: The determination was on the inside, not the outside.[16]

Riley's investment soon began to pay dividends. About a year after he began his paternalistic training of Jesse, he timed him in the 100-yard dash at 11 seconds. Astounded, he couldn't believe his stopwatch, so he found another one, only to clock Jesse once again at 11 seconds. Then in 1928 Owens set his first two of innumerable records: 6 feet in the high jump, and 22 feet, $11\frac{3}{4}$ inches in the long jump. Both were new world marks for junior high school athletes. Yet quick results were not Riley's main concern. His motto, "Train for four years from next Friday," meant patient work for the sake of long-range goals. "Where do I go from here?" the young Owens once asked after slipping back from a prior level of performance.

"Keep training," Riley replied.

"For what?"

"Why, for four years from Friday, of course." [17]

In his quest for the perfect technique and consistency of performance, Riley taught Jesse to run as if he were dancing on hot coals, "like the ground was a burning fire" that he should touch as lightly as possible. He demanded concentration and classic simplicity of form. "All good runners look alike. They have to follow the same principles," Owens observed years later. "We all ran the same way at my junior high school, because that was the way our coach taught us to run. You could watch 500 kids from Cleveland, Ohio, run, and you could pick out the ones who'd been trained by Coach Riley. They ran with their heads held firm and straight; they didn't look around." The smooth, fluid style of Jesse Owens that still captivates the viewer of Leni Riefenstahl's *Olympia* can largely be traced to the tutelage of Charles Riley. [18]

So, to some degree, can Owens's social vision. His inability ever to view the world in simple racial terms—black *versus* white—flowed out of his relation to his white mentor. "He was the first white man I really knew," Owens said, "and without ever trying, he proved to me beyond all proof that a white man can understand—and love—a Negro." They never discussed racial issues, but on those Sunday afternoons at Riley's home after lunch they did talk about values, manners, and dreams. "He trained me to become a man as well as an athlete," Jesse recalled. By his own account, his Irish "father" kept him off the ghetto trash heap. "Coach Riley taught me to behave. His influence on me and many other boys kept us out of trouble. Without his guidance, we could very easily have become wards of the state." [19]

Riley introduced Jesse to yet another white exemplar, the world-renowned track star Charley Paddock. Virtually unbeatable as a varsity sprinter at the University of Southern California in the early 1920s, Paddock at one time held every important sprint record. At the Antwerp Olympics in 1920, he won the gold medal in the 100-meter dash; from Paris four years later he came away with a silver medal. In that early age of journalistic hype, he was one of the first runners to be dubbed "the world's fastest human." Late in the decade his records began to topple under the fast feet of little Eddie Tolan of the University of Michigan, but not before Paddock made the rounds of American schools and civic groups, telling of his Olympic exploits.[20]

In 1928 Riley arranged for him to address the youngsters at Fairmount Junior High. After his speech, Paddock was led to Riley's office to sign autographs, and there Riley personally introduced him to the fifteen-year-old Owens. After the crowd cleared from the office Riley, Paddock, and Owens stood talking. As the two older men dominated the conversation, little did the awestruck Owens know how altogether different he and the accomplished Paddock were as runners. Jesse's style was already smooth as silk; Paddock's was the unorthodox driving thrust of a heavily muscled torso, high knee action, a wildly flailing arm motion, and a final frantic leap to break the tape. His form was no model to imitate. Yet he was a winner, an Olympic champion, and on that point alone he bowled the impressionable young Owens off his feet. Shortly after Paddock left Fairmount for his next speaking engagement, a wide-eyed Jesse told Riley that he wanted to be "like Charley Paddock," a champion. Riley assured him that he could, if he worked hard enough for that goal. To his dying day, Owens recalled his boyhood "idol," Charley Paddock, as a man who first made him aware of the Olympic Games and inspired him to set his sights high.[21]

Not once in all his later writings, public addresses, and interviews did Jesse ever mention any black track star who influenced him as a youth. Prior to the 1930s there were pitifully few nationally recognized black track-and-field athletes. Binga Dismond of Howard University, Sol Butler of Dubuque, Howard P. Drew of the University of Southern California, Edwin O. Gourdin of Harvard, DeHart Hubbard of Michigan—the list is brief. Not until 1920 did any black athlete make the United States Olympic team. Two went to the Antwerp Games but returned home empty-handed; of three others at the Paris Olympics in 1924, Hubbard and Gourdin finished first and second in the long jump. But then not a single black made the Olympic team in 1928. Eddie Tolan failed even to qualify for the final trials.[22]

DeHart Hubbard's failure to impress the young Owens is

particularly puzzling, for Hubbard set up a dentistry practice in Cleveland after earning his degree at the University of Michigan. In addition to his Olympic gold medal, Hubbard in 1925 set the world record in the long jump with a leap of 25 feet, $10\frac{7}{8}$ inches at the National Collegiate Track and Field Championship in Chicago. A laureled athlete, a college graduate, and an accomplished professional, the black Hubbard surely would have been a marvelous role model for Jesse and his friends.[23]

Instead, Jesse's adolescent hero was a white athlete from California about whom he knew little and with whom he had scarcely anything in common except athletic enthusiasm. In their brief encounter at Fairmount Junior High School, Paddock's color was irrelevant. His athletic reputation alone dazzled the young Owens, for Jesse was already beginning to perceive sport—in Harry Edwards's cogent phrase—as "an escalator up and out of poverty and nobodiness." Momentary contact with Charley Paddock clarified that vision.[24]

Somewhere along the way, though, Owens attached his personal aspirations to the principles of a black folk hero, Booker T. Washington. The late president of Tuskegee Institute had recommended education and hard work, humility and patience, pragmatic accommodation and gradual progress for blacks. More militant black spokesmen—such as Marcus Moziah Garvey, who preached racial pride and separatism, and W. E. B. DuBois, who urged active resistance to racial discrimination—held little appeal for the mild-mannered Owens. "I know that the name of Booker T. Washington will live forever in the memory of the colored people," Owens told an audience in 1936. "I would like to become a little bit like him." In fact, he had become more than "a little bit" like his hero.[25]

East Cleveland teachers shaped him in that direction. They taught him to respect the rules, to assume responsibilities, to stay out of trouble, and to lead others along the same path. One elementary school teacher, unable to discipline her class, capitalized on Jesse's being older and taller than his classmates by making of him "an example of what should be done." Charles Riley required good behavior in the classroom before any of his pupils could participate on the track team. Of Jesse he demanded "leadership" in both spheres. Years later Owens acknowledged that he was always "the teacher's pet," but that meant responsibility as well as special favors. So did his appointment as a School Guard and his election as a student council leader and captain of the track team. Those were honors, of course; they were also formative factors. They made Jesse feel, as he recalled years afterward, "like you were somebody."[26]

☆ ☆ ☆

Well before the stock market crash of 1929, Cleveland's economic cycle turned downward. By 1928 fewer employment opportunities and the continuing flood of blacks moving from the South created a situation where the Urban League could place fewer than one-third of its job applicants. The case of Henry Owens and his older sons reflected the problem. Their work in the steel mill was cut back to four days a week, then to three. The boys scrambled for whatever extra work they could find: unloading freight cars, shoveling manure in the stockyards, doing janitorial chores. The father languished, his agrarian experience working to his disadvantage in industrial Cleveland. Too many years of backbreaking toil in the fields of Alabama made him effectively much older than his years. He had to compete with younger, stronger men for unskilled jobs. Brief stints at loading 100-pound crates and collecting garbage proved too much for him.[27]

In the autumn of 1929—the time of the Crash—Henry Owens stepped off a curb into the path of an onrushing taxi. He was fortunate to suffer only a broken leg in the accident, but after several months away from his steel mill job he had to undergo a physical examination before resuming work. The exam revealed that he was blind in one eye (which was, in fact, the reason for his accident in the first place). Never again was he able to find regular employment. While he stayed at home, his wife and daughters had to take in laundry and hire themselves out as maids to affluent whites in the western and northern suburbs of Cleveland. Emasculated, Henry Owens sat staring at the wall. He personified the Depression woes of the early 1930s.[28]

So did his children. One by one they dropped out of school to take whatever work they could find. Except for Jesse, none of the Owens children finished high school. As the older sons married, they moved their wives into the large house rented by their parents. At one time more than a dozen people lived in the one house, unable to afford anything else. All the while, Jesse found extra after-school jobs delivering groceries and working in a greenhouse. By 1930 he was the only child of Henry and Emma Owens still in school.[29]

As the Depression deepened, the Urban League made the best it could of a bad situation. Long having urged blacks to "think industrially," it began campaigning vigorously for "a more serious emphasis upon vocational training and guidance" for black youths. For young Jesse Owens the dolorous spectacle of his unemployed father and brothers was all the prod he needed. In September 1930 he enrolled at East Technical High School, within walking distance of his home. Black students at the time numbered less than 5 percent of the student body, a figure that would rise dramatically in the following decade as blacks sought to equip themselves for skilled trades.[30]

The pattern was not confined to Cleveland. The secondary education of several outstanding black athletes of the interwar era illustrate the trend toward vocational training. In addition to Owens and Dave Albritton at East Tech, Eddie Tolan attended Cass Technical High School in Detroit, Ralph Metcalfe graduated from Tilden Tech in Chicago, and Mack Robinson went to Muir Tech in Pasadena, California. Three decades later John Carlos and Vincent Matthews attended Manhatten Vocational and Technical High School in New York, which the outspoken Matthews described as "one of those places that teaches you a lot about machine and metal trades but never bothers to teach you how to read."[31]

Cleveland's East Tech was one of those places in the 1930s. Years later a teacher there recalled Jesse Owens as a student "of even temperament, who applied himself to his studies as best he knew how." But there was the problem. From a home bare of books, and from a mediocre junior high school, Jesse entered East Tech not knowing how to study. Unfortunately, he never learned. A homeroom teacher, Ivan Green, took a personal interest in him, but primarily because of his athletic ability rather than his academic promise. Hammers, lathes, and welding tools dominated the curriculum. Like Harry Edwards in East St. Louis in the 1950s, Owens at East Tech "never seriously cracked a book" and thus got through "all but completely unscathed by formal schooling at the high school level." Highly verbal and physically active, he never learned to read well. To the end of his life he read little, and poorly. At East Tech he developed a keen interest in ceramics and presumably did well enough in his vocational courses. In academic subjects, however, he struggled to keep up.[32]

His interest lay elsewhere. A handsome young man, he attracted girls with his spontaneously warm smile and his vulnerably shy, modest demeanor. Already distinguished from the pack by a budding athletic reputation, he also early displayed a fastidious attention to personal appearance. Despite his family's poverty, he always wore clean, neat clothes, freshly ironed each day by his doting mother. Athletic but modest, friendly but shy, poor but neat, he was an irresistible combination. Only a cute charmer such as Ruth Solomon could have held onto her prize. While other girls drooled and flirted, Ruth remained Jesse's steady girlfriend in school and out. Sport was her only serious competition for his attention.[33]

In the autumn of his sophomore year, Jesse went out for the East Tech football squad, and three months later he tried out for the basketball team. In neither sport did he last for more than a week or so. An ankle injury in basketball prompted his principal to urge him to put all his ambitions into track, and Jesse complied. In the East Tech track coach, Edgar Weil, he met a man whom the *Cleveland Plain Dealer* described as a coach "with experience and feeling similar to [Charles] Riley." Perhaps the feeling was there; the experience was not. Weil was new to the job, just out of college, where he played football. He had never even competed in track, much less coached it. Wisely he asked Riley to assist him in his efforts, and Riley jumped at the chance to continue grooming those athletes whom he had identified and nourished in junior high school. The arrangement worked greatly to Jesse's advantage. In the spring of 1932, his junior year, the Cleveland black press lauded him as East Tech's "one-man team," "a marvel," "the outstanding individual track man in northeastern Ohio."[34]

His reach exceeded his grasp in the summer of that year, however, when he attempted to win a place on the United States Olympic team. Arriving at Northwestern University's Dyche Stadium for the preliminary trials, he found scores of black athletes, like himself, competing *en masse* for the first time in an arena traditionally dominated by whites. They were participants in what one historian calls "something vital" that began happening to blacks in the 1930s: "Negro expectations rose; black powerlessness decreased; white hostility diminished." That new vitality first manifested itself in the entertainment industry, then in sports. From the various preliminary Olympic trials scattered around the country in 1932, eighteen black athletes won their way to the finals at Stanford University. Finally four blacks—Eddie Tolan, Ralph Metcalfe, Edward Gordon, and Cornelius Johnson—won places on the track team representing the United States in the Los Angeles Olympics.[35]

Young Jesse Owens read about it in the newspapers, for he did not get past the Midwestern preliminaries at Evanston. He competed in the long jump, the 100-meter sprint and the 200-meter sprint, but he lost in all three events. According to his own admission, he "tightened up" under the pressure of competition against older, more mature athletes. Yet something good came of that disappointment. In both sprints, Jesse's conqueror was Ralph Metcalfe. An undergraduate at Marquette University, Metcalfe was older than Owens by a couple of years, taller by a couple of inches, and maturer by a couple of miles. He owned or shared nineteen track records in the course of his illustrious career. At Los Angeles he lost narrowly to Eddie Tolan in the 100 meters, then finished third in a controversial 200-meter final. From Evanston he and Owens carried away a competitive respect that would later develop into a warm, if not intimate, friendship.[36]

Shortly after the Los Angeles Games, several European athletes on their return home stopped over in Cleveland for an afternoon track meet against some American Olympians and the best local talent available. Although none of the better foreign sprinters competed, young Owens salved his pride by winning the 100-meter and 200-meter races. In the long jump he finished second to Edward Gordon, the American Olympic gold medalist. Good for the ego, those performances did little to solve a personal problem. The eighteen-year-old Owens was suffering a mild case of shock. As of August 8, 1932, he was a father.[37]

Ruth Solomon named her healthy daughter Gloria Shirley,

turned to her own father and mother for support, and dropped out of school to work in a beauty parlor. Years later, tales of an immediate marriage circulated freely. According to sworn affidavits submitted by the family to the FBI for a security clearance of Jesse Owens in 1956, he and Ruth were married in July 1932. One witness recalled July 5; another cited July 15. Jesse later insisted that he and Ruth eloped to Erie, Pennsylvania, in the spring of 1932 to get married by a Justice of the Peace. The story has an element of plausibility, as Pennsylvania's more lax marriage requirements made Erie a favorite destination for hasty young lovers from Cleveland in the 1930s.[38]

In Jesse's embellished explanation, his friend David Albritton drove him and Ruth to Erie in an old Model T Ford, and for their wedding dinner all three shared a single hot dog stuffed with all the relish the vendor would allow. He told an interviewer in 1961 that he gave his father a "cock-and-bull story" to conceal the marriage, but his father-in-law found out the truth and had the marriage annulled. That is a charmingly simple, romantic account. But apparently the whole thing was a cock-and-bull story. Jesse's several different versions of the event are riddled with inconsistencies, and Dave Albritton adamantly refuses to comment. The marriage license bureau in Erie has no record of any application submitted by James Cleveland Owens or Minnie Ruth Solomon. When they finally got married amid much publicity three years later, no mention was ever made of any previous legal union, annulled or not.[39]

The adult Owens seems simply to have covered up his youthful indiscretion. Presumably he did so in order to protect the feelings of his family, and certainly to protect his All-American image in the 1950s and 1960s. Most of all, his fabrication served an inner need of a man-child from an earlier era. He was a modern American hero, but he was not a "modern" man. Never could he have admitted, as Sugar Ray Leonard did recently in a *Parade* magazine article, that his first child was born out of wedlock. Between Jesse Owens and Sugar Ray Leonard lay an enormous cultural revolution in sexual mores, public candor, and hero worship.[40]

☆   ☆   ☆

Married or not, at the outset of his senior year at East Tech High, Jesse was elected president of his student council. As neither scholastic nor national politics ever interested him, one can assume that the office was more honorary than active. His election to the captaincy of the track team meant much more. With guarded optimism for a future in intercollegiate athletics, he fixed his mind on the spring track season. He need not have worried. From one meet after another he emerged without a single loss. In the final account, he finished first in 75 of the 79 races he ran in high school. Recovering quickly from a slight knee injury incurred in long-jump practice, he swept the state interscholastic finals on May 20, 1933. His long jump of 24 feet, $3\frac{3}{4}$ inches broke the schoolboy record by more than three inches.[41]

More impressive than the records, however, was the emergence of a personal magnetism that was fast becoming an Owens trademark. He performed seriously and quietly, without any hint of demonstrative gesturing; spectators responded boisterously, watching his every move. "Wherever Owens went, Saturday night he commanded attention," the Cleveland *Gazette* commented after an indoor meet in late March. "When at the far end of the hall, competing in the high jump, he stole the spotlight from the races and when racing he was the recipient of cheer after cheer from the extraordinarily large crowd." At an outdoor meet two months later, the *Gazette* deemed Owens so graceful and dominant "that the spectators scarcely realized that anyone else was on the field."[42] When Jesse electrified 100,000 spectators at Berlin three years later, his acclaim scarcely surprised those Clevelanders who had witnessed his high school feats.

Nor did the effusive prose of sportswriters in 1936 appear new to those black journalists who struggled to put together metaphors and adjectives that would adequately convey the graceful prowess of the high school senior in 1933. In early June, at a championship meet in Cleveland, Owens turned in record-breaking performances in the 100- and 200-yard dashes, and again in the long jump, before anchoring his 880-yard relay team to victory. On the long jump, a visiting reporter for the *Chicago Defender* almost drowned himself in wordy prose: "Owens was away with the rush of an airplane, but the grace of a fawn, streaking down the runway faster and faster, until it appeared he would be forced by his own momentum to continue on into the air." As Jesse left the ground from the takeoff board, the Chicago sportswriter imaginatively soared with him in the air: "Higher than usual he was, but shooting through space faster, too. He came down just three-fourths of an inch short of 25 feet, and before he could reach his feet he was all but ground into the dirt by the hero-worshipers."[43] The athleticism of the young Owens left little room for dispassionate journalism.

In mid-June 1933 Owens capped his remarkable high school career at the National Interscholastic Championship meet at Stagg Field, Chicago. Once again he soared gracefully through the air in the long jump, winning with a leap of 24 feet, $9\frac{5}{8}$ inches. In the 220-yard dash he set a new world mark of 20.7 seconds, and in the 100-yard dash his 9.4 seconds tied the world record. East Tech won the meet with 54 total points; Owens accounted for 30 points on his own.[44]

On the following Tuesday, the city of Cleveland proudly produced a victory parade, taking Jesse with his family and friends in open cars from the East Side downtown to City Hall. Charles Riley beamed with satisfaction in the procession just behind the Owens car. Cleveland's mayor and several city councilmen met the entourage at City Hall and delivered laudatory speeches.[45] At nineteen years of age, scarcely a decade removed from the fields of Alabama, Jesse Owens first tasted the fruit of celebrity status. By no means would it be his last taste.[45]

CHAPTER 3

College Pride and Prejudice

DURING THE GREAT DEPRESSION, fewer than 15 percent of American youths pursued a college degree. The percentage of black collegians was tiny. Had Jesse Owens not made a sterling high school athletic reputation for himself, he would never have even considered the possibility of further education. His parents were too poor to pay his way; his academic record was too weak to gain admission to a university program.[1]

Outside of football, athletic scholarships in present-day terms were simply unavailable in the 1930s. Even football scholarships were forbidden in several conferences, though they were granted quietly, sometimes secretly, throughout the United States. Track was another matter altogether. It was not a money-making sport; only in the upper Midwest and on the West Coast did it carry any campus prestige. For track athletes, money to pay for tuition, room, board, and books had to be earned at menial jobs—"handing out towels, digging out dandelions on the football field, sweeping the stadium, preparing the track, that type of thing," one black college athlete of the era recalls. A track "scholarship" was, in fact, an informal remunerative arrangement made by the coach and his staff.[2]

Many colleges made overtures to Jesse Owens during his senior year in high school, not a single black college among them. With few exceptions, black colleges had inferior coaching, poor facilities, and inadequate budgets for their track programs. Until the late 1930s they sent no teams to major track meets such as the Drake Relays, the Millrose Games, and the Penn Relays. Football, not track, dominated the black college athletic agenda, especially at Wilberforce, Howard, and Morgan State, whose proximity to Cleveland might have attracted Jesse Owens. Even their football teams necessarily played only against other black colleges, making them virtually invisible to the larger American public. When Mel Walker, a bright, well-read black athlete graduated from a Toledo high school in 1933, he never considered going to a black college. Another black high school star in New Jersey, Eulace Peacock, received offers of two dozen or so football and track scholarships, but not a single one from a black institution. Neither did Jesse Owens.[3]

At a National AAU track meet in July 1933, Ralph Metcalfe barely beat Owens in the 100-meter dash and afterward urged him to attend Metcalfe's alma mater, Marquette. Shortly thereafter Jesse reportedly visited the campus of Indiana University. In the end, though, he decided to enroll at his own state university. State pride supposedly prompted the decision. "What I really wanted to do was to go to Ohio State," he later insisted, crediting his mentor, Charles Riley, with making the arrangements for a work scholarship and a job for his father. In all his later explanations, Owens merely elaborated upon the simple account given by the *New York Amsterdam News* in 1936: "Owens was champ in high school and all the big universities wanted him when he was ready for college. But, an Ohio-bred boy, he would go nowhere but Ohio State—and that was that!"[4]

The truth was not so simple. Ohio State was actually Jesse's second choice at best, a result of bungled negotiations elsewhere. Had his black friends had their way, in fact, he would never have even considered being a Buckeye. Ohio State had a notoriously bad reputation for racially prejudicial attitudes and policies. In 1931 a sociology professor was dismissed from the university because of his unorthodox ideas and teaching methods; he particularly made the mistake of taking a class of students to visit Wilberforce College, encouraging them both to eat and to dance with black Wilberforce students. Such interracial experiments were unacceptable to Ohio State authorities in 1931. In that same year the solitary black player on the football team, a tackle named Bill Bell, was kept out of a game against Vanderbilt in Columbus because, as the *Chicago Defender* caustically put it, "arrangements had been made with Buckeye moguls whereby the Commodores' bigoted wishes would be respected." Knowledgeable blacks had little respect for Ohio State.[5]

In a highly publicized case, the NAACP filed a racial discrimination suit against the university early in 1933, accusing administrators of having denied campus housing to two black female students enrolled in a home economics residential program of study. No doubt Jesse Owens heard about the case during his senior year in high school. One of the women, Doris Weaver, was from Cleveland, and the local black press covered the controversy from beginning to end. Ohio State's president, Dr. George W. Rightmire, played into their hands with a tactless defense of his university's supposed separate-but-equal policy. "Knowing the feelings in Ohio," he insisted, "can the administration take the burden of establishing this relationship—colored and white girls living in this more or less family way?" In February 1933 the state's Supreme Court ruled in favor of the university, but the incident merely confirmed what blacks already believed: Ohio State was an unacceptable place for Jesse Owens and his kind.[6]

Owens's choice of a college became a hotly debated issue in the black press. "He will be an asset to any school," the *Chicago Defender* editorialized, "so why help advertise an institution that majors in prejudice?" For Jesse to choose Ohio State would mean that he sanctioned "hate, prejudice, and proscription" of the type suffered by Doris Weaver. "You must realize that in the age in which you are living, a militant spirit against prejudice in all of its forms must be shown," added the *Defender*, one of the more "radical" black newspapers of the era. It pulled no punches in its message to Jesse Owens: "The day has passed for turning the other cheek. We must either fight or perish under the iron heel of the oppressor."[7]

That was a heavy burden for any high school boy to bear, and all the more so for a person so athletically oriented and politically unaware as the young Owens. To demand of him "a militant spirit" was to command the sun to stop shining. He was no political fighter. He had learned long before to survive by turning his head, not merely the other cheek. Twice in the summer of 1933 he was quoted in the *Defender* as saying that he would not attend Ohio State because of its record of racial discrimination, but those lines were either concocted by the press or extrapolated from Jesse's apparent intention to go elsewhere to college.[8]

He almost went to the University of Michigan. Owens later praised Charles Riley for making him a Buckeye, but actually Riley had urged him to be a Wolverine. Riley was rumored to have earlier been on the coaching staff at Ohio State, and to have harbored ill-will over being dismissed. The rumors had no basis in fact; he never coached at Columbus. Quite possibly his aversion to Ohio State resulted from the manner in which he or some of his athletes had been treated by the coaches there. At any rate, he knew that the University of Michigan had a strong tradition of accepting African and black American track athletes long before other Big Ten schools did so. The great DeHart Hubbard, Eddie Tolan, and Willis Ward all wore the blue and maize.[9]

Whatever his reasons, Riley asked a Cleveland alumnus of the University of Michigan to arrange a visit to Ann Arbor. The alumnus offered ten dollars for gas and oil, whereupon Riley and his prize athlete set out in his old Model T. The visit was highly successful. Riley and Owens toured the campus, marveled at the athletic facilities, and met the track coaches. With a promise of a job ("scholarship") in hand, Jesse returned to Cleveland determined to enroll at the University of Michigan in the fall. It seemed that he had finally taken to heart at least one of the admonitions of the *Chicago Defender:* "Owens, if you wish to attend a Big Ten school, draw up a list of the various members leaving Ohio State off completely. Then take your pick of the other nine institutions."[10] He picked Michigan.

In a radio interview several nights later, however, Jesse announced that his going to college depended on his father's securing a job. The point was plain. He would enroll at the university that came up with the best offer. Detroit alumni of the University of Michigan immediately offered Henry Owens a position as caretaker of an apartment building at sixteen dollars a week. Then Henry Owens himself balked, demanding a better salary. "The old boy was just plain out looking to sell Jesse to the highest bidder," a Michigan alumnus later complained. The peeved Michigan group withdrew altogether from the bidding.[11]

A Cleveland owner of a sporting goods chain, Richard Kroesen, stepped into the breach on behalf of Ohio State. Kroesen's motives were unclear. Possibly he acted out of state pride; probably he envisaged obtaining future Ohio State orders for athletic equipment. Whatever the mixture of interests, he pulled strings to obtain for Jesse a political appointment operating an elevator in the State House in Columbus. Presumably the job was easier and better paying than anything Michigan offered. Years later Jesse claimed that he went to Ohio State because his father was given a permanent position as groundskeeper and maintenance man on the campus, but once again Jesse's memory failed him. Henry and Emma Owens never moved to Columbus. Having rejected the Michigan offer, Henry Owens remained in Cleveland, unemployed.[12]

His decision sealed, Jesse set his sights on Columbus. Unfortunately, a minor impediment stood in his way. He had finished his senior year at East Tech High with a marginally acceptable 73.5 grade average but lacked a couple of credits required for graduation. His closest friend, Dave Albritton, had the same problem and decided to stay in Cleveland for the fall semester, take a required course in auto mechanics, and get ready to go to college the following year. Ohio State coaches wanted Jesse immediately, however, so they arranged for him to take special tests to gain admission in the fall of 1933.[13]

In late August one of the two black Cleveland newspapers, the *Gazette,* reported that Owens was registering at Ohio State within the week and editorially commented: "Education, it seems, does not always engender self and race respect." In the following issue the *Gazette* curtly observed that Owens would be attending Ohio State "in spite of the protests of his people at home and the country over." If the black press was indicative of opinion in Cleveland's black community, the protest lingered. Fully two years later Cleveland's other black weekly, the *Call and Post,* recalled that when Jesse went to Columbus, "Many and long were the outcries against his decision."[14]

☆ ☆ ☆

Prior to entering Ohio State, Jesse spent much of the summer pumping gas at Alonzo Wright's Sohio service station on
the corner of East 92d Street and Cedar Avenue in Cleveland.
Perhaps part of his earnings went to Ruth Solomon and their
baby girl, but at this distance the terms of that relationship are
unclear. Both Jesse and Ruth later recalled that her father angrily forbade them to see each other for a while but then soft-
ened in his resolve, allowing Jesse to visit each evening. Ruth
would continue working as a hairdresser in a local beauty
shop, and she and the baby would remain in Cleveland while
Jesse went off to Columbus. Baby Gloria saw much more of her
grandmother than she did of her parents. From as early as she
can remember, she addressed Jesse and Ruth by their Christian names, not as Father and Mother. She still does.[15]

As classes in Ohio State's quarter system did not begin until early October, Jesse took off to Canada to compete in two
track meets in September. To both events Charles Riley took
him in his faithful old Ford, first to Toronto on September 2,
then to Hamilton, Ontario, on September 16. At the Toronto
meet, held in conjunction with the Canadian International Ex-
position, Jesse won the 100-yard dash. There he also competed
in his first of innumerable stunt exhibitions, with two runners
placed several yards ahead of him at the start. Both beat him to
the tape. Jesse at that time was a *wunderkind* but not an
übermensch.[16]

With Charles Riley at his side, he found Toronto a racially
tolerant place. Alone a month later in Columbus, he encountered quite a different situation. Housing was his first problem. On the campus of Ohio State, only two dormitories were
available for women and one for men; most of the student
body, about 14,000, lived in off-campus apartments. The men's
dorm, finished in the summer of 1933 in the southwest tower
of the football stadium, held only seventy-five occupants. Like
Doris Weaver just a year earlier, Jesse was barred from that
"cooperative dormitory" because of his color. He shared a
boarding house with several other black students on East 11th
Avenue, where a cluster of black families lived about a quarter
of a mile from the campus.[17]

He and his housemates cooked their own meals and

sometimes ate in the campus union building. No restaurants along High Street, adjacent to the university, would allow them entrance. Nor were they admitted into the movie theaters, except to the dingiest one in town, where they were required to sit in the top six rows of the balcony. Yet never once did Jesse later recall that dismal treatment; his selective memory blocked it out. His black classmates remember clearly. They still vividly think of Columbus in the 1930s as "a cracker town," a place "just like Jackson, Mississippi."[18]

Jesse had, after all, been warned. In building its case against his going to Ohio State, the *Chicago Defender* had argued that not only was the university "guilty of Jim Crowism" but also Columbus was "almost unbearable" for a black. The *Defender* was right on both counts. Racial discrimination extended even to the job that lured Jesse to Ohio State. He operated a freight elevator in the rear of the State Office Building, away from public view. The front passenger elevator was manned by white athletes, mostly football and basketball players. "There weren't any black boys out there on the front elevator," recalls Mel Walker, himself a black track athlete who was given the even more menial assignment of mopping floors in the same building.[19]

As usual, Jesse saw a flower on the dung heap and cultivated it to his advantage. Ignoring the racial affront of being placed out of sight in the freight elevator, he found a table and chair for himself, creating his own private cubbyhole for study. Only once every hour did the elevator have to move, to take the cleaning crew from floor to floor. For the rest of his evening shift, Jesse studied without interruption. The superintendent of the building, an Ohio State athletic booster, cooperated with the arrangement. He even instructed the night watchman to take the front passenger elevator on his rounds in order not to disturb Jesse's concentration.[20]

Jesse later recounted that he "studied hard" to pull a 3.2 average during his freshman year, "better grades than I ever did at any other time in college." Maybe he did study hard, but his performance fell far short of a 3.2 average. By the end of his first term he was reported already to be suffering "scholastic deficiency." At the end of his second term, in March 1934, he was placed on academic probation because of low grades. From a disadvantaged home and an academically weak high school, he would never be anything but a marginal college student.[21]

The fault was not entirely his own. Unfortunately, just when he enrolled at Ohio State, its administration, faculty, and maintenance staff were in turmoil, suffering the trauma of Depression economics. Since the Wall Street crash, legislative support had plummeted annually, from $10 million in 1929 to $6 million in 1933. In 1931–32 the Legislature imposed a 20 percent reduction in funds, and the Governor added another 7 percent cut, requiring the termination of ninety-one faculty positions. For five consecutive years, dozens of faculty had to be dismissed annually, with the survivors taking pay cuts each year. In January 1934, during Jesse's freshman year, the entire faculty suffered a midyear reduction in salary.[22]

When President Rightmire wrung his hands over his "shrunken institution," however, he had not merely diminished funds and faculty positions in mind. In those hard times the curriculum was decimated. In 1932–33 no fewer than 337 courses were withdrawn from the undergraduate catalog, with sixty-nine others offered only in alternate years. Yet low fees kept the number of students relatively stable. While the budget, faculty, and course offerings almost halved, the student body fell off only about 10 percent—to 13,500 in 1934 from a previous high of 15,126 in 1930. Despite all its cutbacks in funds and personnel, Ohio State remained the fourth largest state university in the United States.[23]

The inevitable result was larger classes, nullifying the conscious efforts of past Ohio State presidents to make classes smaller and more intimate during the decade prior to 1929. For Jesse Owens's undergraduate generation, huge classes meant impersonal lectures and little or no student–faculty interaction. To complete the vicious cycle, heavier student loads combined with regular salary cuts to produce low faculty morale, making teachers all the more inattentive to student needs. For needy students such as Owens, the combination was disastrous. Years later he awkwardly recalled his college experience as one that was "not sort of partial." He meant that it was impersonal, lacking the paternalistic care to which he had been accustomed in high school. "Even though people knew you," he remembered, "you were more or less on your own."[24] He could not make it on his own.

Without close supervision, he was easily distracted by concerns other than classroom lectures and assignments. In the autumn of 1933 the campus was rocked by several mass demonstrations against compulsory military drill, resulting in the suspension of seven students for the remainder of the term. Of greater interest to the apolitical, athletically minded Owens was the abysmal performance of the varsity football team. A barrage of student and alumni criticism of the head coach, Sam S. Willaman, mounted throughout the fall. The Buckeyes' 13–0 loss to arch-rival Michigan sealed Willaman's fate, causing him to resign in order to avoid being fired at the end of the season. Jesse's interest in that issue paled beside his own intense athletic ambitions. Until winter closed in on Columbus, he daily worked out on the track, preparing for his freshman debut in the spring.[25]

Yet his greatest distraction came from quarters off the track, and off the campus. He was a young man marked for athletic success, so both as a perquisite and as a public relations ploy his track coach arranged for him to address local schools and service organizations in the Columbus area each Wednesday at noon. That was no small honor for a freshman, especially a black freshman in Columbus in 1933. "We would talk about Ohio State, about our programs, about athletics and things of that nature," Jesse later recalled. In those sessions he quickly learned to correct his bad grammar and to conceal his limited experience with personal anecdotes, charm, and wit. The pattern started early; it would last a lifetime. Each speech came easier and was more polished than the one before.[26]

Money, too, came easily. As Owens later recalled, he received fifty dollars in "expense money" for each of those weekly noonday sessions. He also claimed that he worked occasionally in the library and cleared tables in the cafeteria for extra money. He estimated his income at $350 a month, a very substantial figure for that day. As Jesse told it, he monthly sent $150 to his mother and the same amount each month to his "mother-in-law" for the upkeep of Ruth and the baby. All those figures seem exaggerated, if not imagined, but the distinction between fact and fiction is lost in the mists of time. Amidst the uncertainties, however, several facts are sure. Far from being a poor Negro college boy barely able to make ends meet, Jesse Owens enjoyed a measure of financial security during his undergraduate days at Ohio State. He paid for his material comfort in time and attention stolen from the classroom. Athletic promise was his golden egg; it was also a potential millstone around his neck.[27]

☆　☆　☆

Sports figured prominently in the life of Ohio State University. When science and humanities faculty salaries were being slashed repeatedly at the outset of the Depression, athletic department salaries remained steady. They depended largely on gate receipts rather than legislative funds. The big moneymaker was football. Despite a decade of mediocre teams, spectators still filled the large horseshoe stadium that was built in the early 1920s, just after three conference championships. King Football reigned supreme over its Columbus fiefdom, aggressively supported by intercollegiate teams in baseball, basketball, track, and several lesser sports.[28]

Since 1912 the Athletic Director, L. W. St. John, had headed the entire athletic, physical education, and intramural program, women's as well as men's. Originally he combined his administrative duties with coaching baseball, basketball, and football, until his empire grew to such an extent that he had to devote full time to administration. In athletic expansion and specialization, Ohio State was little different from other colleges and universities in the United States just after World War I. On the eve of the stock market collapse in 1929, the Athletic Board proposed and the University's trustees agreed to set aside a huge area around the football stadium for "field houses, natatorium, playing fields, etc." To the youthful Jesse Owens, social and academic difficulties seemed inconsequential beside the athletic hothouse that was Ohio State. At the beginning of his second term he received word of his election to the 1933 All-America Track and Field Team named by the Amateur Athletic Union. He and Ohio State were made for each other, All-Americans all.[29]

In the spring of 1934 he came under the tutelage of the varsity track coach, Larry Snyder. Scarcely ten years older than Owens, Snyder himself had starred as a track athlete at Ohio State in the early 1920s. Only an injury kept him from making the Olympic team in 1924. He captained the Ohio State squad in both his junior and senior years, stayed on after graduation as an assistant coach, and in 1932 took over the reins of the track program. He was only in his second year as head coach when Owens arrived. Snyder felt himself on the spot. "Every coach in the Big Ten was watching me with a critical eye," he later recalled, "to see how I would handle him." He handled him exceedingly well.[30]

Snyder quickly discovered that the earlier tutelage under Charles Riley was both a blessing and a bane. On the one hand, from the day Jesse first stepped on the track at Ohio State, he displayed quick feet and legs trained to react instantly to the touch of the ground. Fashioned by Riley, his footwork was a model for the "bounce" technique espoused by another prominent track man of the day, J. Kenneth Doherty:

> As the toe first strikes the ground, the ankles must be completely relaxed, thus cushioning the landing and permitting the foot to drag down for a full forward and upward swing at the end of its stride. This requires great explosive force in the relevant muscles and great elasticity in foot and ankle tendons. Only months of precise conditioning can produce them.[31]

Under Charles Riley's watchful eye, Jesse had spent six years perfecting the art of the "bounce."

By Snyder's standards, though, he had developed some bad habits. He ran with weak arm motion and tended to stretch his fingers awkwardly as he sprinted. He required practice in dropping his hands naturally as he ran. Worst of all, his start was slow. He lacked concentration on the starter's gun, and his starting stance, as taught by Riley, was too elongated for Snyder's taste. Instead of the customary spread of eighteen inches between the front and back foot, Snyder taught a tighter crouch that crowded the starting line. For the long jump, too, he altered Jesse's style, insisting on a hitch-kick—vigorous movement of the legs—in midair.[32]

Although he was not eligible to compete in varsity meets as a freshman, Jesse participated in various open meets, exhibitions, and freshman contests in the spring of 1934. Twice he ran against Ralph Metcalfe, losing both times. On February 24 he first visited New York City for an indoor AAU tournament and did so well that he was asked back for a Knights of Columbus meet on St. Patrick's Day. A month later he was scheduled for an exhibition in Mansfield, Ohio, but had to withdraw because of a spiked ankle suffered in the final preparatory workout. Late in the spring he was forced to reflect upon his earlier decision to enroll at Ohio State rather than the University of Michigan, when the Wolverines came to Columbus for a varsity dual meet. Jesse sat in the stands and watched as Willis Ward and his mates won every event except the 2-mile run. Michigan almost doubled Ohio State in total points.[33]

Owens's exhibitions once upstaged a varsity meet. In Columbus on May 5, about 6,500 fans watched Ohio State defeat Notre Dame in a dual meet but left the stadium buzzing more about their freshman sensation than about the varsity. As a warmup, Jesse set a new Ohio record with 23 feet, $10\frac{3}{4}$ inches in the long jump. For his featured event, he ran 120 yards against the clock, with timers stationed at 90, 100, and 120 yards. At two of the three distances, he broke long-standing records. His 8.6 seconds at 90 yards cut two-tenths of a second off the mark set by Charles Paddock in 1921; his finish of 120 yards in 11.5 seconds topped the record held for many years by Howard Drew of Southern California. Larry Snyder arranged the stunt. As a suspicious black journalist put it, Snyder shrewdly used Owens "as a magnet" to attract crowds "to Ohio State's track carnivals, thus enabling the cinder-path team to earn a profit."[34]

But Larry Snyder was interested in much more than short-term profits. In Owens, he envisaged a golden future for his track program: Jesse would put Ohio State and Larry Snyder on the map. The potential benefits were mutual. In Snyder, Jesse found a new mentor, younger, less patriarchal, and more ambitious than Charles Riley. Once again the racial difference bore upon the athlete–coach relationship. Years later Owens remembered Snyder as "another white man who proved to me again that prejudice is a matter of choice, not coloring." Other black Buckeyes remember him differently—as a conservative man whose racial views had been forged in an earlier era, before any blacks wore the Ohio State colors.[35]

In truth, Snyder held a complex set of attitudes toward his black athletes. His opinions emerged in a debate fashionable among whites of that day, some of whom attempted to explain black athletic prowess in terms of physical and psychomotor factors that were supposedly unique to blacks. Typical of the era was a Cleveland doctor who examined the young Owens's body to see if an exceptional anatomical structure held the key to his speed and leaping abilities. He x-rayed the leg bones and carefully measured the arms, trunk, and legs, only to arrive at the sensible conclusion that Jesse's physical advantages derived from arduous training rather than racial inheritance. Speculative German scholars were not so sure of that. In true fascist form, they insisted that Negro athletic excellence resulted from "a certain conformation of their bones" and from high levels of animalistic horsepower generated by racially determined muscular energy.[36]

Those conjectures were not confined to German Nazi circles. With a characteristic touch of Social Darwinism, track coach Dean Cromwell of the University of Southern California argued that the Negro athlete excelled because he was "closer to the primitive" than the white athlete. "It was not so long ago that his ability to sprint and jump was a life-and-death matter to him in the jungle. His muscles are pliable, and his easy-going disposition is a valuable aid to the mental and physical relaxation that a runner and jumper must have." Cromwell recognized Charles Paddock, Eddie Tolan, Ralph Metcalfe, Percy Williams (a Canadian), and Jesse Owens as the five best sprinters of the day. "Practically all good sprinters," he observed, "are of the nervous, high-strung type."[37] Except for Paddock, all his examples were black.

Another notable track coach of the day, Lawson Robertson of the University of Pennsylvania, reasoned along the same thin line: "Nervous energy makes for great speed and explosive energy. These are racial assets of the Negro. The average Negro track and field athlete is built for speed. The legs are symmetrical, the muscles are tapering and seldom bunched." Jesse Owens's spectacular physique reduced Robertson's reflections from the general to the specific: "Owens has the finest pair of legs I have ever seen. They would inspire any sculptor." In all fairness, Jesse's best friends—black as well as white—often said much the same thing, in awe of Jesse's matchless physical gifts. But in the context of his times and his own assumptions, even Robertson's praise of Owens smacked of the old racial determinist argument.[38]

To his credit, Larry Snyder usually avoided such pseudoscientific explanations. In Jesse Owens he saw the finest athletic body imaginable but reasoned that it was the product of many years of hard training as well as chance inheritance. Snyder well knew that certain social forces were propelling black athletes to the forefront in the 1930s. Although still few in number, more blacks than ever before were in college, training under expert coaches. Moreover, black athletes of Jesse Owens's generation now had a few track stars to emulate. "They want to be another Tolan or Hubbard," Snyder reasoned. "If Tolan and Hubbard and Metcalfe can do it, they can do it, they figure."[39]

Yet for all his reasonableness, Larry Snyder shared with Dean Cromwell and Lawson Robertson the assumption that "the cell structure of the nervous system" was different in blacks and whites. For sprinters and long-jumpers, especially, a "strong stimulus, that energy released all at once, must come from an extra-sharp nervous impulse." Black athletes, Snyder believed, were ideally gifted with "a high tension system capable of carrying a strong stimulus to the muscles." Snyder could as well have been speaking about a thoroughbred race horse. In one sense, he was. He primarily had a thoroughbred in mind: Jesse Owens.[40]

Snyder's ambivalent racial opinions manifested themselves in his coaching style. During the spring of 1934 he had three blacks on his squad: the sprinter Fred Thomas, an upperclassman, and Owens and the high-jumper Mel Walker, both freshmen. Snyder happily attended to them because, as he later noted, they were easily coachable. Hungry for success, they followed instructions carefully, even if the instructions made no immediate sense. In other words, they obeyed orders without talking back. Although Snyder was always fair and tactful, he never let his blacks forget who they were and what he expected of them. They were his boys; he expected obedience. He and Jesse Owens got on famously.[41]

Within the final week of his freshman year, Owens competed in a Big Ten freshman meet in Columbus. He won all three of his events, and set new conference frosh marks in each: the 100-yard dash in 9.6 seconds, the 220-yard sprint in 21 seconds, and a long jump distance of 24 feet, 10 inches. Finally, after regional and national AAU meets during the second half of June, a Cleveland black newspaper reported that Jesse was shortly "expected home for the summer."[42]

☆ ☆ ☆

Home meant familiar food, mother's care, and long talks with sisters and brothers. But home, for Jesse, was not for lounging about. As he put it years later, "being in motion—moving—was always what made me tick. It's what made running so natural to me, those long hours and years of practice you have to put in. . . . I hated to sit or to stand still." He never could remain inactive for long; idleness made him edgy. So in July and August he eagerly served as the star attraction for several local picnics and sports carnivals organized by various political and church groups. Each night he returned to his old job at the gas pumps of Alonzo Wright's Sohio service station.[43]

Apparently his nocturnal activities involved more than pumping gas. In the veiled terms of one report, he was regularly distracted "by the spectacle of feminine pulchritude on parade" near the gas station. Just a couple of weeks before he returned to Ohio State, however, Jesse announced that he was getting married. According to the local press, he and Minnie Ruth Solomon had "kept company" for several years; now he was applying for a marriage license. Ruth planned to continue living with her parents and working in Cleveland while he returned to college. "She's going to stay home, work, and save some money, so that we'll have something when I get out of school," Jesse told a reporter. "Of course," he dutifully added, "I'm going to save all I can, too." But those plans for a late-summer marriage did not materialize. Impatiently, Ruth later announced that Jesse talked her out of marriage. Whatever the circumstances, he never returned to the marriage bureau to pick up the license. In early October he returned to begin his sophomore year at Ohio State, unattached.[44]

The autumn proved uneventful, and early in 1935 Jesse plunged enthusiastically into his varsity track career. First came the indoor season, from February through March, with the Buckeyes traveling to Chicago, Ann Arbor, Champaign, Indianapolis, and Bloomington for conference meets, and twice to New York City for special events in Madison Square Garden. On road trips, the team packed into three large old cars, a Sterns Knight, a Cadillac, and a Packard, each carrying seven passengers. For black Buckeyes, however, the physical fatigue of cramped, long trips did not compare with the emotional tensions generated upon arrival, when the white members of the team settled into a hotel while the blacks were shuttled off to the nearest YMCA. In liberal New York City, blacks were allowed to room at the Hotel Paramount with the rest of the team, but only on the second floor and with the proviso that they would use a freight elevator instead of the public passenger elevator.[45]

In New York Jesse found consolation in postmeet parties arranged by a former black track star, Dr. H. Binga Dismond. Recently divorced, the affluent Dr. Dismond catered to visiting black athletes ready to "bust loose" from the pressures of competition. Coach Larry Snyder liked the arrangement. "Put on your glad rags and get going," he told Owens. "This is your night." Dismond provided girls for the occasions. As friends recall the scene, Jesse always paired off with a neat, attractive girl, not particularly the best-looking one available for the evening. "Why don't you take pretty girls?" one friend asked. "Yeah, you take your pretty girls *out*," Jesse replied, "but I take mine *to bed*." The friend remembers simply that Owens was "a champ" at partying as well as running.[46]

At his Big Ten varsity debut in Bloomington on February 9, Owens won three of his four events, finishing second in the 70-yard high hurdles. A week later at the University of Illinois, he finished first in all four events he entered. But as Ohio State had no indoor training facilities, Jesse occasionally faltered. At Ann Arbor Willis Ward trounced him in the 60-yard dash, the high hurdles, and the long jump. At Madison Square Garden a month later, Ben Johnson of Columbia University edged him in the finals of the 60-yard dash. Still, in the semifinals Jesse had finally got the best of the famous Ralph Metcalfe for the first time. Somewhat prematurely the Cleveland *Gazette* crowed that its local hero had now seized "the mantle worn by Ralph Metcalfe as the greatest of all track and field athletes."[47]

Metcalfe had seemed invincible. Despite his notoriously slow start, he had dominated the sprint events since the retirement of Eddie Tolan from amateur competition in 1932. Just a month prior to his first defeat by Owens, Metcalfe finished second in an indoor meet in Morgantown, West Virginia, prompting one reporter to predict that he would probably "not taste defeat again this season."[48] That prediction proved wrong, but not because Metcalfe had lost any speed. Rather, he was now being overtaken by three swift and eager college sophomores, Owens, Ben Johnson, and Eulace Peacock.

Next to Owens, Peacock posed the greatest challenge. Born in 1914 in Dothan, Alabama, he had moved north with his family to Union, New Jersey, about the same time the Owens family moved from Alabama to Cleveland. While Jesse concentrated on track, Eulace starred as a halfback on his high school football team and as a strong sprinter and long jumper in track. In the same year that Owens enrolled at Ohio State, Peacock went to Temple University intending to play football for the famous Glenn "Pop" Warner, who had just come to Temple from Stanford, and to run track for coach Ben Ogden. But Ogden forbade the dual involvement. He saw Peacock as a natural long jumper, but as a sprinter in need of much practice to achieve quick starts and relaxed leg and arm motion. Like Metcalfe, Tolan, and Paddock, Peacock was what Dean Cromwell called a "driver" rather than a "floater" on the cinders. He relied on strength, not smoothness.[49]

Vastly different in style, Peacock and Owens ran remarkably even in head-to-head competition during the indoor track season of 1935. They alternately beat each other in the 60-yard dash and long jump. Once the outdoor season began, they went their separate ways to different meets. Their parity continued at a distance. In late April, on the very same day that Owens won the long jump and 100-yard dash at the Drake Relays, Peacock did the same in the Penn Relays. Their paths would cross frequently within the next year.[50]

Just before the Drake Relays, Larry Snyder arranged for Jesse to perform another of his exhibition stunts for a small gathering of Ohio State students and local newspapermen. Beginning his run twenty yards or so behind the starting mark for the 100-yard dash, Owens was going full speed when he reached the point of being timed. Three watches clocked him at 8.4 seconds over the hundred yards. The feat was widely publicized, stirring spectator interest in Columbus. Two weeks later 12,000 people turned out to witness a dual meet between Ohio

State and Notre Dame, in which Jesse won all his three events. "Owens' popularity here," reported a Cleveland sportswriter, "can hardly be overestimated."[51]

Local popularity turned to international fame a month later at the Big Ten Championship meet in Ann Arbor. The day was May 25, 1935. To the astonishment of track-and-field enthusiasts everywhere, Owens broke three world records and tied one within the span of a single hour. His feat was all the more startling because each of the records had been on the books for several years. Since 1924 the name of Roland A. Locke of the University of Nebraska had stood at the head of the list of all 220-yard sprinters; Owens replaced it with a performance of 20.3 seconds. His long jump of 26 feet, $8\frac{1}{4}$ inches toppled the mark set by a Japanese athlete, Chuhel Nambu, in 1931. In his normally weakest event, the 220-yard low hurdles, Jesse's 22.6 seconds surpassed the standard long held jointly by C. R. Brookins of Iowa State and Norman Paul of the University of Southern California. Finally, his time of 9.4 seconds in the 100-yard dash tied the world record held since 1930 by the Californian Frank Wykoff. An observation by a Cleveland reporter is altogether believable: "The 12,000 spectators were alternately stunned into silence and then moved to tremendous salvos of applause when the Buckeye ace staged his almost unbelievable show."[52]

Most of those spectators were unaware that Jesse's show was almost canceled before it began. In a mini-drama that was to become an integral part of the saga of the poor boy overcoming adversity, he arrived in Ann Arbor with his back extremely sore from an injury sustained several days earlier. According to some reports, he had wrenched his back in a touch football game; others said he had fallen awkwardly down some steps while horseplaying with friends. Whatever the cause of the injury, it placed in jeopardy Jesse's chance to compete, much less to excel. Only several soakings in a tub of hot water loosened him up enough to qualify in the preliminary trials. Then the back stiffened again, requiring heat pads and rubdowns intermittently throughout the night. Fortunately, the day of the finals broke bright and sunny, the first really warm day of the spring.[53]

Some of Jesse's teammates think "the bad back story" has been overdone in order to romanticize his struggle against the odds. Arguably the injury worked to his advantage. As only an athlete knows, an injury forces him to concentrate, to reach within himself for strength, making opponents and spectators irrelevant. That was Owens's experience at Ann Arbor. Years later he confided to an interviewer that once he warmed up and got into position for his first sprint, he "ran the entire day without a pain anywhere." Best of all, his timing seemed perfect that day, better than on any other day of his life. "I was off with the gun. My knees were working perfectly, my arms were synchronized with my legs. The body position that we worked so hard for was there." Adrenaline carried him.[54]

The two glamor events, the long jump and the 100-yard dash, attracted the most attention. As the long-jump pit stood directly in front of the stands, every eye in the stadium was on Owens as he dramatically asked a friend to place a handkerchief at the 26-foot mark. Without apparent strain, he charged swiftly down the runway and left the board with a strong kick, soaring several inches beyond the handkerchief. That one jump was enough for the world record. Jesse refrained from jumping again in order to protect his back from further strain.[55]

Cautious officials probably robbed him of a new world record in the 100-yard dash. The starter, W. J. Manilaw, required runners to hold their "set" position for at least two seconds as a means of preventing a "flyer" from beating the gun. Greater difficulty came from conservative timers. Today a runner is clocked when he breaks the tape; in the 1930s the "center of gravity" customarily had to cross the line before the timer pressed his stopwatch. The head timer at Ann Arbor, Philip Diamond, was even more demanding. "Watch for the back foot," he instructed his crew of timers; "see it cross the finish line, and then press the old forefinger." His reason was simple: "If a new record shows on the watch dial, you can be sure the former record holder was given a fair deal." A fair deal indeed. For Jesse's 100-yard sprint at Ann Arbor, all three official timers stopped their watches between 9.3 and 9.4 seconds, with all three nearer the lower time. But the fashion of that day called for the higher tenth of a second to stand. Rightly did one witness recall, almost twenty years later, that "Owens' performance that day was even greater than we now officially recognize."[56]

Although the general public remembers Jesse Owens primarily because of his dramatic victories at Berlin in 1936, knowledgeable track people still look to Ann Arbor, May 5, 1935, as the greatest single day in the history of track and field.[57]

☆   ☆   ☆

White-haired Charles Riley sat in the stands that day, shedding a few tears of joy over Jesse's success. After the final event, he saw his protégé mobbed by admirers on his way to the dressing room. Jesse showered and dressed quickly, then climbed out through a back window in order to avoid more autograph-seekers. Behind the stadium, Riley had his Model T Ford cranked and ready to go. They drove most of the night to arrive at Owens's home in Cleveland early Sunday morning.[58]

Shortly after breakfast, proud neighbors and friends began dropping by to offer congratulations for the feats that were making the front page in all the Sunday papers. Reporters came for interviews. "Well," asked one, "how does it feel to be the world's fastest human?" In an answer worthy of the satirical Oscar Wilde at his best, the young Owens replied innocently, "I think the praise is a little too high." At noon he was rescued once again from the crowds by his mentor, who took him to the Riley home in Lakewood for a quiet Sunday dinner.[59]

The Ann Arbor achievements brought more than acclaim to the Owens family. When reporters discovered and publicized the fact that Henry Owens was still without a job, offers poured in from all quarters—from the Mayor of Cleveland, from the manager of the local Sears Roebuck store, and from the owner of Loews' Theatre chain. Finally the elder Owens, now nearly sixty years of age, accepted a menial but easy permanent position at the Rockwell garage of the Cleveland Electric Illuminating Company.[60]

Having completed his second year at Ohio State, Jesse momentarily rested on his laurels. They were many. His few defeats had merely spurred him on to greater heights, culminating in his pinnacle of success at Ann Arbor. Now he received word of his election as captain of the Ohio State track squad for the next year, making him the first black ever to captain a team in the Big Ten. Only one dark cloud hung over his past

year's efforts. His classroom work toward his physical education degree remained unsatisfactory. Although he had taken
the easiest courses he could find, avoiding tough science and
mathematics requirements, he had still not done well. He concentrated better on athletics than on books. Especially during
the winter and spring terms, when he was often on the road and
always under pressure to perform athletically, his grades suffered.[61]

At home for a week in the early summer of 1935, he was
momentarily free of academic pressures. His mind turned to
happier subjects. Ruth Solomon and three-year-old Gloria required attention. Important athletic events lay in the future.
On the immediate horizon was a team trip to California; at a
year's distance were the Olympic Games in Berlin. Despite bad
grades, the future seemed bright, the shadows insubstantial.

CHAPTER 4

Coping with Pressure

AT ANN ARBOR ON MAY 25, 1935, Jesse Owens ceased being merely a promising young athlete. Now he was accomplished; his name was in the record books. Never again would he be able to compete casually and anonymously. He now had a reputation to maintain. Henceforward he would be a marked man, expected by sportswriters, opponents, and spectators to run faster and leap farther than before. Every outing would be a highly publicized test. "People come out to see you perform," Owens recalled years later, "and you've got to give them the best that you have within you on that particular day." The Ann Arbor victories represented promise fulfilled; they also intensified the spotlight, raised the level of expectations, and increased the pressure on the twenty-year-old Owens.[1]

Off the track, too, his life suddenly became "more serious" after Ann Arbor, like "living in a glass bowl." As coach Larry Snyder reminded him, athletic success meant "an obligation to fulfill." Taking up a theme emphasized earlier by Cleveland teachers, principals, and coaches, Snyder urged Jesse to translate his athletic fame into a socially useful model of proper behavior, wholesome attitudes, and good interracial relations. "He was constantly on me," Owens later recalled, "about the job that I was to do and the responsibility that I had upon the campus. And how I must be able to carry myself because people were looking." Not only was Owens expected to be a great athlete, bringing honor to his city, state, and university; he was also expected to be an exemplar, "a credit to his race." As Jesse remembered the pressure, "Everybody's eyes were upon you. And they would scrutinize everything that you did and so you had to be very careful of the things that you did."[2]

But the young Owens was no more careful than most college sophomores. As he packed his bags for a western tour with the Ohio State team in early June 1935, he didn't know he would face a series of crises within the next several months. Some were caused by his own indiscretion and poor judgment, others by bad advice and circumstances beyond his control. From one tense situation to another, his character and budding reputation would be severely tested.

The team stopped over in Chicago for an open meet, then traveled on by train to Los Angeles. On June 14–15 it competed in a dual meet against the University of California. Jesse took first place in all four of his events, but Southern Cal won the meet, 9–6 (with only first places counting). On the following weekend the Buckeyes were in Berkeley, competing before 18,000 spectators in the NCAA championships. Again Jesse won his four events, scoring forty of his team's forty and one-fifth points, but yet again Larry Snyder's squad lost to Dean Cromwell's strong USC team. Just five days later, at the Far Western AAU meet in San Diego, Owens beat Eulace Peacock in both the 100-meter dash and the long jump. Within a span of two weeks he had competed in ten events and had taken first place in every one.[3]

Disappointed that he failed to break any records, California sportswriters nevertheless raved over their first exposure to Owens's relaxed, graceful style. In Los Angeles he seemed, to one reporter, to win "so easily that it was hard to believe what your eyes told you." His technique over the low hurdles left something to be desired, but it scarcely mattered: "Jesse doesn't bother to skim the barriers, he just soars over 'em." Most impressive of all was the timing of his efforts. In preliminary heats he paced himself, saving his energy for the finals "when it really meant something." Foy Draper of Southern Cal beat him in one of the trial heats in the 100-yard dash; in the finals, Owens finished first, Draper fourth. Jesse's uncanny ability to rise to the occasion stamped itself indelibly on the memory of his opponents and friends.[4]

So did his crowd appeal. At all his California meets, he was mobbed by hero-worshipers, "a tidal wave of Owens rooters," according to one journalist. One little girl got his autograph, and her friend was reaching out for one just as a policeman whisked them away. The one without an autograph was heard to say, "Well, I got to touch him anyway." In order to avoid the crush of the crowds, when Jesse made his last run or jump, he kept on going into the locker room.[5]

His failure to evade the charms of a Los Angeles socialite, Quincella Nickerson, set in motion a chain of events that ultimately led to marriage. Miss Nickerson, the daughter of an affluent insurance and real estate man, appeared at a picture-taking session on the first day the Ohio State team worked out briskly before its first meet. She and Jesse "got to talking," as he put it years later, and she invited him to her home for dinner. He got on well with her two brothers, who were keenly interested in athletics and with her father, who was no doubt interested in his daughter's future. After practice each afternoon, she picked Jesse up in her new convertible. Occasionally Jesse's friend Mel Walker, the only other black making the trip with the Ohio State team, went along for the ride. But the evenings were Jesse's and Quincella's alone, partying and dancing from one night spot to another.[6]

They made a dazzling couple. He was athletically trim, handsomely dressed, and famous; she was black and beautiful, immaculately attired, and infatuated. Her father paid their bills, putting Jesse in touch with a classiness he had never known. Not surprisingly, photographers dogged their heels, once catching them in a cuddle, another time snapping them looking at wedding rings in a jewelry store. Years later Jesse insisted that the entire episode "was blown out of all proportion." Perhaps it was, but rumors of an engagement quickly traversed the continent, making front page copy in the black press in the East. Calling attention to the stories was a huge picture of the two supposed lovers, she snuggling close with an arm around his shoulder. "So important is this man," the editor of the Cleveland *Call and Post* commented, "that his love affairs have become front page news in the daily papers."[7]

Minnie Ruth Solomon's injured pride quickly turned to anger. A patient woman, she now had been pushed too far. She wrote to Jesse immediately, threatening to sue for breach of promise. The letter arrived just as the Ohio State team was finishing its last California meet. At the time Jesse was rooming with fellow Buckeye Charles Beetham, with whom he remained in California for a couple of days—along with several other athletes from the East—before taking a train to Lincoln, Nebraska, for another track meet. Mildly concerned, the young Owens dismissed the threat as he showed the letter to friends.[8]

But the issue would not die. Upon arriving in Lincoln on the eve of the AAU championships, Owens had a long-distance telephone call awaiting him. Ruth Solomon had a few choice words to say. Only she now knows the gist of that conversation, and she understandably refuses to divulge it. More sobering still for Jesse, early the next morning he was met by a representative of a Cleveland newspaper, who had traveled all the way from Cleveland with an unambiguous proposition: that either Owens marry Ruth Solomon or a picture of their child would be published on the front page of the weekend edition. When Jesse took the field that day, July 4, 1935, he was a shaken young man.[9]

He performed miserably. In front of 15,000 spectators in the University of Nebraska's Memorial Stadium, he finished behind both Eulace Peacock and Ralph Metcalfe in the 100 meters. Then Peacock beat him again in the long jump. A columnist for the *Los Angeles Times*, having been highly impressed with Owens's easy, fluid style during his sweep of California, conjectured that "Jesse wasn't at his best" in Nebraska because he had been overworked on the West Coast: "Running all those heats in three events of previous meets took the fine edge off." He was half right: Jesse had been overworked on the West coast, but not on the track. At any rate, his problem in Lincoln was mental, not physical. His distractions made him uncharacteristically tight. According to one close observer, he showed "marked tension in his entire upper body" throughout the meet. Nor did the tensions abate at the meet's end. Not in a festive mood, Jesse spent a restless Fourth of July night in Lincoln.[10]

Early the next morning he boarded a train for Cleveland. Arriving in the late afternoon, a Friday, he made his way to Ruth's home by taxi. They called the marriage license clerk, Frank Zizelman, from his dinner to obtain the necessary legal papers. Before the marriage license could be issued, however, Zizelman, Jesse, and Ruth had to hurry over to the home of a probate judge, Nelson Brewer, to persuade him to issue a waiver of Ohio's law that required a wait of five days. Nothing came easy. Ruth's minister was not in town, so she turned to the assistant minister, the Reverend Ernest Hall, to perform the ceremony. Hall was busy with choir rehearsal, and refused to cut it short. Finally, in the middle of the evening of July 5, 1935, the marriage rite was performed in the living room of Ruth's parents.[11]

Quincella Nickerson had had her fling, but won no ring. At least not a wedding ring from Jessie Owens. She later married and moved to San Diego. According to Jesse's later reminiscences, whenever he was in California "she and her husband" would drive to wherever he was for a visit. In 1935, though, "Minnie Ruth Solomon won the Cupid's Sweepstakes, walking off with the prize, a yearling, one Jesse Owens," commented the Cleveland Call and Post with heavy-handed humor. "Quincella of the Los Angeles Nickersons finished out of the money. A baseball scorer would be forced to credit the California lass with an assist, for she certainly helped no end in Jess making up his mind to enter the Matrimonial Derby."[12]

Jesse and Ruth spent their wedding night at her parent's home at 9118 Beckman Avenue, a deadend street. But not for long would the yearling remain in the stable. Early the next morning he went alone by train to Buffalo to compete in the New York Police Club Games. Within the week he was in New York City, then up at Crystal Beach, Ontario, for more track meets. He had tied the knot, but never would he be tied down.[13]

☆ ☆ ☆

At all three of those track meets in the week after his wedding, Owens lost to the hard-charging Eulace Peacock in the 100-yard dash. Those defeats, added to the dismal day in Lincoln, meant that within a two-week period Peacock had beaten Jesse five straight times. The press made much of Peacock's emergence. "Swing wide the gates for a new sports hero," a columnist for the *Los Angeles Times* announced just after the Lincoln debacle. Although Owens's prospects could not be easily dismissed, it now appeared that he and Peacock would be "the Metcalfe–Tolan combination for 1936."[14]

Fully a year ahead, conjectures flourished over Owens's and Peacock's prospects for the forthcoming Berlin Olympics. The former Olympian Charles Paddock, Jesse's childhood idol, publicly placed his bet on Peacock. Unaware of Jesse's personal problems, Paddock thought he seemed "pretty well burned out." As that negative assessment from distant California made the rounds through the wire services in the East, the Cleveland press entered the debate in defense of its hometown boy. Peacock's recent string of victories came as no surprise, insisted the editor of the *Call and Post,* because Owens and Peacock were too evenly matched for either of them to win "every time they meet." The *Call and Post* had long recognized Peacock's excellence. His emergence now simply meant that he and Owens would probably lead a strong contingent of black athletes to Berlin a year hence.[15]

The Berlin games were far from Owens's mind when he returned home in mid-July to Ruth and their daughter in the Solomon home. The future Olympic immortal once again pumped gas on the night shift at Wright's Sohio station and occasionally officiated at local playground meets. Before he returned to Ohio State in the fall, his past rather than his future became an issue, thrusting him into a controversy that had much more to do with politics than with athletics. Ohio party politics, university athletic department politics, and Amateur Athletic Union politics all came to bear on the case. Caught in a squeeze among many conflicting interests, Owens's athletic future hung in the balance for several months. At issue was his "job" as a page boy in the Ohio House of Representatives, which provoked AAU officials to suspect that he had broken the strict amateur code espoused by the AAU. Salary received for a legitimate job was acceptable; money accepted without services rendered was not. Suspension—athletic ineligibility—was the penalty for willfully violating this code.[16]

Coming to the surface in August 1935, the problem had originated eight months earlier, when Owens had relinquished his job as a service elevator operator for an easier, better-paying, more socially respectable assignment as a page boy in the State House. This political appointment came largely from the patronage of the Governor's executive secretary, Dan Duffey, a seasoned Cleveland politican who had obtained his own position by having successfully managed Governor Davey's campaign in Cuyahoga County (Cleveland). One of Owens's sisters had served under Duffey as a ward captain, and she in turn approached him once he was in Columbus to request that her brother be made a page in the lower house. Duffey placed the proposal before the Governor, who routinely approved it. Such appointments were common, especially for Ohio State athletes. Requiring little time or effort, the job paid three dollars a day plus expenses for travel on matters of state interest. The latter clause was interpreted liberally: Jesse had his expenses paid to and from California with a check drawn on the state treasury in the early summer of 1935.[17]

Even that bogus travel allowance would not have alarmed the watchdogs of the AAU had Jesse not been made a page *ad interim* for the summer months of 1935. As the regular session of the Legislature drew to a close in June, Jesse's sister once again approached Duffey, urging that Jesse be one of the twenty or so young men assigned to summer committees. Pages *ad interim* drew salaries of twenty-one dollars a week but were required to be in Columbus only if and when their committees met. Because of Jesse's full athletic schedule through mid-July, no one really expected him to return to the State House until the autumn.[18]

Made privately, these arrangements came to public attention when a member of the Legislature introduced a resolution to make Owens an "honorary" page in recognition of his achievements, which meant paying him a stipend without requiring him to serve. The wording of the resolution proved important to the case once the AAU began its investigation:

Whereas, Jesse Owens . . . has distinguished himself and the General Assembly by his remarkable world record breaking achievements in track and is recognized as the greatest track athlete in the country, be it resolved that Owens is hereby appointed honorary page . . . to serve from the sine die adjournment until the Fall session of the legislature.[19]

Apparently a generous gesture, the resolution blew the cover off a prior measure that was marginally acceptable by the amateur standards of the day. The sponsor of the resolution was Grant Ward, a former football coach and director of intramurals at Ohio State. His impolitic motion stirred rumors of base motives. Some accused Ward of seeking to win black votes for himself by posing as Jesse's benefactor. Others thought he was using Owens to get at L. W. St. John, the Ohio State athletic director, with whom Ward had long been at odds. Ward reportedly wanted St. John ousted and to replace him as athletic director. To expose Jesse Owens under the pretense of honoring him seemed, to Ward's critics, a devious way "to discredit folks at Ohio State, posing all the time as being tremendously interested in Ohio State athletes and athletic affairs."[20]

If it was a ruse, it almost worked—to Owens's great detriment. An anonymous individual in Columbus immediately reported the case to Judge Jeremiah T. Mahoney, the tough president of the AAU. Once again politics extraneous to Owens threatened his future. Bad feelings existed between Ohio State and AAU officials. Recently St. John had infuriated the AAU as chairman of a Basketball Rules Committee jointly representing the AAU and the NCAA by restructuring the committee to give the NCAA the larger representation. Now Ohio State officials feared that the Owens case would serve as an occasion for revenge. Their fears seemed warranted when Mahoney ordered an investigation by the Northeastern Ohio AAU Eligibility Committee.[21]

On August 12 the committee summoned Jesse and Dan Duffey to appear before it and to explain the terms of the honorary page appointment. Jesse admitted to having received $159 between June 9 and July 31 without ever going back to Columbus. He insisted, however, that he had conferred with his Ohio State coaches before accepting the appointment, and that they had advised him to take it. Duffey conceded that the case looked suspicious, but he maintained that it was neither unique nor illegal. Fortunately, he could report in all honesty that the summer legislative committee to which Jesse had been assigned had not yet convened in any special session.[22]

Fortunately for Owens, the hearing was held in Cleveland, with several Cleveland AAU members present. Officially they represented the amateur principles of the AAU; emotionally their sympathy lay with their hometown hero. "He is a Cleveland boy," one member of the committee explained. "I have know him for eight years, and in that time I have never known Jesse Owens to do anything that really discredits him." In the committee's deliberations, Jesse's recent controversial marriage came up only to be dismissed as having no pertinence to "the situation at hand." From the evidence presented, the committee reported to the national office of the AAU that Jesse Owens's amateur status was "not in doubt." "We fail to find that Owens is paid because of his athletic ability."[23]

Emerging from that meeting somber but optimistic, Jesse told a reporter that he would return the $159 to the state in order to protect his amateur standing. Twice in September the Northeastern Ohio AAU convened again to consider further evidence. Uneasy Big Ten and American Olympic Committee officials, fearing the loss of their most attractive performer, kept abreast of the proceedings. Finally in early December the AAU rendered an indecisive judgment: that Owens had acted unwisely but not in willful contempt of AAU rules. As one AAU spokesman concluded, "Knowing the facts as we do, we have considered Owens to be a victim of circumstances and offended, rather than offending against any of the provisions of the AAU."[24]

Whether Jesse was a victim or an offender, his case exemplified a larger, more pervasive problem afflicting American intercollegiate athletics in the 1930s. In a tradition uniquely American, zealous alumni and local partisans secretly gave money, clothes, and occasionally even automobiles to college athletes. When caught in the act, they either covered their tracks or shrewdly rationalized their bending of the rules. Some institutions quietly waived tuition and room-and-board fees, especially for football players, the unrivaled aristocrats of the college campus. When the Owens case first became public, Big Ten Commissioner John L. Griffith pompously announced, "I do not know of any Big Ten athletes who get a salary without working for it, and I do not think Owens does." But not a single college coach came forward with such a myopic pronouncement.[25]

Scarcely was the Owens case closed when, in late December 1935, the annual gathering of the NCAA debated a resolution introduced by the football-mad Southeastern Conference to make athletic scholarships legal. The purpose of the proposal was by no means to entice athletes to rich institutions. The "scholarships" would be equal in size and uniformly limited in number for all colleges and universities. Certainly the intent was not primarily to reward athletes for their arduous efforts. Rather, athletic scholarships, it was believed, would regulate the shady deals and sham jobs provided by coaches and athletic boosters.[26]

Unfortunately, no athletic scholarship was available for Jesse Owens's generation of track athletes. For receiving $159 from the state of Ohio in the summer of 1935, he had his wrist slapped by the AAU.

☆ ☆ ☆

In October Jesse left Ruth and Gloria in Cleveland with the Solomons and returned to Columbus to begin his junior year at Ohio State. With his marital status settled, and without the constant demands of track practice and meets, he now had an opportunity to redeem himself in the classroom. But once again he struggled unsuccessfully against distractions. The controversy with the AAU dragged on throughout the term. Worse still, in the late autumn of 1935 athletes all over the United States had come under a barrage of arguments, pleas, and shrill demands for them to join a boycott of the 1936 Olympics, scheduled to be held in Germany. Because of his prominence, Owens could not avoid the issue.[27]

The origins of the boycott movement went back to 1933, when Adolph Hitler, shortly after seizing control of the German government, began setting in place his discriminatory policies against German Jews. One of his first measures was to bar Jews from all German sports clubs and public sports facilities, thus effectively excluding them from Olympic participation. At that time Jesse Owens was a senior in his Cleveland high school. During his first quarter at Ohio State, AAU delegates voted overwhelmingly to withhold American athletes from the 1936 Games unless the Nazis altered their policies against German Jewish athletes "in fact as well as in theory." But the American Olympic Committee was of another mind. Committed to the principles of peaceful international competition as espoused by the idealistic founder of the modern quadrennial games, Baron Pierre de Coubertin, they adamantly opposed mixing politics and sport.

In 1934 and 1935 several leaders of the American Olympic Committee went to Germany to see for themselves if Nazi anti-Semitic policies were as bad as depicted in the American press. For each visit, a Nazi host adroitly controlled the investigation. Each visitor gave Germany high marks for orderliness, relative prosperity in the midst of the world depression, and reasonable adherence to the spirit of Olympism. One of those visitors was Avery Brundage, a proud, self-made millionaire and forceful president of the American Olympic Committee. Upon his return to the United States, Brundage persuaded his colleagues to place themselves on record as supporting American participation in the forthcoming winter Olympics in Garmisch-Partenkirchen and the summer Olympics in Berlin.[28]

Yet the debate continued to simmer, heating to a boiling point after Hitler issued his famous Nuremberg Laws on September 15, 1935, depriving German Jews of their citizenship and equal protection under the law. American Jewish organizations rose up *en masse* to accuse Brundage and his committee of political naïveté, insensitivity, and lightly veiled anti-Semitism. Nor did American Jews stand alone in their opposition to the "Nazi Olympics." From all quarters, Protestant and Catholic Churches, labor unions, city councils, and civic groups insisted that American athletes should not honor the Nazis with their presence in 1936.

The black press saw more than anti-Semitism at stake in the issue. Black editors were quick to remind their readers that German Jews were by no means the only non-Aryans suffering under the heel of Nazi racism. Blacks in Germany—mostly African troops from World War I who had remained in the Ruhr Valley, married to German women—also suffered legal and social discrimination because they failed the test of Nordic purity. More physically visible than Jews, blacks were all the more vulnerable. Several large antifascist rallies were held near Jesse Owens's home in Cleveland in 1934 and 1935.[29]

The rhetoric at those gatherings reflected the source of black ambivalence toward the Olympic boycott. Orators castigated racist attitudes and practices as being no less fascist in the United States than in Nazi Germany. The black press joined the chorus, indicting boycott spokesmen for their concern for fair treatment of minority groups abroad while making little effort to stop lynchings, racial segregation, and even athletic apartheid at home. Why all the furor over the possibility that the Nazis might not allow Jews on their Olympic team? Not a single black could be found on major league baseball or football teams, and pitifully few on university teams. In unison the black press concluded that the boycott movement contained a strong element of hypocrisy on the part of American whites. In aligning themselves for or against the boycott, however, black editors parted company. Some supported the boycott as a means of protesting racism "in its every manifestation." Others looked eagerly toward the Berlin games as an opportunity for black athletes to display their prowess, thus striking a blow against both German and American racial arrogance.[30]

The spotlight inevitably fell on the black athlete and his intentions. If an American team went to Berlin, would he join it? In late August 1935, the *New York Amsterdam News* addressed an open letter to all would-be Olympians, urging them not to go. But older editors were not speaking the young athlete's language. Athletes who had trained for years would now scarcely forgo the opportunity to compete in the international arena. The politics of the situation meant little to them. They wanted merely to go to Berlin, beat the Germans and all the others, and proudly claim their laurels. In several interviews with the press, black athletes overwhelmingly affirmed their determination to compete in Berlin if they made the American team.[31]

In early November, however, Owens publicly announced during a radio interview that "if there is discrimination against minorities in Germany then we must withdraw from the Olympics." When Larry Snyder heard about the statement, he immediately advised Jesse to refrain from taking any position on the issue. Word of Snyder's intervention leaked out, provoking a group of concerned citizens to visit his office and urge him not to apply a "gag rule" on Owens. They were wasting their breath. "Jesse Owens is sitting on top of the world today," Snyder impatiently explained. "If he continues to participate in this activity he will be a forgotten man." He then unwittingly turned the dominant complaint of the black press on its head: Jesse Owens and other black athletes had not been invited to the forthcoming Sugar Bowl meet in New Orleans, but no one was suggesting that those games be canceled. "Why should we oppose Germany for doing something that we do right here at home?"[32]

Jesse's two hometown black weeklies, the *Gazette* and the *Call and Post*, remained in opposition even after the AAU narrowly decided, on December 8, 1935, to reverse its earlier decision to keep American athletes away from Berlin. Fully a month after the AAU's capitulation, the editor of the *Call and Post* protested that Cleveland's young star should still "stay away from the Olympic games which are being staged this year by the world's outstanding criminal gang, the Nazis."[33] Never having taken the advice of his hometown press very seriously, Jesse was not now ready to start.

Just before the end of the year 1935, he took two severe body blows from other quarters, both related to the tensions of the past several months. In early December he received word from the headquarters of the AAU that his name had been removed from the list of ten finalists for the prestigious Sullivan Memorial Award, honoring the year's best amateur athletes, because of his dubious employment as an honorary page during the summer. Shortly thereafter his case was dismissed by the AAU, but too late for him to be reconsidered by the Sullivan committee. There was slight consolation in his being named to three places on the All-American track and field team selected by *Spalding's Athletic Almanac* for 1935.[34]

Worse still was the news that arrived in Owens's mailbox a few days after Christmas from the office of the registrar at Ohio State University. In the fall quarter Jesse had done poorly again in his class work. He had failed a psychology course outright. He would therefore be academically ineligible for the forthcoming winter indoor track season and would have to bring up his grades in the second quarter even to be eligible for the outdoor season.[35] As Jesse Owens celebrated the New Year, 1936, memories of his sterling athletic moments of the past year mingled with the traumas of more recent personal crises, hard decisions, and disappointments.

☆ ☆ ☆

While he fretted over his ineligibility and trained as best he could without the impetus of indoor meets, his friends teased him for his appearance in Ripley's nationally syndicated comic page feature "Believe It or Not." On January 21, 1936, Ripley featured the record-breaking 8.4 seconds in the 100-yard dash (with a 20-yard running start) set in a stunt performance the previous spring. That item turned out to be a good omen, for 1936 was destined to be Jesse's year of unbelievable success and fame. Few other signs pointed in that direction during the early months of the year. Restless with his enforced inactivity, Jesse one day borrowed a car from a friend for a weekend visit home to Cleveland. In Mansfield, Ohio, he was arrested for speeding and reckless driving. He pleaded guilty to both charges and was fined.[36]

Even two road trips to indoor track meets turned out badly, marred by ugly scenes of racial discrimination. Although he was ineligible to compete, Owens went with the team to the University of Indiana at Bloomington. On the return home he and the two other blacks on the team were refused admission to a restaurant in Richmond, Indiana. His friend, David Albritton, wanted to fight the proprietor. "Now Pappa," Owens reportedly cautioned, "just take it easy." Jesse's own patience was tested on yet another excursion into Indiana. On the way to the Butler Indoor Relays in Indianapolis—an "open" meet in which Owens could compete—he and his black friends were forbidden to enter a roadside café. They waited in the car for white teammates to bring them food, only to have the enraged owner of the café come out hollering that he didn't want "to feed no niggers" on his premises. Once again the pugnacious Albritton threatened retaliation, and once again Owens talked him out of it.[37]

One of Jesse's finest gestures came in an indoor track meet a week later at Cleveland's Public Hall. For the first time since his disastrous string of defeats during the previous summer, he and Eulace Peacock lined up with two other sprinters for the finals of the 50-yard dash. From crudely built starting blocks, all four men burst away at the gun. In the words of one journalist, Jesse left his blocks "with the grace and poise of a deer," but Peacock's starting block slipped, almost throwing him to the floor. He recovered his balance, but was so far behind that he simply stopped and watched as Jesse easily won the race. When Owens saw what had happened, he trotted back to Peacock (by now a close friend as well as his keenest competitor), insisting that they run the race again. After a brief rest and a repaired starting block, Peacock finished in 5.5 seconds, inches ahead of Owens. About 6,000 hometown fans saw that race, in which Jesse won more respect than he had ever won in his many previous victories.[38]

Although momentarily sidelined from varsity track competition, Jesse Owens was a name readily recognized by black youths everywhere. As his period of ineligibility drew to a close, he was invited by the Supervisor of Negro Schools in West Virginia to visit ten high schools and four colleges in the state, speaking to students during National Negro Health Week, March 29–April 5. In addition to those engagements, he also extolled the virtues of physical fitness in four radio addresses of fifteen minutes each in Charleston, Huntington, Bluefield, and Fairmount.[39]

Larry Snyder accompanied Jesse on the tour, supervising his daily workouts in preparation for the outdoor track season. Owens was still "in scholastic troubles," as the *Chicago Defender* tactfully phrased it, but Jesse's grades came up enough to make him eligible for the spring quarter. For his Olympic ambitions, of course, top-flight competition was imperative, especially as he had been largely inactive since the previous summer. His place on the Olympic team was by no means assured. Of his six major races since July 4, 1935, he had lost five, all to Eulace Peacock.[40]

The gods dealt cruelly with Peacock. At the Penn Relays on April 24–25, Jesse's first important outing of the year, Peacock suffered an injury that prevented his even making the Olympic team, much less winning one or two of the gold medals that in all probability would have been his. For several days prior to the event, the press promoted the meet as a clash of titans:

Peacock versus Owens. Unfortunately, Peacock never made it to the finals. Having suffered a leg injury in a tour of Italy late in the summer of 1935 just after he had trounced Owens in four straight meets, he had entered the 1936 season ten pounds over his normal running weight of 179 pounds, which to begin with was heavy for a sprinter slightly less than six feet tall. Only a month before the Penn Relays, Peacock's heavily-muscled legs had carried him to his last indoor victory over Owens. Now they failed him.[41]

In a preliminary heat for the 400-meter relays, Peacock received the baton as the anchor man, with his team far behind. He put on a tremendous burst of speed, but about fifteen yards from the finish he grabbed his right leg and hobbled in behind the winner. Some journalists reported a leg cramp, others a strained muscle. Peacock knew better. He had snapped a hamstring. From Franklin Field he went directly to the Temple University Hospital, where he stayed several days undergoing physical therapy. As 40,000 spectators watched the finals, Owens won the 100-meter sprint with a new Penn Relays record of 10.5 seconds, the long jump with a modest leap of 23 feet, $\frac{5}{8}$ inch, and the relays as anchor man for his Ohio State team. Jesse's star rose as Peacock's dipped.[42]

It continued to rise in five successive dual and triangular meets between Ohio State and other Big Ten schools. On all but one of those occasions, Jesse broke world, conference, or local meet records. Against the University of Wisconsin, at Madison on May 16, he ran the 100-yard dash in 9.3 seconds, shattering the world mark he equalled at Ann Arbor a year earlier. This year the Big Ten finals were held on May 22–23 at Columbus, and once again Owens won all four of his events, setting new records in two of them. His most impressive victory, by far, was in the unlikely 220-yard low hurdles. He got off to an atrocious start, knocked over the first hurdle, lost his stride, and by the fifth hurdle was running last in the field. Then he surged past one hurdler after another, beating Bob Osgood of the University of Michigan to the tape. "The part about Owens we like most is his fighting spirit," his hometown press raved. "Unlike many, he isn't just 'a front runner'."[43]

By early June 1936 Jesse was once again a favorite for Olympic laurels. In Ohio State's final dual meet of the season, he captured first place in all four events in Columbus against another strong University of Southern California squad. Just a month earlier Larry Snyder had publicly admitted that he doubted "very much whether Jesse's idleness during the winter season did him any good." In fact, that idleness had rested him physically and fired his determination. During workouts prior to the Southern Cal meet, he suffered a slight muscle strain in a leg, but he recovered quickly to compete at top form. With his various personal, legal, and academic trials behind him, Owens confidently faced the Olympic tryouts.[44]

☆ ☆ ☆

While Jesse easily qualified in three events at the regional tryouts in Chicago, Eulace Peacock struggled to recover from his hamstring injury. A veteran Newark Athletic Club trainer, Maney Gordon, worked daily on the damaged leg, but with no great success. Peacock pulled up lame at a New Jersey AAU meet on June 27. A week later, at a regional Olympic tryout at Harvard Stadium, he again failed miserably in the 100-meter dash, and in the long jump he barely cleared 22 feet. As one reporter observed, Peacock's right thigh was "taped up like a baseball bat." He was so obviously below par that Olympic officials invited him to try again at the semifinal trials two weeks later in Princeton.[45]

The semifinals were scheduled for July 4, exactly a year after Peacock had conquered a shaky Owens in two events in Lincoln, Nebraska. But Princeton was another story. Jesse beat Peacock in the long jump and Ralph Metcalfe in the 100 meters. Once again Peacock received special consideration from Olympic officials, who allowed him to withdraw from the 100-meter sprint and give himself one last chance in the tryout finals on July 11–12 at Randall's Island, New York.[46]

In a new stadium hastily constructed for the event, the final trials for the United States Olympic team seemed to have been organized, in the vivid words of one journalist, "about as systematically as the potato races at a church bazaar." Although the new Triborough Bridge had just been opened, scarcely half of the 22,000 seats were filled for the first day's events. Loudspeakers broke down. A thunderstorm interrupted activity midway through the program of the preliminary heats.[47]

Undistracted, Owens finished first in the finals of the 100-meter and 200-meter sprints and in the long jump. Ralph Metcalfe came in second in the 100 meters, thereby qualifying for Berlin. The runner-up in the 200 meters was Mack Robinson, an unknown junior college freshman from California. By the end of the day, ten black males won places on the Olympic track-and-field team bound for Berlin: Owens, Metcalfe, and Robinson in the sprints; Cornelius Johnson and David Albritton in the high jump; Californians Archie Williams and Jimmy LuValle in the 400 meters; John Woodruff, a freshman from the University of Pittsburgh, in the 800 meters; Fritz Pollard, Jr., from the University of North Dakota, in the 110-meter hurdles; and John Brooks, a Chicagoan, joining Owens in the long jump.[48]

In addition to those ten males, two black females, a hurdler named Tidye Pickett and the sprinter Louise Stokes, made the track team. Five black boxers and two black weightlifters won berths on the ship bound for Berlin. Those nineteen athletes, almost four times as many blacks as had competed for the United States at the Los Angeles Olympics in 1932, represented a breakthrough of no small proportion. "Those who mourn the defeat of Joe Louis at the hands of the determined German, Max Schmeling," the *Amsterdam News* commented, "can find not only solace, but also genuine pride and appreciation in the results of the Olympic selections."[49]

For every success, several failures went home disappointed. No fewer than five former world record holders came up short in the Olympic trials. Jesse's close friend, the high jumper Mel Walker, who had to cross a drainage ditch to reach the high jump pit from his unorthodox straight-ahead approach, lost when thrown off balance. His white Buckeye teammate, Charles Beetham, broke stride and lost in the 800-meter semifinals when someone stepped on his heel at the first turn. Saddest of all was Eulace Peacock, whose heavily taped leg kept him far back in the pack of the 100-meter finals.[50]

Years later Owens recalled a banquet shortly before the team left for Berlin. As he told it, he sat beside the great Babe Ruth, the retired Yankee immortal.

"You gonna win at the Olympics, Jesse?" the Babe asked.

"Gonna try," Owens replied.

"Trying doesn't mean shit," retorted Ruth in his high-pitched voice. "Everybody *tries*. I succeed. Wanna know why?"

Owens nodded.

"I hit sixty home runs a few years back because I *know* I'm going to hit a home run just about every time I swing that frigging bat. I'm surprised when I *don't!* And that isn't all there is to it. Because I know it, the pitchers, *they* know it too."

Then the Babe dropped his voice to a mischievous whisper. "They're pretty sure I'm going to hit a homer every time," he said, breaking out in a belly laugh.[51]

In the wake of the Olympic trials, American athletes, track officials, and the press were "pretty sure" of a good showing at the Berlin Olympics. For Jesse Owens, especially, they predicted great success. His year of personal and athletic trials was past. Glory beckoned.

CHAPTER 5

Bound for Glory

JESSE OWENS'S RISE TO PROMINENCE coincided with the emergence of another black athlete, Joe Louis. While Jesse blazed his trail at Ohio State, Louis turned from a highly successful amateur boxing career to enter the professional ranks. By the summer of 1936 he had made quick work of black and white opponents alike. Jesse Owens and Joe Louis stood together as stellar black athletes, exceptions to the rule of white dominance in the mid-1930s.

Their backgrounds were remarkably similar. Born within a year of each other, both were sons of Alabama sharecroppers. As children both moved north—Louis to Detroit—with their families, and in sport found a means of excelling in the white man's world. Even in sport the options were limited. By the 1930s, rigid social barriers kept outstanding black baseball and football players racially segregated from white teams. Boxing and track were nominally open to blacks, but ever since the controversial reign of Jack Johnson (1908–1915), contention for the heavyweight championship had been denied to blacks. Only a paucity of good white heavyweights gave Louis his chance. He seized the opportunity. As Jesse Owens prepared himself for Olympic laurels, Joe Louis set his sights on the heavyweight crown.[1]

America's black community fixed its attention on both men, viewing them as leaders on the road to a new era of black achievement and recognition. Their prowess, according to one spokesman, would alter "the usual appraisal of Negroes by the rank and file of the American public." Whites might continue to ignore the talents of such artists and intellectuals as Paul Robeson, Louis Armstrong, Langston Hughes, and W. E. B. DuBois, but they could not, and would not, fail to appreciate the athletic feats of Joe Louis and Jesse Owens. "If these two mere boys have done nothing more than just awaken curiosity in Negroes in millions of white minds," a black journalist noted in 1935, "they have served their race well."[2]

Black hopes of social acceptance depended not on the perception of their racial opposites alone. Black self-confidence had to be aroused if dreams of equality were to be realized. Authentic heroes helped build that confidence. "The Negro youth has been starved for their own heroes a mighty long time," lamented the editor of a black newspaper. "Everything they have seen glorified in the past has been white. They have heard of Babe Ruth, Jack Dempsey, etc. But deep down in their little hearts, they have gone to bed and reflected that, after all, these fellows are white. A hero of their own flesh and blood, they have lacked." Until Louis and Owens hit the scene, that is. In winning "the praise and admiration of sport lovers of all races and groups," they instilled racial pride and self-respect, inspiring "countless thousands of little lads of our race to emulate them."[3]

Just six weeks before the Berlin Olympics, Joe Louis fell from his pedestal. In view of a stunned partisan crowd at Yankee Stadium, he suffered a savage thrashing at the hands of the German heavyweight Max Schmeling. In the twelfth round he went down for the count. "There was something terrible—something fascinating, too," the black *New York Amsterdam News* commented, " in watching a great idol fall to the ground and break up in pieces." Louis would soon rise from the rubble to reign for more than a decade as the unrivaled king of the ring. But for the time being, his star was eclipsed. His momentary failure left Jesse Owens alone to carry his people's hopes.[4]

☆　☆　☆

While Louis fell dramatically in full public view, two mini-dramas played themselves out in the athletic corridors of Ohio State University. Both were quiet, private affairs whose details can now be reconstructed only from notes and correspondence in the university's archives. Neither episode would deserve mention were it not for the fact that each contributed to the manner and means of Jesse Owens's going to Berlin and to his controversial return home.

The first issue pertained to the funding of the Olympic team's trip to Berlin. In 1936 large corporate donors had not yet entered the Olympic fundraising picture, so money came largely from athletic organizations such as the Amateur Athletic Union and the National Collegiate Athletic Association. The AAU was financed primarily from gate receipts at AAU-sponsored track meets. The NCAA, on the other hand, turned directly to individual colleges and universities for contributions. Fully a year before the Berlin Olympics, Avery Brundage, President of the American Olympic Committee, urged the NCAA to collect $100,000 toward the Olympic effort. By November 1935 Frank G. McCormick, Athletic Director at the University of Minnesota, had been appointed chairman of the national committee. He in turn instructed each athletic conference to set up an Olympic Finance Committee.[5]

McCormick's job was not easy. The controversy over American participation in the Berlin games hindered his efforts. Moreover, the appeal to district coordinators by the NCAA president, John L. Griffith, was exceedingly vague: to collect "such contributions as the colleges and the college men may care to make to the Olympic Fund." His instructions to McCormick were more specific: to pressure universities into contributing more than they had given for the Los Angeles Olympics of 1932. The money could come directly from university and athletic department coffers; solicitations from alumni, faculty, and students; the sale of Olympic emblems and pins; special benefits and concerts; and even "passing the hat" at regularly scheduled athletic events. Despite the difficulties, by mid-May 1936 the total exceeded the amount raised by the NCAA in 1932.[6]

Although both leaders of the national fundraising effort were Big Ten men—McCormick of Minnesota and Griffith, the conference commissioner—the Big Ten lagged behind in its gifts. As of May 20, only Wisconsin and Minnesota had surpassed their 1932 totals. Embarrassed, McCormick leaned heavily on his conference athletic directors. Presumably he wrote several letters like the one that survives in the Ohio State archives, addressed to L. W. St. John:

> Up to the present time, I have received no report of contributions from the Ohio State University. I will greatly appreciate it if you will let me know what plans you have made to make some contribution from your institution. We are not asking for large contributions. If your athletic funds are in such shape that no direct contribution is possible, I suggest that you pass the hat at one of your track meets or baseball games or that you solicit small personal contributions from members of your staff, students or others interested in athletics.

Finally, within a month of the Olympic team's departure for Europe, Ohio State came through with a contribution of $504.60, less than half of the total it had given in 1932.[7]

Fortunately, this lackadaisical effort was not characteristic of the larger fundraising drive. For the American track-and-field team, the original proposed budget was $43,000; in the final tabulation, the NCAA and the AAU raised $60,000 to pay the expenses of seventy-one track and field athletes, three coaches, and five "managers" (trainers and chaperones) for the Berlin games. On the other hand, the original estimate of cost for each individual was only $500, but in the end the expenses turned out to be about $650 per person. The budget was tight at best.[8]

The slow pace of the fundraising drive prompted the AAU to schedule several post-Olympic track exhibitions in Europe to ensure that the Americans' bills would be paid. By the time a marginally comfortable level of funds had been collected in the United States, the contracts for those barnstorming exhibitions had already been signed. The tardy, penurious contribution of his own institution contributed to the post-Olympic troubles of Jesse Owens.

A briefer, much more secret little controversy in the spring of 1936 also pertained to Owens's trip to Berlin. The editor of the *Cleveland News*, Earle Martin, and his sports editor, Ed Bang, decided that they would publicly solicit funds to send Charles Riley with Jesse. They knew that Ohio State coach Larry Snyder was already planning to go; Riley would "give him a helping hand . . . in prepping Owens." Before announcing their plans, however, Martin and Bang asked a local AAU representative, Floyd A. Rowe, to check with the Ohio State athletic director to make sure Riley would be welcomed. The answer was unequivocal: Riley's presence was most decidedly not desired. The whole idea was a "far fetched" one, St. John informed Rowe, for "in place of being a source of any help to Jesse, it probably would be a source of danger in upsetting Jesse to have Riley attempting in any way to advance some of his silly ideas." Rowe agreed, recalling that Riley had been a disruptive voice in Jesse's ear in both high school and college, criticizing first Ed Weil and then Larry Snyder for their handling of Owens. "Without going into the relative merits of the abilities of the two men [Riley and Snyder]," Rowe wrote to Bang, "I would say that it would be upsetting to any athlete to have two coaches trying to tell him what to do."[9]

The scheme died in embryo, without Riley or Owens ever hearing about it. "We only wanted to be helpful," Bang informed St. John, "but . . . we have concluded 'too many cooks might spoil the broth'."[10]

☆ ☆ ☆

In the early morning of July 15, 1936, the *S.S. Manhattan* sat in New York Harbor receiving eight hundred passengers bound for Europe. Onlookers spotted the actresses Mary Astor and Helen Hayes boarding the ship, but the moment belonged to American Olympic officials, coaches, and athletes. Journalists mingled with the crowd, conducting hasty interviews that they would later edit and embellish for their story lines. Photographers laden with bulky equipment snapped pictures frantically, from every imaginable angle. When Jesse Owens appeared, smartly dressed in a dark blue pinstripe suit, he was immediately surrounded by reporters, photographers, and well-wishers. According to Jesse's later recollection, that handsome suit was the only one he owned.[11]

He made his way to his assigned quarters, Room 87 on Deck D, along with 382 athletes in the two lower decks beneath the waterline—"in the hold of the ship," as one athlete recalls. Physically segregated by a sealed door were a few wives and parents who were making the trip, whose section divided male from female athletes. Regular passengers nearly filled the two upper decks to capacity. Among them were American Olympic officials and coaches, who traveled first class. To one of their own members, they seemed like "a bunch of junketeers taking the gravy that should have gone to the athletes."[12]

Unaccustomed to anything different, most athletes scarcely noticed the contrast. For nine days they regularly stretched, jogged, and walked each morning on the top deck, then whiled away the afternoon at games of shuffleboard and cards. Some wrote letters home; a few read light novels. Owens kept a brief diary of the trip. Each night they enjoyed a movie, then danced to live music before turning in. When the *Manhattan* hit a fierce storm on the second night out of New York, several athletes became frightfully seasick from the tossing and rolling of the ship. Owens himself became sick, then caught a cold that required medical attention. By the fifth day at sea he was feeling better but was bored with confinement and routine. He slept one afternoon away. Two days later he noted briefly in his diary: "The day as a whole was very dreary & nothing exciting happened." The passage to Europe for those American Olympic athletes in 1936 seems to have been little different from most other transatlantic crossings of the day.[13]

But these were athletes on a mission, not tourists on vacation. As athletes they were accustomed to vigorous exercise that normally burned away the calories consumed by gargantuan appetites. Rich ship food and limited physical activity proved to be a disastrous combination for several unwary individuals. Years earlier, when Avery Brundage himself was an athlete bound for the Stockholm Olympics of 1912 aboard the *Finland*, he had seen several of his comrades destroy their chances at Olympic laurels by eating too much. "Exposure to the unlimited menus on shipboard was fatal to some," he observed, "and several hopes of Olympic victory foundered at the bounteous dinner table." On the second day at sea aboard the *Manhattan*, Brundage addressed the athletes now under his supervision. Perhaps he warned them of shipboard gluttony, but if he did, some paid him no mind. Bored and inactive, several athletes gorged themselves. A 5,000-meter runner from the University of Indiana, Donald Ray Lash, gained more than a pound a day, 10 pounds in all, and embarrassingly finished at the rear of his pack of runners two weeks later in Berlin. Even worse was the case of Ellison "Tarzan" Brown, a Narraganset Indian, who gained no less than 14 pounds at sea. Once on land he injured his achilles' tendon, partly because he was overweight, and lasted less than 2 miles in the Olympic marathon.[14]

Owens dealt with his boredom, homesickness, and anxiety by sleeping, not by eating foolishly. His seasickness worked to his advantage, requiring him to avoid heavy quantities of rich food. Yet for him, too, the dining room represented one of his more memorable experiences of the trip. On the first evening at sea he went to his assigned table only to find all three of his dining mates to be outspoken, wisecracking Southerners—the hurdler Glenn Hardin and the shot putter Jack Torrance from Louisiana State University, and the hurdler Forrest "Spec" Towns from the University of Georgia. All were whites, and to Jesse their necks appeared red. For all his easy-mannered adaptability, he could not cope with that situation. He found another table. Ever afterward Towns would tease him for his prejudice against white Southerners.[15]

A moment of drama occurred midway through the voyage when a middle-distance runner, Harold Smallwood, came down with signs of appendicitis. Doctors put him in sick bay, packing him in ice in order to avoid an operation at sea. Rumors of surgery circulated freely when the *Manhattan* slowed to a snail's pace, until the captain announced that the ship was only trying to avoid a school of whales. Smallwood, in fact, recovered sufficiently to qualify for the 400-meter semifinals in Berlin, only to fall ill again. He finally had his appendix removed in a Berlin hospital.[16]

The most dramatic—or melodramatic—episode at sea involved Eleanor Holm Jarrett, a brash, free-spirited backstroke swimmer. In Los Angeles in 1932 she had won the 100-meter backstroke in almost three seconds below the previous Olympic mark, and by 1936 she held world records in all the backstroke distances for women. Her athletic prowess was beyond dispute; her Berlin prospects were pure gold. But she was a maverick. After the Los Angeles Olympics, she had remained in Hollywood on a handsome contract, married a bandleader, and toured the country singing, all the while carefully abstaining from swimming-for-pay arrangements that would have made her ineligible for the Berlin games. Compared to the great majority of the team, who were young and socially sheltered, Eleanor Holm Jarrett was worldliness incarnate. She trained, as she often said mockingly, "on champagne and cigarettes."[17]

Champagne was her undoing. On her first night at sea, she joined several journalists at the bar, becoming so tipsy that she received a reprimand from the heads of the Olympic Committee for flagrantly violating the official handbook's prohibitions against "smoking and the use of intoxicating drinks and other forms of dissipation while in training." She responded haughtily with further indiscretion rather than abstinence. Her lively participation at parties in private staterooms became the talk of the trip, provoking further warnings. On the final night before the *Manhattan* docked in Bremerhaven, as she staggered back toward her quarters she encountered one of the women chaperons in the hall. Both the team doctor and the ship's physician were called to examine her, more to verify her intoxication than to assess her wellbeing. Her game was up, her Olympic career finished. Early the next morning Avery Brundage summoned reporters, several of whom had been partying with the sociable Eleanor the night before, and announced that she was forthwith dismissed from the team.[18]

Never once in his brief diary entries did Jesse ever mention the antics of Eleanor Holm Jarrett. His mind was elsewhere. "While I was going over on the boat," he recalled years later, "all I could think about was taking home one or two of those gold medals." The presence of Larry Snyder helped him concentrate. So did the quiet influence of Ralph Metcalfe, the senior statesman of the 1936 Olympic team. Several years older than most of his teammates, Metcalfe was one of the few members of the squad who had any previous Olympic experience. He walked and spoke with authority. While Eleanor Holm Jarrett self-destructed on the last night aboard the *Manhattan*, Metcalfe called a meeting of all the black track and field athletes, urging them to resist emotional involvement in the political atmosphere they would soon encounter. They were going to Europe to run and jump, not to debate politics. Their goal was both clear and simple: to win for themselves, for their schools, and for their country. "That led to our success," Owens remembered almost half a century later. "He calmed our fears. He was the guy who did it for us."[19]

Just before they disembarked, the Olympic team played a high-schoolish game of choosing superlatives. They voted Glen Hardin as "most handsome" and Glenn Cunningham, the Kansas distance runner, as the "most popular" shipmate, with Jesse coming in second. For "best dressed," however, Owens took the laurels. If his handsome dark pinstripe suit was the only one he owned, he apparently had a quite sufficient wardrobe of similarly neat other clothes. Even on the eve of his greatest athletic moment, he attended carefully to his appearance.[20]

☆ ☆ ☆

At the break of dawn on June 24, the *Manhattan* finally docked at Bremerhaven. In nearby Hamburg the Olympic coaches and athletes were given a brief formal reception, then put on an express train to Berlin. Arriving in midafternoon, they were paraded down the main thoroughfare, Unter den Linden, with thousands of Berliners lining the sidewalks. Earlier, Larry Snyder had warned Owens to be prepared for a cold, stony reception, but quite the opposite occurred. For the past year or two, Berlin's illustrated tabloids had acquainted their sports-minded readers with the dominance of black American athletes. Physical, racial differences merely heightened the fascination. Now Germans young and old clicked away with their cameras, directing them primarily at blacks. Boys ran alongside the athletes, asking for autographs. They mobbed Jesse. "Enthusiasm about the Negro contingency centers mainly around Owens," the *New York Times* reported. "None of the others enjoy anything approaching his popularity."[21]

Berlin glistened—old but clean, large but colorful and warmly receptive. The Nazi swastika flew from most shops and homes, but in 1936 its crooked black cross on a blood-red background had not yet become a sinister symbol for American youths. A few shops displayed the white Olympic flag with five interlocking rings. As Owens and his friends were unlikely to have known, an Olympic flag often masked the premises of Jewish families, who had been forbidden to fly the Nazi flag. No anti-Jewish placards or graffiti could be seen, for Hitler had expressly ordered them removed for the duration of the Olympics. To the outsider newly arrived, Berlin seemed relaxed and wholesome.[22]

A band led the American party up Unter den Linden to the city hall, where the Mayor of Berlin and several German Olympic officials gave brief welcoming speeches. Finally the athletes were put in buses, the women to be taken to a spartan dormitory near the Olympic Stadium, the men to be transported 15 miles west of the city's center to an Olympic Village, where they would reside for the next three weeks. Hitler Youths greeted them at the Village and led them to their quarters while a band played waltzes. Similar hospitality greeted the arrival of each Olympic team. A French journalist commented only half in jest, "They do things thoroughly, these people."[23]

They certainly planned the Olympic Village thoroughly and well. Eager to outdo the simple housing provided for athletes at the Los Angeles Olympics in 1932, Hitler ordered that no effort or expense be spared in the project. His subordinates found a beautiful forest of birch trees just beyond the western outskirts of Berlin, exquisitely landscaped the area, and added an artificial lake to several small ponds. Army engineers built 160 sturdy houses of brick, stone, and cement, each to hold about two dozen athletes, two to a room. English-speaking stewards were assigned to each house inhabited by Americans to serve as messengers, guides, and interpreters. Setting a high standard for all future Olympic Villages, this one was a kind of temporary self-contained town. At the athletes' disposal were a library, hospital, theater, barber shop, and swimming pool. Jesse Owens found it all "very interesting" and impressive, especially the little television screen—the first one he ever saw—set in one of the central buildings for the transmission of the Olympic events. For his first evening, however, he was most impressed with the cool night air, which afforded solid sleep at the end of a hectic day.[24]

He awoke to a clear, sunny sky, virtually the last full day without rain during his two weeks in Germany. By the end of the second day a cold rain was falling. "The weather in Germany is some what funny," he noted in his diary. "In the morning the sun is shining beautiful and suddenly it will rain." Rain or shine, though, he found the food to his liking: "steaks and plenty of it . . . bacon, eggs, ham, fruits, juices," everything to which he was accustomed, and more. He ate with his teammates but quickly expanded his circle of acquaintances. "Met many people from strange lands," he noted in his diary on the evening of July 25, "& most of them could speak some English." He found the Australians to be particularly entertaining. "Sitting around listening to a Victrola having a bull session with some of the boys," he observed on July 27, "What liars they are," he said of the Australians.[25]

For a week before the opening of the Berlin games, Jesse and his track teammates worked out daily "to get the sea legs off" on specially prepared tracks adjacent to the Olympic Village. The official American coaches were Lawson Robertson of the University of Pennsylvania, Dean Cromwell of the University of Southern California, and William "Billy" Hayes of Indiana University, but Larry Snyder arrived daily from his Berlin hotel (where he stayed with his Ohio State track assistant, William Heintz) to work with Jesse and his Buckeye friend, high jumper David Albritton. As Snyder had feared, Robertson tried to change Jesse's form—his arm action as well as his starting stance. Snyder quickly intervened, and Owens carried on as usual.[26]

More upsetting to Snyder were the distractions of photographers and autograph seekers on the practice field. For all their efficient organization, the Germans did not limit access to the Olympic Village, largely because security was not then deemed a problem for Olympic athletes. So "hordes of spectators," as one American journalist put it, descended on the athletes, especially around Owens. "It seemed to me," Snyder complained, "that Jesse spent most of his time in Berlin smiling at the birdie, with a dozen or so foreign athletes clustered around him or hanging on him, so that they might have a souvenir to take back home." Understandably concerned about the disruption of his star athlete's concentration, Snyder talked Dean Cromwell into banning all amateur photographers and autograph seekers from the field.[27]

Once Snyder returned to his hotel room in the late afternoon, however, Owens was again easy prey for his German admirers. Women slipped notes under his door at night, often with marriage proposals. Several times Jesse was awakened in the early morning by people shoving autograph books through his open window. One night he closed the window even though the room was too stuffy to sleep soundly, but awoke to early morning sounds of clicking camera shutters as people took pictures through the windowpane. When Jesse stepped outside of the Olympic Village, he was immediately recognized and lionized. Once he and Dave Albritton went out for a night to Shebini's Bar in Berlin to hear a black trombonist. There Albritton drank his first champagne, which tasted to him like ginger ale. According to his recollections, neither he nor Owens had difficulty finding dance partners. Men came up asking them to dance with their wives.[28]

Even Maximilian Schmeling sought Jesse out in the Olympic Village shortly before the opening of the Berlin Games. Only a month earlier Schmeling had demolished Joe Louis and had returned home to Germany to accolades from all quarters. When he met Owens, one of his eyes was still puffy from his brawl with the Brown Bomber. He and Owens chatted briefly, but years later Jesse vividly recalled that he and his black teammates were incensed at the proud manner in which the Nazis paraded Schmeling around the Village. If Jesse's memory served him correctly, "inwardly many of us were trying to atone for Joe's loss."[29]

Larry Snyder was trying to achieve something more immediately practical. Aboard the *Manhattan* he had learned that Owens had brought one old pair and two new pairs of running shoes to the final Olympic trials and Randall's Island but had lost both new pairs. Fearing that the one remaining set of spikes would not hold up for all the long jump and sprint trials in Berlin, Snyder urged the American Olympic Committee to order a new pair from England. Two days before the games were to open, the new shoes had not arrived. So Snyder combed the streets of Berlin for a sporting goods store and bought Jesse new shoes with his own money. Still, he fretted that as Jesse had not the time to break them in slowly, he would develop blisters. According to Snyder, Owens had the final word: "They'll make me jump farther when they begin to hurt."[30] Apparently they hurt nicely, for he jumped far and ran fast in them.

A black welterweight boxer, Howell King, needed no new shoes, gloves or anything else, for he and a white featherweight, Joe Church, were dismissed from the Olympic Village and sent home. A spokesman for the American Olympic Committee announced that King and Church were too "homesick" to compete in the games, but rumors circulated to the effect that they had been caught stealing a camera from a German shop. King countered with the accusation that he was dismissed because he refused to use inferior headgear in sparring sessions. Whatever the truth of the matter, as tales of this little episode made the rounds of the Olympic Village, they added another element of distraction to a situation in which mental concentration was already extremely difficult for Jesse. He welcomed the opening of the Berlin Games on August 1.[31]

☆　☆　☆

Despite an overcast sky, crowds began arriving early on the day of the opening ceremonies. People came from outside the city by train, bus, and automobile. Berliners took the subway or walked to the stadium, set on the western edge of the city amid a vast complex of sports fields, tracks, indoor gymnasiums, and officials' buildings. The newest and largest of its kind, Olympic Stadium held 110,000 people, 5,000 more than the Los Angeles Coliseum. As the huge airship *Hindenburg* hovered overhead trailing the Olympic flag, the stadium was virtually filled by noon. A festive mood prevailed.

While the athletes assembled at midafternoon on nearby fields preparing for their grand entry, Hitler and his official entourage pulled up in a caravan of shiny black Mercedes convertibles. Beside Hitler was Count Henri Baillet-Latour, the Belgian president of the International Olympic Committee, and Dr. Theodor Lewald, the president of the German Olympic Committee. They paraded past the assembled athletes, leading various heads of state, members of the International Olympic Committee, and Hitler's ranking military officers and government officials. Thirty amplified trumpets announced their entry through the wide tunnel at the western end of the stadium. Then a huge orchestra and chorus broke out with "Deutschland über alles," followed by the "Horst Wessellied" and a new "Olympic Hymn" written specially for the occasion by the aged German composer Richard Strauss.[32]

Finally came the athletes, marching in teams representing fifty nations variously attired in colorful uniforms. Some gave the Nazi salute, others the Olympic salute (which was unfortunately strikingly similar). The British team simply gave an "eyes right" gesture as they passed the reviewing stand. Every team except the Americans dipped its flag. Not since the London Olympics of 1908—when Anglo-American tensions provoked the famous line, "This flag dips to no earthly king"—had Americans lowered their flag in honor of the host ruler. A ripple of displeasure swept through the crowd as the Americans walked past, but that negative reaction was immediately swamped by the emotional entry of the large German Olympic team. The vast majority of the entire stadium rose to its feet in the "Heil Hitler"salute. Hitler's presence, German pride, and Nazi symbols dominated the opening ceremonies.[33]

Oratory flourished. A recorded message from the absent, ailing "father" of the modern Olympics, Pierre de Coubertin, reminded the audience of his lifelong dream: "The important thing at the Olympic Games is not to win, but to take part, just as the most important thing about life is not to conquer, but to struggle well." A long-winded, self-serving address by Dr. Lewald effectively drowned out Coubertin's idealism in a flood of patriotic platitudes. Finally Hitler officially announced the opening of "the Games of Berlin, celebrating the eleventh Olympiad of the modern era." More trumpet flourishes accompanied the raising of all the national Olympic flags and the release of a thousand doves, symbols of peace.[34]

A unique twist was given to the igniting of the Olympic flame, a feature introduced just four years earlier at the Los Angeles Games. In a wholly new ceremony, the flame was lit at the sacred altar amid the ruins of Olympia, then relayed to Berlin by more than three thousand runners covering a kilometer each. At precisely the right moment, the last torchbearer—blond and slender, an ideal Aryan—entered the stadium and made his way to a huge brazier atop a tripod at the east end of the stadium. Almost half a century later a similar "torch run" would serve American patriotic and economic interests at the 1984 Los Angeles Olympics; in 1936 it served Nazi interests. In Dr. Lewald's words, it symbolically sealed "a real and spiritual bond between our German fatherland and the sacred places of Greece founded nearly 4,000 years ago by Nordic immigrants.[35]

That dramatic moment was preserved for posterity by yet another innovation that was destined to become an integral part of future Olympics: a full film record of the ceremonies and athletic contests. Commissioned and extravagantly financed by Hitler, Leni Riefenstahl directed dozens of cameramen and assistants to station themselves on the field, in the stands, and even in a dirigible overhead to take a prodigious amount of film footage. In the end, no less than 1,300,000 feet of film were developed and edited to make Riefenstahl's *Olympia*. Consciously artistic, she sought unusual angles, varying shades and shafts of light, alternate closeups and panoramic effects. The festive pageantry as well as the athletic performances of the Berlin Olympics still live largely because of her thorough, efficient artistry. Perhaps Jesse Owens noticed her cameramen during that afternoon of the opening ceremonies; certainly they noticed him throughout the following week.[36]

Another innovation pointed to a more distant future of Olympic spectatorship. Several bulky cameras relayed electronic images of the opening ceremonies, and later of the athletic contests, to several thousand people in the Olympic Village and in eighteen halls scattered around Berlin. Televised sport was born, but barely. "Unfortunately, the results are very close to zero," a reporter for the *New York Times* commented. "You cannot see Olympics by television yet. All that you can see are some men dressed like athletes but only faintly distinguishable, like human beings floating in a milk bath." White athletes, especially, fared poorly through the earliest television lens, for "white objects" were "divined, rather than seen, in vague blurs in a milky mess."[37]

Aglow with the spectacular opening ceremonies, the athletes returned to the Olympic Village to await their various contests. Now they, not Hitler and his Nazi pageantry, would become the center of attention. For the next two weeks, August 2–16, daily athletic contests would be held. As a rule, preliminary events were scheduled for the mornings, with the finals in the afternoon. The premier events, track and field, would all be crowded into the first week.[38]

Richard Mandell imaginatively suggests that the athletes

"endured the inevitable, gnawing anguish" of anticipation, twisting restlessly in their beds and staring open-eyed at darkened ceilings on the eve of their great test.[39] But Jesse and his roommate, David Albritton, avoided such free-floating anxieties by fixing their minds on Albritton's forthcoming morning preliminaries and afternoon finals in the high jump. While Jesse would run only two trial heats in the 100-meter dash, Albritton would complete his entire purpose for coming to Berlin on the very first day of competition.

His toughest opponent was a fellow black American, the Californian Cornelius Johnson, who had barely but consistently beaten him in most of their previous encounters. Now Jesse suggested that his roommate employ an old trick that he himself had used earlier in the year to defeat a favored hurdler at an NCAA meet. He had delayed at the start, tying and untying his shoes to make his opponent lose his concentration. As Cornelius Johnson was a notoriously fast jumper, Albritton should slow him down, Jesse counseled. Years later he recalled that he and his best friend lay talking until late in the night, refining a strategy whereby Albritton could win a gold medal the next day. Their ploy failed, but the scheming relaxed them for sound sleep in the cool night air of the Village quarters.[40]

The stage was set. Owens's proven skills made him confident of his own prospects. Equally important in his winning of Olympic fame would be Hitler's daily presence, a stadium filled with enthusiastic spectators, an exceptional filmmaker, and a curious world.

CHAPTER 6

The Berlin Blitz

THE BERLIN OLYMPICS TOOK PLACE against a backdrop of momentous world events. Just a year earlier Benito Mussolini had announced the annexation of Ethiopia and promptly unleashed his Italian army against that ancient but fragile African state, driving Emperor Haile Selassie into exile. More quietly but no less ominously, in the early spring of 1936 Hitler's army moved into the previously demilitarized Rhineland, causing tremors of anxiety within an unstable French government. Except for the authoritarian regimes of Germany and Italy, instability seemed the rule of the day. England endured almost a year of constitutional crisis before King Edward VIII abdicated his throne to marry an American divorcée, Wallis Warfield Simpson. Greece and Austria seethed with internal strife, Communists vying with fascists for power. Even distant Brazil suffered turmoil as two rival factions sent separate athletic teams to Berlin, requiring Olympic officials to weigh conflicting claims of legitimacy. Unable to decide, the International Olympic Committee finally rejected both teams.

Gone were the days—if ever they existed—when sport and international politics could remain separate. In the wake of the furious debate over the participation of athletes from Western democratic nations in Nazi Germany, alternate games—"the People's Olympics"—were planned for July 19–26 in Barcelona, Spain. Supported by a liberal-socialist host government that in 1930 had replaced an old autocratic regime, those games were canceled at the last minute. On the very morning of the opening ceremonies, reactionary forces led by General Francisco Franco plunged Spain into a civil war. Born of political idealism, the People's Olympics were the victim of political crisis.

The Berlin Olympics reeked of politics—of Hitler's designs and calculations, of the hopes and fears of the German people, and of the anti-Nazi bloc throughout the Western world. Little wonder that the very first day of athletic competition produced a controversial episode that within the week would turn into a most memorable and politically useful myth: Hitler's legendary "snub" of Jesse Owens. In truth, the yarn was a fabrication that originally had nothing whatsoever to do with Owens.

On the first afternoon of the games, Hitler excitedly watched two German athletes, Tilly Fleischer and Hans Woellke, win gold medals, and summoned them to his box for personal, public congratulations. Shortly thereafter, he did the same for a Finnish victor. Then late in the afternoon, as drops of rain began to fall from a darkened sky, Cornelius Johnson barely beat his teammate, David Albritton, for the gold in the high jump. Just before the playing of the American national anthem announced the awarding of Johnson's medal, Hitler and his entourage left the stadium.

Did they make a hasty exit so Hitler would not have to shake hands with the black Johnson? Maybe they did. A Nazi spokesman explained that Hitler's party always entered and left the stadium on an exact prearranged schedule, but it is difficult to imagine *Der Führer* publicly congratulating a black man, whom he considered only slightly less odious than a Jew. But if he snubbed any black American athlete, it was Cornelius Johnson rather than Jesse Owens. Not until the next day did Owens win his first gold medal. By then the president of the International Olympic Committee, Henri de Baillet-Latour of Belgium, had gotten word to Hitler that as the head of the host government he must be impartial in his accolades—congratulating all or none of the victors. Hitler stopped inviting winners to his stadium box. He was much too sensitive to world opinion,to leave himself open to negative publicity.[1]

But Hitler had not banked on the ingenuity of the American press. "Hitler greets all medalists except Americans," the front page of the *New York Times* announced the day after the first competitive events; "Hitler ignores Negro medalists," ran the headlines the next day. Not by coincidence, the *New York Times* had earlier led the movement to boycott the Berlin Games. Still, after those initial barrages, the *Times* largely ceased mentioning the "snub" story. Other newspapers picked it up with a new twist. "HITLER SNUBS JESSE," read the huge, bold headlines of a black Cleveland paper, the *Call and Post*, the day after Owens won his first medal. Ignorant of Baillet-Latour's instructions and confident of its ability to read Hitler's motives, the American press shifted the focus of the snub yarn away from Cornelius Johnson onto Jesse Owens. Every new medal won by Owens enhanced his appeal as the target of Hitler's supposed insult.[2]

Yet Jesse denied it to interviewers at Berlin and to reporters on his return home. He would soon find, however, that the constant denial was too much of a bother and that to claim the "snub" for his own would work to his advantage. "And then," as Bud Greenspan says it simply, "Jesse kept on using the story." Especially in his postwar public addresses, newspaper articles, and ghosted books, he would make much use of Hitler's refusal to shake his hand, and his "leaving the stadium in a tantrum."[3]

☆   ☆   ☆

In the real world of competition, on the first morning of the Berlin Olympics sixty-eight runners competed in twelve preliminary heats in the 100-meter dash. Running in the final heat just before noon, Owens turned in a time of 10.3 seconds, tying the world and Olympic records. Shortly after lunch he ran in the semifinals, breaking the world and Olympic mark with a time of 10.2 seconds, only to have the record disallowed because of a following wind. The American press immediately showed its patriotic colors, accusing German officials of bias, but Owens himself had only praise for the German starter, Franz Miller: "He's soft-spoken and soothing, which is a mighty big help to a fellow like me who's so nervous his legs shake in the starting pits. He gave me the best starts in my life," Jesse told reporters.[4]

German spectators gave him the warmest ovation of his life. Just before he entered the stadium, Larry Snyder warned him to be ready for a hostile reception: "Don't let anything you hear from the stands upset you. Ignore the insults and you'll be all right." Little did Snyder know that German admiration for athletic achievement transcended racial prejudice. From the moment Owens first appeared on the track, curious German athletes and coaches milled around him. Erich Borchmeyer, who had competed at Los Angeles in 1932, chatted with him briefly in broken English. One German coach seemed, to Snyder, intensely interested in Jesse's graceful legs, studying them "like a scientist studying a rare specimen of fauna." Then, after Jesse won his first heat, the entire stadium burst out in thunderous applause. From then on he received a loud ovation every time he walked onto the track.[5]

In addition to Owens, the qualifiers for the finals the next day were the Americans Ralph Metcalfe and Frank Wykoff, the German Borchmeyer, Hans Strandberg of Sweden, and Martin Osendarp of the Netherlands. A reporter for the *New York Times* predicted an easy outing for Owens: "Victory for him tomorrow in the finals seems to be his merely for the asking."[6]

It was not so simple as that. Two obstacles stood in the way as potential disrupters of Jesse's concentration. One was the infrequency of the shuttle bus from the Olympic Village to the stadium. In the early morning buses delivered the athletes to the stadium, then at noon took them back to the Village for lunch with no intervening shuttles to and from the stadium. After lunch, buses returned to the stadium, not to return to the Village until the day's end. Regardless of an athlete's scheduled time of competition, he had to stay all morning or all afternoon at the stadium, awaiting his event. For athletes competing in only one event, as most did, those arrangements posed no problem. But for Owens, who was originally scheduled for three events, several preliminaries and finals required him to be at the stadium virtually all the time for the first three days.

The awkward logistics of his situation became apparent on the very first morning. He arrived early but had to wait around three hours before his quarterfinal heat just before noon. Immediately after his winning sprint, he rushed to catch the bus for a forty-five minute drive back to the village for lunch, then returned in the afternoon for his 100-meter semi-finals. After that first day's rush, Jesse and Snyder decided that he should bring sandwiches and milk for lunch, avoiding the tiring noonday jaunt back and forth from the Olympic Village. Cold, soggy sandwiches were better than the bother of the shuttle bus.[7]

Cold, damp weather posed another problem. As extensive warmup exercises were necessary before each event, Owens's multiple schedule made him uniquely susceptible to fatigue. But to warm up inadequately was to court disaster in the form of a pulled muscle. The sad memory of Eulace Peacock loomed in Jesse's mind. For his first trial runs and jumps, he followed the example of Cornelius Johnson in keeping on his entire sweatsuit.

A noonday cloudburst almost placed him at a dire disadvantage for the 100-meter finals on the afternoon of August 3. Jesse drew the inside lane in a six-man field, putting him on the portion of the cinder track that had been churned up by distance runners. Fortunately, German officials moved all the sprinters over one lane to avoid "the heaviest section of the track." Still, the foul weather tested character. Faced with unsatisfactory conditions, some athletes grumble and fear the worst start imaginable; others concentrate all the more on their goal. Jesse Owens concentrated. Years later, when he was asked the stock question about Hitler's treatment of him, his answer could as well have been in reference to the weather as to the Führer. "See, we weren't there to worry about Hitler." Or the weather:

There was something very big. When I lined up in my lane for the finals of the 100 meters, I was looking only at the finish line, and realizing that five of the world's fastest humans wanted to beat me to it.

There were six of us finalists, all with a gold medal ambition. Yet there could only be one winner. I thought of all the years of practice and competition, of all who had believed in me, and of my state and university.

I saw the finish line, and knew that 10 seconds would climax the work of eight years. One mistake could ruin those eight years. So, why worry about Hitler?[8]

Or about a cold rain, or a heavy track?

At the starter's gun, all six men broke cleanly out of the little starting holes they had dug with trowels in the wet cinders. After ten meters or so, Owens was in full stride, smoothly moving ahead of the field. Then three-quarters of the way to the finish, Ralph Metcalfe put on a burst of speed to finish second, three meters behind Owens. Osendarp of Holland won the bronze. When Jesse's world-tying time of 10.3 seconds was announced, the packed house of almost 110,000 spectators burst into an ovation, as a black correspondent for the *Chicago Defender* put it, "seldom equaled in these days of mighty ovations."[9]

On the victory stand to receive his gold medal, Jesse was overcome with the quiet emotion that is now visibly apparent in televised closeups of victorious Olympic athletes. In photographs he appears calm, but years later he recalled, "My eyes blurred as I heard the Star-Spangled Banner played, first faintly and then loudly, and then saw the American flag slowly raised for my victory." Ever afterward he remembered that brief ceremony as the "happiest moment" of his entire career.[10]

From the victory stand he was called to the press box to make a brief statement over an international radio hookup to American listeners back home. On his way up the stadium steps, he thought he saw Hitler smiling and waving to him. Jesse waved back. Whatever that transaction, the *Chicago Defender* reported that "in due fairness to Hitler," it had to be noted that he did not publicly receive any Olympic victors that day, not even the famous German hammer thrower, Karl Hein, who had just won a gold medal.[11]

☆ ☆ ☆

Jesse scarcely had time to savor the thrill of winning his first gold medal. Early the next morning he was once again on the shuttle bus from the Olympic Village to the stadium, first to run in two 200-meter preliminary heats, then to qualify for the long jump finals in the afternoon. In both races he turned in identical marks of 21.1 seconds, a new world and Olympic record for 200 meters around a turn. Fellow American runners Bobby Packard and Mack Robinson also qualified for the semifinals that would be held the next day. Having finished, they relaxed, watching other preliminary trials while waiting for the noon bus to take them back to the Olympic Village. Jesse, on the other hand, went directly from the track to the long jump area for yet more preliminary competition.

To qualify for the afternoon finals, he had only to leap 23 feet 5 inches, a distance he had exceeded during his senior year in high school. He was, in fact, clearly favored to win the gold medal. Except for a Swede's victory in 1920, Americans had seized first place in every long jump since the beginning of the Olympic Games in 1896. In recent years blacks had utterly dominated the event in the United States, winning all but three national championships since 1920. Two of the three Olympic golds prior to 1936 had gone to American blacks, DeHart Hubbard and Edward Gordon. Owens seemed destined to follow easily in their train, especially since his Ann Arbor leap of 26 feet, $8\frac{1}{4}$ inches still stood as the world record.[12]

He did win in the end—but violations in the morning's first two preliminary jumps left him momentarily tottering on the brink of total failure. His own later accounts sadly misrepresent the facts. Tacitly playing upon the myth of Hitler's snub, in 1960 Owens recounted that he was so upset by Hitler's master race theories that he angrily leaped "from several inches beyond the take-off board" on his first jump, then "fouled even worse" on his second try. Later he claimed that Hitler had walked out on him just before he jumped, making him so "mad, hate-mad" that he lost his self-control. Both stories are less than credible. The athlete's utterances in 1936 contain nothing to indicate that Hitler's "master race theories" were of concern to Jesse Owens at that time, and Hitler was not even in the stadium for the morning preliminaries. Even when Owens dropped Hitler from his account of his difficulties, he still got the facts wrong. In his favorite version of the event, he stepped across the front edge of the take-off board on his first attempt, then was so careful not to scratch on his second try that he made a mediocre leap, too short to qualify.[13]

Aided by Paul Neimark, Jesse Owens was always strong on

imagination, weak on literal truth. Contemporaries in 1936 described his first two futile jumps altogether differently from what Owens later remembered. All agreed with Arthur Daley's account in the *New York Times:*

> Owens strolled over to the runway and, still in his pullover, raced to the pit and ran right through, a customary warm-up gesture. But the red flag was raised in a token greatly to the Buckeye Bullet's astonishment. That counted as one of his three jumps.

Apparently a practice run through the long jump pit was customary only in the United States, not in other parts of the world. Daley continued his narrative:

> On his second try, which he made in earnest, Jesse hit the take-off board cleanly and sailed through the air. Again the red flag was raised. . . .

Owens had stepped over the front edge of the take-off board.[14]

One more "scratch" would disqualify him, placing the world's greatest long-jumper on the sidelines for the afternoon finals. As he pulled on his sweatshirt to wait for his third and final turn to jump, he was an anxious young man. For his Olympic coaches and teammates—not to mention Larry Snyder—his final qualifying leap would be a heart-stopper. Out of that critical moment came a story that is a heart-warmer for Olympic enthusiasts.

As Owens later told the story with various embellishments and varying degrees of consistency, his reveries of self-disgust were interrupted by a German competitor, Lutz Long, who came to his rescue with words of consolation and advice. An inch or two taller than Owens, Long was blond, lean, and blue-eyed, a walking advertisement for Hitler's Aryan ideal. According to Owens's reminiscences, Long initiated a conversation. They exchanged small talk, and Long's awkward use of American idioms momentarily amused and relaxed Owens. Then Long reportedly suggested that Jesse make a mark 6 inches back of the take-off board (as one version of the story has it) or that he place a towel 6 inches back of the board (according to another of Owens's accounts) in order to avoid fouling.[15]

If Long did, in fact, make a helpful suggestion, no one but Owens heard it. No one else even observed the two men in conversation at that time. The doyen of American sportswriters, Grantland Rice, was in the press box with binoculars trained on Owens between his second and third attempts to qualify. Rice was "searching for some telltale sign of emotion" in Owens but saw only a calm mask of a face as Jesse walked down the sprint path to the take-off board, retraced his steps, then "anteloped" down the path to make his final jump. Arthur Daley picks up the action: Owens "sprinted carefully, left the ground with a half-foot clearance at the take-off and went past 25 feet to safety."[16]

Whether or not Lutz Long assisted Jesse in the qualifying trials, Long was the only serious challenger in the finals. He was not fast afoot, as most good long-jumpers need to be, but he had excellent form and good elevation. Four other finalists lagged far behind, as Owens held a narrow lead after their first jumps, only to see Long equal his mark with a leap of 7.87 meters (25 feet, $9\frac{3}{4}$ inches). Jesse then exploded beyond 26 feet, and Long faltered on his final jump. Having already officially won the gold medal, Owens nevertheless gave his best at the last. "As he hurled himself through space," noted Rice, the master of colorful prose, "the Negro collegian seemed to be jumping clear out of Germany. The American cheering started while Jesse was airborne." And for good reason. That final majestic jump, captured memorably by Leni Riefenstahl's cameramen, carried to a new Olympic record of 8.06 meters (26 feet, $5\frac{1}{4}$ inches).[17]

Jesse's record-breaking victory came as no surprise. Lutz Long's response, however, was most unexpected: Long rushed up to congratulate him. Years later, for select audiences, Owens indicated that this was, in fact, the first time Long and he ever spoke to each other, which is probably as near to the truth of the Lutz Long myth as one can get. For popular audiences, however, Owens not only set their initial exchange earlier—in the preliminaries—but also dramatized Long's public gesture in the finals. As Jesse told it, Long took his hand, held it high, and shouted to the huge crowd, "Jesse Owens!

Jesse Owens!" and the entire stadium reverberated with a chant that sounded like "Jaz-ee-ooh-wenz." The scene makes good Hollywood drama, but is best left to that. According to all firsthand accounts, the two men merely walked arm-in-arm off the field toward the dressing room. That was enough.[18]

In the hands of a postwar scriptwriter, Hitler would have been enraged at Lutz Long's demonstration of respect and affection for a black American athlete. He would have glared angrily, as Owens himself later insisted. In truth, Hitler virtually ignored the incident. He reserved his evil irrationality for Jews, Poles, and foreign foes, not for his Olympic athletes. Proud of Long's valiant effort, he congratulated him privately just before leaving the stadium. As one reporter commented, "his eagerness to receive the youthful German was so great that the Fuehrer condescended to wait until his emissaries had pried Long loose from Owens."[19]

Scarcely could even Hitler have pried the two young athletes apart that night in the Olympic Village. Shortly after dinner Owens went to Long's room to thank him for his generosity, and for two hours they talked as best they could, given Owens's total ignorance of German and Long's limited English vocabulary. Despite their racial and national differences, they discovered some remarkable similarities. They were precisely the same age and of similarly humble origins. They shared an intense competitiveness and also some anxiety over their futures once their athletic careers were finished. They talked briefly about racial prejudice in the United States and then about the same in Germany.[20]

Like their supposed first encounter prior to Jesse's final preliminary jump, that Olympic Village conversation must be reconstructed entirely from Owens's reminiscences. No doubt he again embellished his story, but this one has the ring of plausibility, at least in broad outline. Three days after the long jump finals, the New York Times noted that "Something like a Damon and Pythias friendship has sprung up between Lutz Long, German star, and Jesse Owens, outstanding member of the American team." Years later Owens explained the basis of their "unique friendship": They were "simply two uncertain young men in an uncertain world."[21]

That they were. Long was destined to die in combat, fighting for the Third Reich in World War II.

☆   ☆   ☆

On Wednesday morning, August 5, Jesse awoke emotionally drained from the previous day's tense competition and the late-night conversation with Long. A chill in the air and leaden skies overhead did not lift his spirits. As he boarded the bus for the stadium, rain began to fall.

A large crowd turned out nevertheless, filling two-thirds of the stadium for morning preliminary trials in five events. For Jesse's semifinal heat in the 200 meters, he kept on his sweatshirt for a slow time of 21.3 seconds, but still won easily. The same time placed second in another semifinal heat, won by Mack Robinson in 21.1 seconds. Rain made a mess of the morning's events. American and Japanese pole vaulters ran warily down a muddy approach to the pit; an even muddier hurdler, Forrest Towns, slipped and stumbled midway through his race, barely recovering sufficiently to win.[22]

Despite the rain, Hitler made his usual ceremonious procession to the afternoon finals. The American novelist Thomas Wolfe, himself in daily attendance at the games, vividly recalled Hitler's route from the Wilhelmstrasse to the stadium, a lane "walled in by the troops, behind which patient, dense, incredible, the masses of the nation waited day by day." As the Führer passed in his open black limousine, standing motionless with his right hand extended, palm downward, Wolfe felt that "something like a wind across a field of grass was shaken through that crowd." To the imaginative novelist, Hitler's charismatic appeal seemed reminiscent of the Buddha or the Messiah.[23]

On the field, however, American athletes once again enjoyed the limelight. Ken Carpenter, from the University of Southern California, won the discus throw; his college teammate, Earle Meadows, edged two Japanese competitors in the pole vault. Only Britain's 50-kilometer walker, Harold Whitlock, broke the American streak, with a world-record time of four and one-half hours. Unfortunately for Whitlock, his torturous trek of about 31 miles through the streets of Berlin and the surrounding countryside ended back in the stadium just as the six runners in the 200-meter final were digging their little starting holes in the cinder track. The announcement of Whitlock's world record scarcely caused a ripple of applause among the 110,000 spectators. Their attention was riveted on the sprinters.[24]

The focus was especially on Owens, who was shooting for his third gold medal. Little did it matter that the official Nazi newspaper, *Der Angriff*, had just slurred America's "black auxillaries." Even less did it matter that a rabid Nazi assistant to Foreign Minister Joachim von Ribbentrop had just complained to Martha Dodd, the daughter of the U.S. Ambassador in Berlin, that the United States had taken unfair advantage by letting "non-humans, like Owens and other Negro athletes" compete in the Olympic Games. To Nazis and non-Nazis alike, the advantage was apparent. Before the finals on Wednesday afternoon, August 5, four of the five American gold medalists (in eight events) were black, with Owens leading the charge. His dark features, boyish smile, fluid motion, and record-breaking performances now made him the center of attention. Presumably this would be his last race, and "natives and tourists didn't want to miss the spectacle," according to one American sportswriter. Berliners watched Owens all the more closely because no German runner made the 200-meter finals. Tensely crouched alongside Jesse at the starting line, waiting for the gun, were Martin Osendarp of the Netherlands, Paul Haenni of Switzerland, Lee Orr of Canada, Wynand van Beverin of the Netherlands, and Mack Robinson of the United States.[25]

True to form, Owens was off like a cat shot from springs, to finish in an Olympic record time of 20.7 seconds. Some 3 or 4 meters behind him came Mack Robinson (who seemed destined always to be second best—behind Jesse Owens, behind his younger brother, Jackie, and ultimately behind most of his Olympic teammates in their postathletic careers). Unlike Owens, Robinson had come to Berlin with little prior notice outside southern California. A lowly college freshman, he had had to pay his own way to the Randall's Island tryouts. No Larry Snyder accompanied him to Berlin. No coach or trainer bothered to find him new track shoes when the only pair he owned virtually fell apart in a preliminary heat. Still, he ran the 200-meter final in 21.1 seconds, one-tenth of a second better than the Olympic record established by Eddie Tolan in 1932. Unfortunately for Mack, Jesse finished a full *five*-tenths of a second below Tolan's mark.[26]

Not since 1900 had a track-and-field athlete won three gold medals in a single Olympics. The entire stadium, mostly filled with native Germans, rose in applause. Thomas Wolfe did more than applaud. At Jesse's victory he let out such a whoop that his hosts, the family of Ambassador William E. Dodd, thought—or imagined—they saw Hitler turn in his seat to peer angrily in their direction. Actually, Wolfe's attitude toward American blacks was not altogether different from Hitler's. "Owens was black as tar," Wolfe later explained, "but what the hell, it was our team, and I thought he was wonderful. I was proud of him, so I yelled." Wolfe's patriotism momentarily outweighed his Old South racial prejudice.[27]

Just before Owens, Robinson, and bronze medal winner Osendarp took the victory stand to receive their medals, a steady drizzle turned into a downpour of rain. Spectators hurried for cover. For once, no one complained that Hitler hastily left before Owens received his gold medal.[28]

On the fourth day of competition, Jesse rested. He rose late from bed, then lounged about the Olympic Village receiving congratulations by word and gesture from fellow athletes. In the early afternoon he took the bus to the stadium to watch the finals in the javelin throw, the triple jump (the running "hop, step, and jump"), and the 110-meter hurdles. To no one's surprise, a German and two Finns dominated the javelin contest; Japan claimed both first and second place in the triple jump. In the hurdles, however, the Georgian Forrest "Spec" Towns won the gold medal, and a black North Dakota undergraduate, Fritz Pollard, Jr., took the bronze.[29]

For all their excitement, those finals were overshadowed by the 1,500-meter final, perhaps the most dramatic of all the week's events. Among the twelve starters were the Italian Luigi Beccali, the 1932 gold medalist; the American Glenn Cunningham, the holder of the world record for the mile; John Lovelock, a former Rhodes Scholar from New Zealand, now a London medical student who had soundly beaten Cunningham a year earlier at Palmer Stadium, Princeton; and the only black, Phil Edwards of Canada. From midway through the race to the beginning of the final lap, Cunningham led. On the homestretch, however, he was outsprinted by the spindly Lovelock, whose blob of sandy red hair and unique all-black shorts and shirt made him easily recognizable. Lovelock won in 3:47.8, a full second under the world record, but the next four men—Cunningham, Beccali, Archie San Romani of the United States, and Edwards of Canada—all broke the Olympic record time for the 1,500 meters.[30]

The excitement generated by that dramatic finish scarcely touched Owens, who sat relaxed in the stands beside Larry Snyder. Once again the sky was overcast, but Jesse wore sunglasses in a futile attempt to disguise himself from hero-worshipers. All afternoon he was interrupted with requests for autographs and poses for the camera. He seemed not to mind. His own events finished, he could now savor the fruit of fame without having to prepare himself mentally for another contest. Or so he thought.[31]

☆ ☆ ☆

To his surprise, he found himself as the leadoff man on the 400-meter relay team with Ralph Metcalfe, Foy Draper, and Frank Wykoff. Unfortunately his opportunity to win a fourth gold medal came at the expense of others, creating a bitter controversy that still simmers half a century later. It is an episode steeped in accusations of narrow self-interest, ugly anti-Semitism, and petty pride.

During the Olympic trials at Randall's Island a month earlier, the American coaches announced that the first three runners in the 100-meter trials would represent the United States in that event at Berlin, with the next four finishers making up the 400-meter relay team. Owens, Metcalfe, and Wykoff finished 1-2-3; Draper came in fourth, Marty Glickman fifth, Sam Stoller sixth, and Mack Robinson seventh, presumably ensuring them slots on the relay squad. When Robinson qualified for the 200-meter sprint, however, Wykoff replaced him on the relay team. Wykoff had, after all, successfully represented the United States in the relays at both the two previous Olympics. Moreover, the coach in charge of the relay team was Dean Cromwell, under whom Wykoff had excelled at the University of Southern California. From beginning to end, Cromwell's interests were to be a prominent factor in the story. Of the four athletes originally designated for the relay squad, only Foy Draper competed at Berlin. It was no mere coincidence that Draper, too, was a product of Cromwell's ambitious program at the University of Southern California.[32]

Sam Stoller, on the other hand, was a senior at the University of Michigan, and Marty Glickman a sophomore at Syracuse University. One was from Cincinnati, the other from New York City, but they shared a common ethnic heritage. Both were Jews, the only two Jews on the American track-and-field squad. Having resisted their friends' demands that they boycott the Berlin games, they went to Germany determined to display their athletic talents for all the world to see. Instead, they ended up as the only members of the American track-and-field team who went to Berlin without competing.

Early in the week of the games, Stoller, Glickman, and Draper were taken by coaches Cromwell and Robertson to one of the practice fields adjoining the Olympic Village, where they were instructed to run a trial 100-meter race to decide in what order they would run the relays. Stoller finished first, Glickman second, and Draper third. At the Olympic Stadium the next afternoon, Robertson congratulated Stoller on "a very fine race yesterday." As Stoller put it in his diary that night, Robertson assured him that he would be running the relays. "Had you taken third as Draper did, you would not run. As it is, I'll have to break the news slowly to Foy." Already, it seems, the American coaches were having second thoughts about the lineup for the relays. By Tuesday Owens had won his second gold medal, and perhaps his hot streak bore upon their deliberations. Metcalfe's name also regularly bobbed up as a potential member of the relay squad. Not only had he finished strong in the 100-meter dash, but now he was free to practice passing the baton. Yet Cromwell's concern for his own USC athletes remained a constant factor. If Robertson intended to drop Foy Draper, he first had to deal with Draper's mentor.[33]

Their private conversations are irretrievably lost, as both men have long since died without ever making public mention of their deliberations. On Friday, August 7, the day before the relays, Coach Robertson announced to the press that Owens would be on the squad the next day. As reported by the *New York Times*, Jesse relished the prospect. "That's swell news," he eagerly told his coach. "I haven't known what to do with myself since Wednesday. I'll sure hustle around that corner." That evening Owens confided to Stoller that Robertson had informed him that the relay team would be composed of Owens, Metcalfe, Stoller, and Wykoff. According to Stoller, though,

Draper also heard of the changed lineup and went immediately to Cromwell, who in turn arranged "a nice little chat" with Robertson.[34] The entire episode reeks of backroom politics.

Whatever their motives and sequence of decisions, the coaches called all their sprinters together in one of the Olympic Village rooms early Saturday morning, August 8, the very day of the 400-meter relay trials and finals. Pacing nervously in front of the group, Robertson reported a rumor that the Germans had been hiding their best sprinters for the relays. In order to ensure victory, Owens and Metcalfe would join the team. Then came the bombshell: Draper and Wykoff would round out the squad, to the exclusion of Stoller and Glickman. Although Draper had recently tested out third behind Stoller and Glickman, he, like Wykoff, had "more experience," the coaches explained.[35]

The two Jewish athletes felt they had been slapped in the face. Glickman, the younger, brasher of the two, blurted out, "Coach, this is ridiculous. You can't hide world-class sprinters; they have to race to get experience. Any American relay team you pick will win by fifteen yards—*any* of our runners, the milers or the hurdlers, could run against the Germans or anyone else and win by fifteen yards." To drop both Jewish athletes from competition seemed the height of insensitivity. "Sam Stoller and I are the only two Jews on the team," Glickman continued, "and there's bound to be a furor back home by keeping the two Jews off the team."

"Well, we'll see about that," replied Robertson.[36]

The room smoldered with dissension. As Metcalfe and Wykoff reminisced about the episode years later, they blamed Owens for having selfishly insisted privately to the coaches that he should be allowed to try for a fourth gold medal, and then for not protesting the omission of Stoller and Glickman from the team. "I guess he wanted Number Four that bad," Metcalfe recalled. Glickman remembers the scene altogether differently. He vividly reconstructs Jesse's protest: "Coach, let Marty and Sam run. I've had enough. I've won three gold medals. Let them run, they deserve it. They ought to run." In Glickman's account, one of the coaches shot back at Owens, "You'll do as you're told."[37]

Contradictory memories jostle with each other. Glickman insists that Metcalfe said not a word of protest; Metcalfe, now deceased, is on record as vehemently denying the charge. Despite all their disagreements, however, Metcalfe, Glickman, and Wykoff concur on one point: A strong element of anti-Semitism lay behind the decision to drop Glickman and Stoller. The eloquent Glickman was, and remains, the most outspoken critic of the decision. He suspects collusion between Dean Cromwell and American Olympic Committee president Avery Brundage, both of whom were members of a pro-Nazi organization, the America First Committee. They wanted "to save Hitler and his entourage the embarrassment of having Jews on that winning podium," Glickman insists.[38]

The accusation is plausible but lacks proof. If the coaches and Brundage ever discussed the issue prior to the decision to drop Stoller and Glickman, they did so privately and kept no notes. They could well have aired the matter informally at one of the nightly parties thrown for Olympic officials by their Nazi hosts. Predictably, both Robertson and Brundage declared publicly that the Jewish question had absolutely nothing to do with Stoller's and Glickman's removal from the relays. They convinced reporter John Kieran, who shrewdly observed that the substitution of two blacks for two Jews was "a transfer that would not have sent Herr Hitler off into raptures of delight even if he had paid any attention to it." Kieran ignores the point, however, that Jews, not blacks, were the primary targets of hostility in both Nazi Germany and within American pro-Nazi circles.[39]

Motives are seldom simple. In this case they are multilayered and intertwined. For Dean Cromwell, apparently, paternalistic interests and anti-Semitism worked in tandem to produce his desired results. His promotion of his own Southern Cal athletes was made possible by an anti-Semitic attitude—some of it explicit, more of it latent—in both the Olympic establishment and American society at large. Despite the prior American furor over the German Jewish question, coaches Cromwell and Robertson deemed their replacement of two Jewish athletes socially and politically acceptable. "We'll see," replied Robertson to Marty Glickman's warning of a hostile reaction back home. What they saw was merely a brief, light ripple of press criticism. To their relief, even the *New York Times* declared their decision acceptable for the sake of victory. Today Forrest "Spec" Towns, retired after a long career as track coach at the University of Georgia, is still firmly convinced that the American coaches at Berlin simply did what they felt they had to do to be certain of winning.[40]

To that end, they succeeded. The Owens–Metcalfe–Draper–Wykoff team won easily. In their morning trial heat they equaled the world and Olympic records, and in the afternoon they finished 15 yards or so ahead of their nearest competitors in a new world and Olympic record time of 39.8 seconds. Owens ran the opening leg, presumably in order to avoid receiving the baton, which he had not practiced recently. Several yards in the lead, he passed awkwardly but safely to Metcalfe, whose long legs lengthened the lead so dramatically that audiences still invariably gasp when they watch the spectacle in Leni Riefenstahl's film. "I was mad," Metcalfe recalled years later. Because his two Jewish teammates had been insensitively benched? No, because Dean Cromwell had placed his own man, Wykoff, at the crucial anchor position.[41]

The race was virtually won by the time Draper, then Wykoff, received the baton. In sportswriter Paul Gallico's words, Owens and Metcalfe "put the team so far out in front on the first two legs that the white boys to whom they turned over the baton could have crawled in on their hands and knees." As young Marty Glickman had predicted, the opponents were abysmally inept. Two of the six teams, the Netherlands and Canada, dropped the baton on their final exchange. The "surprise" German squad sprang no surprise at all. They ran strongly and passed the baton carefully to finish second, far off the American pace. An Italian team finished third.[42]

As Metcalfe, Draper, and Wykoff approached the victory stand, they agreed that Owens should take the uppermost platform in honor of his Olympic grand slam. But Jesse refused, generously demanding instead that Metcalfe—who had barely missed winning a gold medal three times previously—should occupy the highest perch. If one can believe the report of a black Cleveland newspaper, Hitler joined in a loud applause for the American foursome.[43]

☆ ☆ ☆

His fourth gold medal in hand, Owens casually watched three long-distance races, including the marathon, on the final day of the track-and-field events, Sunday, August 9. By the end of the program, sixteen Olympic records had been broken and one equaled. Four of those new marks belonged to Owens. In the unofficial point system devised by the American Olympic Committee (ten points for first place, and five, four, three, two, and one for the next five finishes), the American male track-and-field team scored 203 points. Owens alone scored 40, almost two-thirds of the entire German team's total.[44]

Outside of track and field, however, the Germans dominated: 87–1 in gymnastics, 65–6 in equestrian events, 43–4 in canoeing, 34–9 in boxing, 28–10 in weightlifting, 27–0 in cycling, 20–2 in yachting, and 19–0 in fencing. Only in wrestling and basketball did Americans other than the track-and-field athletes make a decent showing. When the president of the International Olympic Committee, Henri Baillet-Latour, finally proclaimed the closing of the Berlin games, both American and German scoring systems accorded the Germans a decisive victory over the United States. The other European fascist power, Italy, finished a distant third in team point totals.[45]

Accounts of those closing ceremonies now seem perversely ironic. As Count Baillet-Latour drew the curtain on Berlin, he called upon "the youth of every country to assemble in four years at Tokyo, there to celebrate with us the twelfth Olympic Games." An American journalist described the scene colorfully: "The five-ringed Olympic flag came slowly down from above a packed stadium, the Olympic flame flickered and went out, and in the twilight at Berlin the true Olympians turned their thoughts toward Tokyo and 1940."[46] The Tokyo Games of 1940 would be canceled, of course. Japanese leaders in the late 1930s planned for military aggression, not athletic contests.

And now, so did the Nazis. Just two days after the closing ceremonies in Berlin, the American press reported that as soon as the few remaining athletes departed, the "once peaceful" Olympic Village would become an infantry training center. The largest restaurant and the music hall would be transformed into a military hospital; another dining hall and lounge were earmarked for an officers' club. Foreign athletes still in the Village could already hear machine guns rattling on nearby training fields. "The army had done its best to help make the

Olympic show a success," one American reporter commented, "but it now is resuming its real job."[47]

Once the glow of the Berlin Games wore off, all of Nazi Germany returned to business as usual. Anti-Semitic signs reappeared in the press and on billboards. By the autumn of 1938, when Leni Reifenstahl finally finished editing her monumental *Olympia* for public viewing, terms such as the anti-Comintern pact, *anschluss,* the Munich crisis, and *kristallnacht* had become common references in the West. Soon *blitzkrieg* and "the final solution" would join the vocabulary of horror, casting the Berlin Olympics into the hinterland of public memory.[48]

CHAPTER 7

A Champion's Reward

THE BERLIN GAMES MADE JESSE OWENS a household name throughout the world. He was America's newest idol. Even Southern newspapers such as the *Nashville Tennessean*, the *Arkansas Gazette*, and the *Chattanooga Times*, which normally ignored black athletes altogether, carried Associated Press wire photographs of Owens in action. Americans, Southerners included, loved a winner, whatever his color. In the *New York Times's* daily front-page coverage of the games, Owens figured prominently in the headlines. For two weeks his name appeared on a Broadway marquee as movie houses ran newsreels of his Olympic exploits.[1]

In Europe, where track-and-field athletes were held in higher esteem than in the United States, Owens was even more acclaimed. Hitler's Minister of Propaganda, Josef Goebbels, instructed the German press to portray the American Negro favorably in order to blunt foreign criticism of the Nazi regime. He need not have bothered: German athletic enthusiasts needed little encouragement. A cigarette company, Reemtsma, produced a popular picture-and-text series featuring seven photographs of Owens. The text lauded him as the

Wunderathlet of the Berlin Games, the greatest of all track-and-field athletes in the history of the Olympics.[2]

Athletic promoters in a dozen or so cities throughout Europe welcomed the publicity, for in each of those cities Jesse and his American mates were booked for track exhibitions shortly after they finished their Olympic events. Months earlier, as contributions to the Olympic effort lagged in the United States, the Amateur Athletic Union had arranged barnstorming tours in order to pay the American team's expenses to and from Berlin. By the time the team left New York, the track budget was oversubscribed, but the deficit for the entire team stood at almost $30,000. Now, despite its own successful (though tardy) efforts at fundraising, the track squad had to make up what the other sports had failed to collect. The schedule called for two groups to fan out all over Northern and Eastern Europe, with a boxing team to join them as soon as the Olympic boxing program was finished.[3]

Anticipating Jesse Owens's dominance at Berlin, promoters tried to book him for each of the local post-Olympic exhibitions. "They demanded a star gate attraction," recalls William Heintz, the Ohio State assistant coach who roomed with Larry Snyder in Berlin. Cologne organizers, for example, offered the AAU 15 percent of the gate receipts if they could have Owens; without him, they would guarantee only 10 percent. They got him, and the AAU in turn got its money. Unfortunately, the entire episode went sour, producing charges of exploitation by the AAU and of selfish insubordination on the part of Owens himself.[4]

In a meeting with the whole track-and-field team on the ship to Europe, Daniel Ferris, the Secretary-Treasurer of the AAU had casually mentioned the AAU's plans for a post-Olympic tour. The athletes, preoccupied with their forthcoming Berlin events, gave the matter little thought. Almost three weeks later, as Owens sat in his dressing room just after his final 400-meter relay race, he was reminded of the Cologne engagement. At his side, Larry Snyder winced when he heard the news. He saw Jesse as bone tired after his many races and long jumps within a week. "About the trip to Cologne," Snyder snapped at an AAU official standing nearby, "that's out. You can't run him on the day after the relay. You can't ask him to do that." Technically, Snyder was right. The AAU would not ask Jesse to run again on the very day after his last Berlin victory; the Cologne exhibition was scheduled not for the next day, but the day after. The AAU would not ask him to run then; it commanded him to.[5]

Years later Owens recalled that he was reluctant to make the exhibition tour for two reasons: He was homesick for his wife and child, and he was physically exhausted from the Berlin games. Both those explanations were no doubt true, but in wanting to return immediately to the United States he was prompted also by more material concerns. As he watched the last track-and-field events on August 9, the day after his relay races, he received a telegram from a California orchestra offering him the mind-boggling sum of $25,000 to appear on stage for two weeks. He reacted with glee, "I'm anxious to finish my college career," he told a reporter, "but I can't afford to miss this chance if it really means big money. I can always go back and get a degree." Larry Snyder agreed. "It would be foolish for me to stand in Jesse's way," Snyder announced. "He's absolutely at the height of his fame now. Nothing that he could do in his remaining year at college competition would lift him to a higher peak in the athletic world than he now enjoys."[6]

From that peak, Jesse tumbled into a valley of hectic travel, frustrated ambition, and personal despair. The California "offer" turned out to be a hoax, the first of many to raise his hopes unrealistically. With that telegram in hand, he returned to the Olympic Village by bus from the stadium, determined to go through with the exhibition tour. Presumably, the train would leave early the next morning and would arrive in Cologne in plenty of time for the exhibition scheduled in the early evening of August 10. Jesse planned to pack his belongings at a leisurely pace, then spend the evening saying goodbye to teammates and various newfound friends such as Lutz Long.

At the Village, however, Ralph Metcalfe rushed up to him with disquieting news: "Forget the packing, Jesse. Just grab spikes and togs and let's get out of here. We've got a train to catch." Hurriedly packing the essentials, Jesse left a note asking his roommate, Dave Albritton, to bring the remainder of his gear and belongings. Early the next morning Albritton left Berlin with Glenn Cunningham, John Woodruff, and several other athletes for a meet in Dresden. Larry Snyder accompanied that group. They seemed "so dead tired," he told a reporter, "they could scarcely drag themselves around."[7]

Certainly no records were in danger of being broken by those touring teams. Jesse, especially, performed far below his normal standards. Under the pressure of the crowds, the numerous contests, and the late-night conversations at Berlin, he had lost ten pounds off his trim, muscular frame. On the tour, he lost his concentration. At Cologne 35,000 spectators saw him win the long jump with a modest leap of 24 feet, $4\frac{1}{2}$ inches; his sprint relay team also won its match, but narrowly. Worst of all was his 100-meter final against Ralph Metcalfe and several other American and German sprinters. "Larry," he told Snyder a few days later, "when I saw Ralph waiting there on the mark and realized what I was up against, and the kind of party that had been arranged for me as a reward, I just didn't care. I hope Ralph enjoyed winning that one. He can have it." He took it—in 10.4 seconds, a step ahead of Owens.[8]

The Cologne meet began at 6 P.M. and ran to 8:30 or so. A banquet then lasted until midnight. Early the next morning, Jesse was put on a plane alone to join Cunningham's group in Prague for another exhibition meet that very night against Czech athletes. Jesse had a little American money in his pocket but no German marks. A man on the plane kindly bought him a sandwich and a glass of milk, or else he would have had no lunch. After a delayed stopover, the plane arrived in Prague at 4:30 P.M. Cunningham's squad had arrived several hours earlier, in time to check into a hotel, but from the airport Owens was rushed directly to the stadium for the six o'clock meet. Although American athletes won all nine events, Jesse's performances once again suggested physical weariness and mental distraction. He won the 100-meter dash in 10.7 seconds, his slowest time in months. His winning long jump distance of 23 feet, $11\frac{1}{64}$ inches scarcely equaled his best high school marks.[9]

Mediocrity turned to inconsistency on the next night, back in Bochum, Germany. Having taken all day to travel by plane from Prague to Bochum, with a long stopover in Berlin, the team finally received "lunch" at 4 P.M. Bumpy plane rides made several athletes too sick to eat. The others wolfed down their food in time to be on the field again at 6 P.M. Still, Owens won the 100-meter dash in 10.3 seconds, tying his own world record. The noisy cheers of 8,000 spectators turned to groans, however, when his best long jump measured an abysmal 23 feet, $\frac{3}{8}$ inch. An unknown German athlete, Wilhelm Leichum, outleaped the world-renowned Owens by almost a foot.[10] The champion's reward was wounded pride.

☆ ☆ ☆

Immediately after the Bochum meet, the team boarded a night flight for a Channel crossing to England. They landed just before midnight at Croyden Airport, near London. Too late to find a restaurant or hotel open, they ate stale sandwiches in the airport lobby, then collapsed on cots in an empty hangar. Two hours later another group arrived from Hamburg, bringing the American party to about fifteen athletes. On Saturday, August 15, they were all scheduled to compete against a combined Commonwealth team of Canadian and British athletes. Rumors circulated that further engagements were planned throughout the next week in Sweden, Norway, and Finland, but no one seemed to know for sure, least of all the athletes. No itinerary was made available. After each meet they were simply herded onto another train or plane for their next destination—like "trained seals," as Larry Snyder caustically put it.[11]

Only youthful vigor, flexibility, and curiosity made the prospect bearable. "We didn't know from one day to the next where we were going. We enjoyed competing and seeing new sights. We just did as we were told," one athlete recalls.[12] For the weary Owens, however, a picture of his wife and child in one pocket and a supposedly lucrative contract offer in another pocket combined to produce serious misgivings about further barnstorming. The prospect of more mediocre, embarrassing performances intensified his doubts.

Jesse found London pleasant enough. Surprisingly, the weather was much better than Berlin's. Londoners were enjoying a mid-August deluge of sunshine. Most of all, Jessie enjoyed being able to speak and understand the language. Communication by gestures and in the broken English spoken by Germans had become tiresome. Yet one thing was no different. In London, as in Berlin, Jesse was mobbed by autograph-seekers every time he appeared on the street. With boys, especially, the fabled English reserve dissolved quickly in the presence of the strangely colored, world-famous American athlete. Jesse responded warmly to his London admirers, but his heart was not in it. In a response to a New York journalist several days later, he unintentionally revealed his preoccupation. Asked if he had signed many autographs, he replied, "If I had a penny for every time I've signed my name, I wouldn't have to work for the rest of my life." On the streets of London his autograph attested to past athletic achievement; internally, he was fretting over future financial security.[13]

Like most of his teammates, he was broke. When not out wandering the streets, they sat around the hotel lobby, unwilling to expose themselves to entertainment temptations that would cost money. In their rooms they played crap games for pennies and wooden matches, not dollars. "Somebody's making money somewhere," Owens blurted out to a reporter in an uncharacteristic expression of anger. His target was the Amateur Athletic Union: "They are trying to grab all they can and we can't even buy a souvenir of the trip."[14]

That sideswipe at the AAU reflected many years of conflict between NCAA and AAU interests. Ever since the founding of the NCAA in 1906, the older AAU (founded in 1888) had jealously guarded its traditional control of amateur athletics in the United States. NCAA officials bitterly resented that dominance, all the more so because of the AAU's weighty representation on the American Olympic Committee. During the 1920s the NCAA attempted to force a change in the ratio of delegates on the AOC, only to have its numbers reduced from sixteen to three, while the AAU kept all its thirty-three seats on the AOC. In 1928, when Avery Brundage became President of both the AAU and the AOC, he readjusted those numbers in order to bring an end to "the war" between the AAU and NCAA. Open warfare did cease for a while, but NCAA enthusiasts continued to chafe at the legislative and financial power of the AAU.[15]

Finally settled in a London hotel free of athletic meets on Thursday and Friday, August 13–14, Owens and Snyder spent many hours discussing Jesse's future in relation to his enforced participation in the AAU's barnstorming tour of Europe. Into their sessions they brought an NCAA administrative official, Alfred R. Masters; the Harvard athletic

PROUD PARENTS. Henry and Emma Owens and Jesse's wife, Ruth, welcome Jesse back home from Berlin in 1936. Originally Alabama sharecroppers, the Owenses moved to Cleveland, where they found irregular employment, in the early twenties. From his mother Jesse inherited an optimistic, determined spirit. *(Chicago Daily Defender)*

CHARLES RILEY, MENTOR. A short, frail Irish-American, Riley taught physical education and coached Jesse in track at Cleveland's Fairmount Junior High School. In addition to honing the young Owens's athletic skills, "Pop" Riley helped to shape his manners and values, and raise his aspirations. *(Personal collection of Harriet Mae Bottorff)*

PAGE BOYS, 1935. Jesse Owens and "Tippy" Dye running errands in the Ohio State Senate, a more pleasant task than Jesse's earlier work of cleaning tables and operating an elevator in order to pay his way through college. *(Ohio State University Photo Archives)*

LARRY SNYDER, COLLEGE COACH. A former track star at Ohio State University, Snyder became head track coach shortly before Owens matriculated. He handled Jesse firmly but tactfully, and accompanied him to Berlin in 1936. At Rome in 1960, Snyder served as head coach of the United States Olympic track team. *(Ohio State University Photo Archives)*

A MEASURE OF EXCELLENCE. The dramatic emergence of black track athletes in the mid-thirties caused physiologists to wonder if unique bone and muscle structure held the key to the athletes' prowess. Here (in 1936) a physician examines Owens, only to find that Jesse possesses no unusual anatomical characteristics that could be considered peculiar to his race. *(Chicago Daily Defender)*

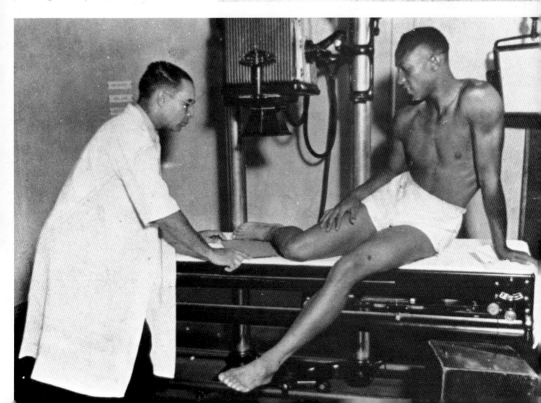

THE NAZI OLYMPICS. Followed by Nazi officials and flanked by Comte Henri de Baillet-Latour, President of the International Olympic Committee (left), and Dr. Theodor von Lewald, German Olympic Committee President (right), Hitler enters Berlin Stadium as the central figure in the opening ceremonies of Olympiad XI. Each afternoon he returned to watch the finals in track and field, in which Jesse Owens stole the show. In legend, but not in fact, Hitler "snubbed" Owens, refusing to congratulate him publicly for his feats. *(Personal collection of George Eisen)*

BATTLING THE BERLIN ELEMENTS. Rain and cold plagued track athletes during the entire first week of the Berlin Games, making it all the more difficult for Owens to warm up and compete in his numerous preliminaries and finals. Here, waiting for his next event, he huddles to the far right with (left to right) American Frank Wykoff, Swiss runner Paul Hänni, and American Ralph Metcalfe. (*Die Olympischen Spiele 1936*)

GOING FOR GOLD. Poised in his classic "tight" starting stance, Jesse awaits the starter's gun for the finals of the 100-meter dash, in which he equalled the Olympic record of 10.3 seconds. This photograph clearly shows the toes of Owens's track shoes sunk in holes dug in the cinders—without benefit of starting blocks. *(Die Olympischen Spiele 1936)*

OLYMPIC FRIENDSHIP. When Jesse beat Germany's best, Lutz Long, in the long-jump finals, Long spontaneously rushed up to congratulate him. Ignoring their racial and national differences, they walked arm-in-arm from the field, and fast became friends. Unfortunately, they never met again after the Berlin Olympics: In 1944 Long was killed in combat, fighting for the German army in Sicily. *(Personal collection of George Eisen)*

UP AND AWAY. Having almost disqualified himself through infractions in the long-jump preliminaries, Jesse soared to a new Olympic record in the finals. To sportswriter Grantland Rice, he seemed to be jumping "clear out of Germany" on his final leap. *(Ohio State University Photo Archives)*

SET IN STONE. At the Games' end, a German artisan renders a reminder of Owens's victories. These engravings, skillfully tattooed into the wall of Berlin Stadium, are still quite legible. *(Die Olympischen Spiele 1936)*

HERO-WORSHIPPERS. After Berlin, never again would Jesse Owens go unrecognized on the street. Here he responds to eager English schoolboys in London, just before returning to the United States. *(Ohio State University Photo Archives)*

MENTOR'S DELIGHT. [Above:] His dream come true, Charles Riley welcomes Jesse home from Europe. *(Personal collection of Harriet Mae Bottorff)*
[Below:] Larry Snyder joins Jesse in a procession of honor—one of the three major victory parades in which Owens participated—through the streets of Columbus. *(Ohio State University Photo Archives)*

LOOKING SHARP. Smartly dressed in the only suit he owns, Jesse boards a train for Cleveland. Enthusiastic crowds, eager reporters, and numerous offers of employment made him beam brightly. Unfortunately, most of the offers proved to be insubstantial. *(Ohio State University Photo Archives)*

HAPPY TIMES. Basking in the glow of Olympic fame, Ruth and Jesse in the autumn of 1936 attend the Ohio State Homecoming football game as honored guests of the president of the university, Dr. George W. Rightmire. Jesse's smart new outfits came from the $10,000 or more he received to stump for presidential hopeful Alf Landon. *(Ohio State University Photo Archives)*

EXPERT ADVICE. After several money-making efforts as a political campaigner, night-club performer, and athletic exhibitionist, Jesse returned to Ohio State in 1940-41 in a futile attempt to win his college degree. To pay for his tuition, he assisted Larry Snyder in the coaching of track. *(Ohio State University Photo Archives)*

FOR A NATION AT WAR. During World War II, Jesse briefly headed a
government program of physical fitness for blacks, then worked as an
executive in a Ford Motor Company defense plant. Like Joe Louis, he served
the purposes of patriotic propaganda, as here indicated in a poster displayed
by former heavyweight champion Jack Dempsey. *(Library of Congress)*

YOUTH WORK. [Above:] Acclaimed for his work with the Southside Boys Club and the Illinois Youth Commission, Jesse also contributed his time and energy to less spectacular projects. In the mid-fifties he headed an anti-polio campaign sponsored by the Jaycees of Chicago. [Below:] In this 1962 scene Jesse awards trophies and certificates to the winners of a local athletic meet. *(Chicago Daily Defender)*

"ONLY IN AMERICA." At the halftime ceremonies of Ohio State's Homecoming game in 1960, Jesse crowned daughter Marlene as Homecoming Queen. Such an event could occur "only in America," he reminded Marlene (left), while Ruth (right) proudly looked on. (*Ohio State University Photo Archives*)

RAPT ATTENTION ON THE ROAD. For the last two decades of his life, Owens stayed constantly on the road addressing civic, business, and athletic groups. An audience in Bangor, Maine, was so captivated that a local reporter observed "You could hear a biscuit land on the floor." Here Bangor High School athletes listen attentively to his informal remarks in 1968. *(Bangor Daily News)*

A DEGREE AT LAST. Having failed to acquire a baccalaureate degree, Jesse was awarded an honorary Doctorate of Athletic Arts degree from Ohio State in 1972. *(Ohio State University Photo Archives)*

AN ATHLETE GROWN OLD. Still going strong at age sixty-five, Owens continued to laud the virtues of athletics, the Olympic Games, and the American way of life. He is shown here in 1978 puffing on a pipe in order to cut down on cigarettes (he had smoked a pack daily for many years). Less than two years later, he died of lung cancer. *(Ohio State University Photo Archives)*

director, William Bingham; and the Indiana track coach, William "Billy" Hayes, all staunch NCAA men. They agreed with Snyder's complaint that "colleges provide 90 percent of the athletes and the politicians run the show," and that the athletes on this barnstorming tour were being treated "like mere cattle being shipped about." Most of all, they agreed on the cause of the problem: "Such things wouldn't occur and couldn't occur if greed on the part of the AAU were more easily satisfied."[16]

Had it not been for their antipathy toward the AAU, those leaders of intercollegiate athletics would probably never have recommended, as they did, that Owens return immediately to the United States to capitalize financially on his Olympic fame. Buoyed by their support, Snyder acted on Jesse's behalf. On Friday afternoon he was approached by a London representative of Swedish promoters, with plane tickets for him and Jesse to fly to Stockholm for the next scheduled meet. Snyder refused the tickets, informing the perplexed Englishman that Jesse would instead be taking the earliest ship available to the United States.[17]

That decision seemed justified by a pleasant surprise early the next morning, the day of the London athletic meet, when a hotel porter delivered to Jesse's door a transatlantic cablegram from Los Angeles. The entertainer Eddie Cantor's agent was proposing a $40,000 fee for Owens to appear with Cantor for ten weeks on stage and radio. Jesse immediately sought out Snyder, who sent a return telegram to Cantor asking for further details. Snyder encouraged his protégé to give serious consideration to the offer. "But I ain't so hot as a tap dancer," Jesse protested. "With your sense of rhythm," Snyder replied, "you'd soon master it." Both men floated giddily to the White City Stadium that afternoon.[18]

Built to hold 90,000 spectators for the Olympics of 1908, White City Stadium on the afternoon of August 15, 1936, bulged at the seams. Thousands of athletics enthusiasts were turned away as the gates closed in their faces just before the meet began. They missed seeing ten records, including four world marks, broken in the fourteen events. Apparently the two days of rest had renewed the strength of the American athletes, who demolished a combined British and Canadian team, 11–3. Owens contributed little to the rout. He ran only one race, and that as the inconspicuous third leg of a relay team with Frank Wykoff, Marty Glickman, and Ralph Metcalfe. Had fair-minded Britons known of the earlier controversy over the relay team at Berlin, they undoubtedly would have given their heartiest cheers to Glickman for his spunky comeback. After the race Owens was heard to say that he was "pretty sick of running."[19]

Little did he know that he would never again run as an amateur athlete. That night Avery Brundage, president of the American Olympic Committee, called Larry Snyder long distance from Berlin. Overseeing the final week of the Olympic Games, Brundage had heard rumors of Owens's disaffection. Now he sought clarification, but Snyder refused to divulge any information. As Brundage later put it, Snyder gave not "an inkling of Owens' sudden shift in plans." Snyder certainly took too lightly Brundage's threat of "dire consequences" if Jesse did not go to Stockholm. Owens had not signed any entry blank for the Swedish meet, Snyder reasoned; according to AAU rules, an athlete had to sign an application form before he could be suspended for not fulfilling his commitment. The legal reasoning was sound. Unfortunately, AAU and Olympic Committee officials were in no mood to abide by the letter of their law. They were political animals, eager to reap the benefits of their Stockholm agreement and unwilling to let an athlete go his own way without punishment.[20]

Larry Snyder should have known all that, for the entire history of the AAU was littered with instances of severe penalties against nonconformist athletes. As early as 1904, at the second modern Olympiad in St. Louis, the marathoner Fred Lorz was suspended for life after he dropped out of the race exhausted, took a ride by automobile to a site near the finish line, and jogged the remaining distance to finish first. Even Jesse's boyhood hero, Charles Paddock, suffered the wrath of the AAU. His gold and silver medals in the 1920 Antwerp Olympics mattered little three years later when he stubbornly competed in a YMCA-sponsored Paris meet that was not sanctioned by the AAU. He was suspended for a year, barely becoming eligible again in time for the 1924 Paris Olympics. The AAU was a tough taskmaster from whom no mercy could be expected.[21]

Jesse chanced it. With Larry Snyder, he remained in his hotel as a plane laden with American athletes and coaches left

London for Stockholm in the early morning of August 16. It was a Sunday, a dismal Sunday. Rolf Dillon, chairman of the Stockholm committee, called long distance to AAU secretary-treasurer Daniel Ferris in Berlin, angrily protesting Owens's withdrawal. Ferris in turn rang Snyder's number in London. As Snyder later reconstructed the conversation, the phone line could well have melted from the heat of mutual hostility.

"What's all this I hear about you and Jesse not going to Sweden?" Ferris asked.

"You heard right," Snyder replied. "Jesse's got a big chance. He's got a break that comes once in a lifetime and never comes at all to a lot of people. It's tough for a colored boy to make money, at best. What kind of a friend would I be to stand in his way?"

"You can't do that," Ferris insisted. "I've signed a contract with these people." The Stockholm engagement was necessary, he added, because the AAU was still "in the red."

But Snyder refused to budge.

"Well, I'll have to suspend him," Ferris threatened.

"You can't suspend him in the Big Ten," Snyder shot back, "because that's one organization you don't run." That salvo off his chest, Snyder flung another, more bitter barb: "And listen, you're spending money on this call that could be spent in making up Olympic deficits." Then he slammed down the receiver.[22]

The enraged Ferris went immediately to Brundage. Together they called a press conference in Berlin's Olympic Stadium, where precisely two weeks earlier Jesse Owens had run his first preliminary heat. The press conference had to be held in the early afternoon in order not to conflict with the closing ceremonies of the 1936 Games. Once again the public images of Owens and Hitler interlocked. While Hitler made his final grand procession to the stadium, Owens's amateur track career came to a crashing halt. With Brundage at his side, Ferris announced Jesse's suspension from all further amateur competition in the United States. "We had no alternative under the circumstances but to disbar Owens," Ferris insisted. Suspension became "automatic," he explained, when Jesse failed "to fulfill his competitive obligations."[23]

By then Jesse had already sent a telegraph message to his wife and parents, informing them that he would return to the

States as soon as possible. Two hours later he received by telegram from Ferris a terse notice of his suspension. Now it was Jesse's and Larry Snyder's turn to make public statements—denunciations of the Amateur Athletic Union. Snyder blasted the AAU for not caring "whom it sacrifices to get its ten per cent." Owens was even more outspoken. On his own predicament:

> This suspension is very unfair to me. There's nothing I can gain out of this trip [to Sweden]. All we athletes get out of this Olympic business is a view out of a train or airplane window. It gets tiresome, it really does.

On the greed of the Amateur Athletic Union:

> This track business is becoming one of the biggest rackets in the world. It doesn't mean a darned thing to us athletes. The A.A.U. gets the money. It gets all the money collected in the United States and then comes over to Europe and takes half the proceeds.

On his own central concern:

> A fellow desires something for himself.[24]

☆ ☆ ☆

Before he and Snyder left London on Wednesday, August 19, Jesse finally received "something for himself" in the form of an international check for two hundred dollars. It came from Cleveland. Jesse's former employer Alonzo Wright, and a black owner of a local barber shop and grocery store, Bennie Mason, had heard that while Owens struggled with Olympic authorities, he was stranded and nearly penniless in London. They had conferred, agreed to give him a hundred dollars apiece, and sent it by wire.[25]

The transatlantic wire service did a booming business that week, as did the porters at the London hotel where Jesse stayed. Several times a day they brought him a fistful of telegrams. Most were flashy commercial proposals that turned out to be unreliable, such as Paramount Pictures' "offer" of a contract for a series of short movies, and a bid from a

Manhattan theater for $10,000 a week. Some were more modest, more tentative, but substantial, such as an invitation from Dr. D. Ormond Walker, president of Ohio's premier black university, Wilberforce, for Jesse to become the head track coach at Wilberforce upon his graduation from Ohio State. "Do not turn professional," Dr. Walker implored. "Wilberforce will take care of you."[26]

At the time Jesse seemed quite well taken care of without having to finish his college degree. The black press in the United States proudly but naïvely reported that his offers amounted to $100,000. The *New York Times* observed merely that the young Owens held "a sheaf of cables from American promoters offering him fantastic prices for personal appearances." The range of apparent possibilities overwhelmed Jesse. "I don't know what I'm going to do," he told one reporter. "All I know is that I want to get back to my family.... I'll be the gladdest man in the world to get there, believe me. All this ballyhoo is getting on my nerves."[27]

Amid the pressures he retained a sense of humor. In response to a reporter's question about his wife's attitude toward his turning professional, he replied, "She's left the whole situation up to me. After all, I'm the head of my house—while I'm away at least." He wouldn't be away for long. On Wednesday morning, August 19, Jesse and Larry Snyder took a train to Southampton to board a large Cunard–White Star liner, the *Queen Mary,* bound for New York. At the dock, Jesse lightheartedly shrugged off a question about the AAU suspension; he didn't care "a couple of hoots" about it.[28]

The American public cared more than a couple of hoots, if its views were accurately reflected in the press. Editorial opinion overwhelmingly supported Owens's refusal to go to Stockholm. As one editor shrewdly commented.

> He may have agreed at one time to join the junket, but he changed his mind. That is an amateur's privilege. It is what distinguishes him from a professional. As he was to receive nothing for his appearance in Scandinavia, no contract binding him could have existed. Somebody should tell the moguls of amateurism about the Emancipation Proclamation.

Those "moguls," of course, were Avery Brundage and Daniel Ferris. "They have pretty well succeeded in making amateurism odious," declared one editor. "Czar" Brundage had stolen a page from Hitler's book, another newspaperman exclaimed. Owens was simply the victim of "hair-trigger action by the bureaucrats of sport," added another. He was "the latest target of the [Amateur Athletic] Union's keenedge axe" that earlier felled the Olympic hopes of Eleanor Holm Jarrett, the *New York Times* noted.[29]

Those shrill indictments of the AAU and American Olympic officials stemmed from an outraged sense of fairness. Owens had represented his country honorably, even spectacularly, and now had every right to translate his athletic exploits into financial security if he could. "If he can make a little honest money," the *Boston Herald-American* commented, "more power to him." The great bulk of editorial opinion saw the issue in terms more practical than idealistic: Jesse's medals and world acclaim would not provide "a nickel's worth of benefit" to him if he remained an amateur. He had enough medals; now he needed a job. That was certainly the position of Jesse's family and friends. "If he fails to get the money now," Ruth Owens told a correspondent for the *New York Times*, "he'll simply be a forgotten Owens in ten years. He should get the money while he can and then finish school." Jesse's past opponent and friend, Eulace Peacock, said it best: "After the glory is gone, what have you? Jesse made a smart move."[30]

Some people were not so sure. Were the offers authentic? Would the money really be forthcoming? As the *Herald-American* tentatively put the case, "We feel he is doing wisely—provided he's going to get the money." The black press especially smelled rats in the cupboard. Familiar with white duplicity, they wisely urged caution on their hero. As events unfolded, the warning of Owens's hometown *Call and Post* proved to be prophetic: "Are all of these offers real? Unfortunately a gang of people like to rush into print with fabulous sums mentioned for the services of reigning popular heroes, without any intention of making good, simply imbued with the idea of gaining free publicity."[31]

Black newspapermen were not the only ones worried about the credibility of the numerous "offers" Owens had received. Ohio State's athletic director L. W. St. John was similarly concerned. He sent separate but almost identical transatlantic cables to Owens and Snyder just before they left London, urging them to return to Columbus before making any decisions. In a more relaxed atmosphere, the three of them should sit down and "determine the authenticity and reliability of some of these offers which are said to have been made to Jesse." St. John instinctively questioned the wisdom of turning professional but assured Owens that this would "not necessarily" be his final recommendation.[32]

Immediately after he dispatched the cables, St. John wrote a more candid letter to Snyder, to be delivered personally by a friend as soon as the *Queen Mary* arrived in New York, before Snyder "gets too tangled up with these promoters." St. John reiterated his insistence on a deliberate course of action: "If it seems best for Jesse to go Pro I can see no reason why he may not do so more safely after looking the thing over carefully— here—and considering with some of us who are so deeply interested in his ultimate welfare." To Coach Snyder, privately, St. John confessed the university's stake in the decision. The presence of Owens on the Ohio State track squad made scheduling easier and the terms of each engagement more lucrative. For example, the athletic director at the University of Southern California was "anxious to have our team back at Los Angeles again next summer," St. John noted. "I am sure he thinks that Jesse will be on the team. If he is not that may make a difference. Jesse would certainly be a great asset and we could probably take pretty good care of him."[33] Self-interest and benign paternalism coexisted comfortably in the office of athletics at Ohio State.

For altogether different reasons, another Ohio State man concerned himself with Jesse's future. On the very day after the *Queen Mary* embarked for the United States, Delbert Oberteuffer, an eminent Professor of Physical Education, in a long, richly detailed letter to the athletic director, expressed his anxieties for Owens's future prospects as a student. It was "well known," according to Oberteuffer, that Jesse had been steered away from the tough basic courses necessary for his degree, principally because of "the desire on the part of his athletic advisors to keep him eligible." Oberteuffer thought that policy a mistake: "I believe that if he had developed an enthusiastic desire to do something besides run foot-races in college, no matter how meritorious an ambition that might be, he could have succeeded satisfactorily to at least an average competency in these avoided fields."

Oberteuffer based his opinion on a firsthand acquaintance with Owens in the classroom. He had taught him in a course during the spring and had found him "intelligently curious" on occasion, but saw him lapse periodically "into that state of indifference in which it was plain to be seen that his mind was on his track career and nothing else." His Olympic fame now made his academic progress all the more imperative: "The world has come to admire him as a beautiful and remarkable animal. He has been on display and has invariably come through. He has reached the top in athletic skill. The world, it seems to me, now is entitled to look upon him as a remarkable man as well as a remarkable psychomotor genius."

Toward that end, Owens's "energies and interests" would have to be "carefully redirected" by his advisers. Otherwise, the university itself would be to blame. "We have been interested largely in keeping him eligible, but beyond that we have been more or less unconcerned," Oberteuffer lamented. "The time has come, in my judgment, when we as a faculty should do what we can to fan the spark of interest into the flame which it can become." Suggesting a series of conferences between Owens and his academic advisers, Oberteuffer closed on a note of "great sympathy" for the problems of "this outstanding athlete as he faces his professional future."[34]

Unfortunately, the prospect that Owens might turn professional bothered the athletic director much more than did the obstacles to his earning a college degree.

☆ ☆ ☆

The *Queen Mary* made the transatlantic crossing in the record time of four days, seven hours, an appropriate feat with the world champion Owens on board. Jesse enjoyed the trip immensely. Unlike his crossing to Europe on the *Manhattan* a month earlier, he was now free of daily athletic workouts and anxieties over forthcoming contests. The hectic barnstorming schedule behind him, he could now rest, sleep late each morning, and eat whatever he liked. He had lost 10 pounds in Europe; on the ship he gained 12.[35]

He traveled tourist class with Larry Snyder, but in the dining room, on deck, and in the ballroom he was a conspicuous figure. Famous, handsome, and sociable, he danced nightly until the music stopped. By the second evening he had paired off with a blonde English beauty, Marjorie Shaw. She dispelled his homesickness. "And my," she announced in her heavy English accent to reporters at the pier in New York, "but isn't he the most perfect gentleman! Perfectly grand!"[36]

Shortly before the *Queen Mary* steamed into New York Harbor, ship-to-shore telephone lines became clogged with calls for Jesse. Bill "Bojangles" Robinson had a brief but urgent message: "Don't do anything till you see me!" He had big plans for Jesse—and for himself. Newspaper reporters, hoping to scoop hordes of competitors waiting at the dock, had only questions. Why didn't Jesse go to Stockholm? Did Hitler really snub him? What did he think of Avery Brundage? Was the suspension final? What about all those offers? The last question evoked the clearest answer by far: "It doesn't make any difference to me what I do as long as I make a lot of money."[37]

His parents, brother, and wife had more modest concerns when they arrived by train from Cleveland on Sunday afternoon, August 23, planning to welcome Jesse at his arrival the next morning. Only after several humiliating rejections did they find a downtown hotel that would accommodate them for the night. The Hotel New Yorker turned them away, as did the Biltmore, the Lincoln, and the McAlpine. The American South had no corner on prejudice in 1936. Only through the intervention of a city councilman from Cleveland, Herman Finckle, were accommodations obtained. Himself in New York representing Cleveland's welcome of its hometown hero, Finckle happened to be staying in the Hotel New Yorker when he heard of the Owens family's difficulties. He immediately vacated his room and transferred to the Hotel Pennsylvania—but only on the condition that the Pennsylvania would admit the Owenses.[38]

The Owenses were up early the next morning and down to the Battery, where they joined several dignitaries aboard a Coast Guard cutter out to the *Queen Mary* anchored offshore. Unaware of the plans for this special delegation, Jesse had to be summoned from his cabin below deck. His mother was the first member of the party to reach him. "My baby, my wonderful boy," she shouted as she smothered him with kisses. "Am I proud of you!" According to one reporter, Ruth then "smudged Jesse with so much lipstick that he blushed and couldn't talk for a few seconds."[39] Presumably, Marjorie Shaw faded into the background.

By the time the *Queen Mary* docked, Jesse had gained his composure. He masterfully handled a barrage of questions from reporters. Everything now seemed "fine." Hitler? "Why, he was fine. . . . Stories about him refusing to cheer for Americans are not true at all." Brundage? "Personally, he is a fine man. I won't comment otherwise." The AAU? It was "a fine thing. It keeps us all together." And so it went, with explanations of why Jesse did not go to Stockholm (he was "too tired" and felt he could not do his best), and with firm promises that he most definitely would return to Ohio State and finish his degree. Roi Ottley, a reporter for the *Amsterdam News,* observed that the positive tone and polished style of Owens's response to reporters could well lead one to believe that he had practiced the right answers in order not to harm his professional prospects. Apparently Larry Snyder coached him in techniques other than track on their Atlantic crossing. Jesse's earlier mentor, Charles Riley, was also present at the pier. Having come from Cleveland with the welcoming delegation, he watched proudly as his protégé adroitly handled each question.[40]

As soon as Jesse finished with the reporters, however, both Riley and Snyder lost their prize pupil to other interested parties. Bill "Bojangles" Robinson took over. The premier tap dancer and stage performer on the black nightclub circuit, Robinson was show business incarnate. In Yankee Stadium five years earlier, at the age of fifty-three, he had run backward in a 100-yard race against three New York Yankees, beating two of them to the finish line.[41] Rich and famous, he still sought fresh ways to attract the public. He found Jesse Owens ripe for the picking. Jesse wanted money, and Bojangles wanted Jesse's spotlight. It was a promising match.

Jesse and his family went to Bojangles's Harlem apartment by motorcade behind a motorcycle escort arranged by Robinson himself. For the entire day, black friends and business associates of the King of Entertainment dropped by to meet America's newest hero, one of their own. They stroked Jesse's ego and spoke glowingly of his professional future. Then Bojangles showed his trump card. He introduced Jesse to his own agent, Marty Forkins. In a party atmosphere, they talked briefly of commercial prospects. When Owens and his family finally left for Grand Central Station to board an overnight train to Cleveland, visions of dollar signs danced in their heads.[42]

More crowds awaited them in Cleveland, where a huge victory celebration had been carefully planned during the past two weeks. Heading the welcoming party at the East Cleveland Station, at 8:15 in the morning, was Cleveland's Mayor Harold H. Burton, who had returned home early from a distant vacation to head the party. At his side were the Lieutenant Governor of Ohio, Harold Masier, and Cleveland's greatest sports luminary, Tris Speaker. They rode with Jesse and Ruth in an open Lincoln convertible at the head of a motorcade on a winding 15-mile route through the East Side ghetto, then to the affluent West Side, and finally to City Hall. In the black districts especially, crowds lined the curbs and waved from windows, showering their hero with confetti and streamers. Rain began to fall just before the parade reached City Hall, and the drivers speeded up to avoid having their passengers drenched.[43]

Inside City Hall, a capacity crowd of 4,000 applauded and whistled as Jesse was showered with gifts and speeches of praise. One of the gifts was a $500 gold watch. The Mayor's speech blended the racial paternalism of that era with a chauvinistic boosterism that seems timeless:

> We are proud of Jesse because he is a clean gentleman wherever he goes. It is indeed an honor to have had him as our representative at the Olympics in Germany. By his high character, his clean living and attention to duty, he has brought this credit and honor to his Race, to this the greatest city of the world, to his alma mater, Ohio State, to our great commonwealth, to this country at large.

Jesse rose to the occasion, thanking Cleveland for its support and assuring everyone that he intended to return to Ohio State. In conclusion, he indicated that most of all he wanted to be remembered as a "worthy citizen" as well as an athletic champion.[44]

Another reception awaited him three days later in Columbus. State offices closed for two hours to allow people to go to Union Station for the arrival of the train from Cleveland. The script was essentially the same: an open motorcade, huge crowds of hero-worshipers, several gifts, and colorful speeches at the end. Only the leading actors were different: Governor Martin L. Davey, Columbus Mayor B. Gessaman, Ohio State vice president Low Morrell, and Arthur L. Evans, the local Chamber of Commerce president. Ruth received an expensive set of silverware; Jesse received extravagant accolades.[45]

Shortly after the reception, Owens finally sat down to discuss his future with Snyder and St. John, as "Saint" had earlier suggested. Assuming the problem with the AAU would be ironed out, St. John insisted that Jesse return to Ohio State for his final year of track eligibility. But Snyder remained firmly supportive of Jesse's pecuniary interest. "He's practical about it," Snyder told the press afterward. "He sure can use the money and he wants to get it now while the opportunities are there." By the very next day Jesse was back in New York announcing to the press that he would not be returning to Ohio State in the fall.[46]

On September 1 he signed an agency contract with Marty Forkins in an office high above Times Square. Forkins mentioned several new offers totaling about $100,000. Jesse beamed. "Even if I make only $25,000," he told newsmen, "that'll be a fine lot of money to begin with after you have had practically nothing all these years." Did that mean his amateur track career was at an end? "If I can make money and still remain an amateur, fine," he replied. "If not, it is just as well, providing I can get the money."[47]

☆   ☆   ☆

He had one more parade to endure. While he returned home on the *Queen Mary*, his Olympic track mates performed poorly in wet, chilly weather in Stockholm. From there they traveled by train to Oslo for a single day's meet, then dashed over to Finland for a whirlwind tour of eight Finnish cities. The AAU got its pound of flesh, and more, from its track athletes. Meanwhile, the rest of the Olympic team returned home on the

U.S.S. President Roosevelt, arriving in New York on August 28, the day Owens was in Columbus. They were quartered in various Manhattan hotels to await the arrival of the track squad on the morning of September 3. The entire Olympic team then rode in a grand open-car motorcade up Broadway to Harlem, back down Lenox Avenue and across the Triborough Bridge to a public reception at the same little Randall's Island stadium where they had qualified for the Olympics two months earlier.[48]

Jesse and Ruth joined them at the Battery, to ride with several New York City officials in the first limousine. The customary shower of ticker tape and confetti rained down upon them as they passed through the financial district, but the enthusiasm seemed forced, "curious rather than excited," not "delirious" by any means, according to one report. The passage of time—almost three weeks—since the end of the Berlin games had apparently dimmed the public's adulation of its Olympic heroes.[49]

The reception in Harlem was even cooler, surprisingly so since this was the first Olympic team with an appreciable number of blacks. "Now, why was Harlem so tame at a time when it should have cut loose?" a reporter for the *Chicago Defender* asked as he sounded out Harlem residents. He found a high level of dissatisfaction with Owens's hasty decision to turn professional. He also uncovered a reluctance on the part of blacks to honor their own in sports other than boxing and baseball. Most of all, he discovered seething hostility toward the manner in which the parade was organized. In the front car with Owens and his wife sat former heavyweight champion Jack Dempsey, who had refused ever to fight a black challenger. Harlem never forgave him. Harlem blacks simply refused to applaud Owens at Dempsey's side. Quite the reverse. "Jesse Owens, Jim Crowed. Jesse Owens, Jim Crowed," several angry blacks chanted as the motorcade made its way through Harlem. It did not escape their attention that all the black athletes except Owens rode together, racially segregated, in several cars far back in the procession. As one oldtimer told an interviewer, all the black Olympians were "literally jim crowed in the parade of honor."[50]

None of those incongruities made much impression on Jesse Owens. Years later, whenever he spoke about the parade up Broadway and through Harlem, he would recall hardly anything but an extravagant gift that literally dropped into his lap that day. As Jesse (and only he) told the story, someone tossed a brown paper bag wrapped with rubber bands into his open car. He carried the unopened little package with him through the Randall's Island ceremonies, the story goes, and finally unwrapped it that night to find $10,000 wadded up inside.[51] In all its particulars, the account sounds fictitious. Coincidentally, $10,000 has been mentioned by some sources as the sum Jesse received shortly thereafter for working in behalf of the 1936 Alf Landon presidential campaign.[51]

At the final ceremony on Randall's Island, 2,000 or so spectators applauded as the Mayor of New York, Fiorello H. LaGuardia, presented special medals to each athlete. Lauding them all as "splendid examples of American youth and American sportsmanship," Fiorello delivered a special little speech in honor of Owens. "Jesse, on behalf of New York City," the Mayor concluded, "I hail you as an American boy. We are all Americans here; we have no auxiliaries in this country." After a long ovation, Jesse called Bill Robinson to the platform and gave him one of his four gold medals from the Berlin games. Apparently Jesse's mind was more on the future than on the past. His athletic career was finished. A professional career beckoned.[52]

CHAPTER 8

Tarnished Gold

Upon his hasty return home from Europe to make the money that seemed to be his for the taking, Jesse got what he said he wanted. He made money, but not in the manner he had anticipated. Most of the "offers" turned out to be tentative queries or unscrupulous grabs for publicity. The apparent $40,000 offer from Eddie Cantor actually came from Cantor's agent without the client's knowledge. It was eventually retracted. Various other propositions from Los Angeles and New York came to nothing. Only Bill "Bojangles" Robinson stood by his promise to teach Jesse to perform on stage, for engagements several months hence. In the meantime Owens found all the quick money schemes to be "just so much hash."[1]

By the second week in September, he was "a sadder but wiser man," the Cleveland *Call and Post* reported. "He has learned a lesson that most of us already know, that 'all that glitters is not gold'," the *Call and Post* editor commented. "A few weeks ago it seemed as if he couldn't get here fast enough to take advantage of all the offers that were pouring in on him. Today he needs a Sherlock Holmes to find a bona fide offer that he can cash in on." In fact, the offer from Wilberforce University remained firm, but Jesse could not "cash in on" it until he finished college. As he recalled several years later, Wilberforce would have paid him $2,800 a year to coach the team, "and that was a lot of money in those days." His hasty decision to discontinue his studies effectively closed the door on that opportunity.[2]

At the time, much larger sums of money seemed available in vaudeville, the movie industry, and the night club circuit. As one bogus prospect after another vanished into thin air, however, Owens decided that he could best translate his fame into financial security by returning to competitive track. Two possibilities beckoned. One was explicitly professional, "a swing around the old big-time Nurmi circuit" of exhibitions and county fairs. According to Marty Forkins, several promoters wanted Jesse to compete head-to-head against the 1932 Olympic champion, Eddie Tolan, and were offering to pay him "far more than $50,000." Yet those schemes turned out to be as insubstantial as the many rumored offers from the moguls of state and screen.[3]

More solid prospects lay in the veiled professionalism that was already available for big-name stars in amateur athletics: padded "expense accounts" for participation in meets sponsored by local athletic clubs. Track men of that era recall that the amount of "expenses" paid to each athlete varied widely according to the individual's reputation. The name of Jesse Owens would have attracted large crowds, assuring Jesse of a reasonable—if not exorbitant—cut of the gate receipts. With those arrangements in mind, he accepted an invitation to compete on September 17 in the New York Caledonian Club meet at Yankee Stadium.[4]

A large impediment stood in his way. However phony its amateurism, the Caledonian Club meet was sanctioned by the Amateur Athletic Union. Ironically, for Jesse to rake in money under the table, he had to be on good terms with the guardians of amateur athletics. His position was untenable, and not merely because of his refusal to complete the European barnstorming tour. With no more occasion than that, the AAU would have come under heavy pressure for reinstatement. But Jesse's signing with a professional agent had sealed his fate. In the rigid amateur code of the 1930s, it mattered little that his "professional intentions" had nothing directly to do with athletics. "The suspension became automatic when Owens said he would turn professional," Daniel J. Ferris announced. Perhaps poor communication caused the Stockholm incident, Ferris admitted, but now the issue was clear: "There is no misunderstanding involved. We wish Owens luck in his new venture."[5]

Jesse ate humble pie. Aware by now that a stage or screen career was simply not an immediate option, he announced on September 12 that he had changed his mind about turning professional. Instead, he wanted to continue competing in track-and-field meets if the AAU would allow it. Marty Forkins complied, announcing publicly that Owens had never signed a contract with him. But the AAU would not budge. Claiming that he had a photostatic copy of the contract in his files, Ferris threatened to suspend any athlete who competed against Owens.[6]

One last scene remained to be played out. On Monday morning, September 12, Jesse arrived home in Cleveland for a noonday interview with the Executive Committee of the Northeastern Ohio Association, a local branch of the AAU. Hometown friends and boosters listened sympathetically to his case for reinstatement but delayed their decision until he left the room. What did he tell them? a reporter asked as Owens emerged from the meeting. "What could I say?" he replied. "I'm no professional. I haven't received any pay. My status is the same as it always has been." Impatiently he added, "I'm getting good and tired of getting kicked around."[7]

As expected, the Cleveland group recommended Jesse's reinstatement as an amateur. Yet the AAU issued a flat refusal from its national headquarters in New York, citing the rule that "an athlete must remain ineligible for a year after he announces his intentions of turning professional." Owens would not be eligible to compete in the Caledonian Club meet or in any other event sanctioned by the AAU. Deprived of its star attraction, the Caledonian Club canceled its meet.[8]

For star-watchers of the era, America's brightest and best Olympic champion seemed to have sold his fame for a bundle of hollow promises and futile hopes of commercial success. Little did they know, as his mother did, that Jesse was "a face boy." As Emma Owens told an inquisitive reporter during one of her son's difficult moments, "Jesse was always a face boy.

. . . When a problem came up, he always faced it." He did just that in early September 1936. Told by Marty Forkins that he would not be going on the stage circuit any time soon, Owens candidly explained the reason to an interviewer: "You see, I haven't any talent. I can't dance. I can't sing." How did he feel about that? "I feel good about it," he answered. "Since you can't do some things, you might as well do the best you can." What he could do, he decided, was peddle his fame to a political party in the presidential campaign of 1936.⁹

☆ ☆ ☆

Both parties courted his favor. By all odds, the Democrats had the inside track, for they had given him the soft page's job in Columbus a year earlier. That patronage identified Owens as "a solid Democrat." Although he demonstrated scarcely any political interests, to his friends he referred to Franklin Delano Roosevelt as a President who was "just perfectly swell." The Democrats were determined to seal Jesse's support for their autumn campaign. The National Democratic Campaign chairman had sent one of his black assistants (who happened to be in Europe on vacation) to the Berlin Olympics to visit Owens. He found a Republican representative already there in the Village, making a pitch for Jesse's support in the fall.¹⁰

The Democrats merely raised the stakes. While Jesse and Larry Snyder returned home on the *Queen Mary*, Ohio's Democratic Governor, Martin L. Davey, appointed a committee to raise funds to purchase Owens a new house in Cleveland. The project seemed wonderfully generous—for Ohio to "give something substantial to its greatest athlete." But the scheme was transparently political. The chairman of the fundraising committee was none other than Francis W. Paulson, the chairman of the State Democratic Committee. A gift of a house was a marvelously respectable means of making Jesse indebted to the Democratic Party.¹¹

In New York, just before the *Queen Mary* landed, Paulson's heavy-handed tactics almost discredited him altogether. Claiming that the Governor of Ohio had instructed him to head the welcoming party, Paulson snatched up all the tickets for the little boat that was to go out into the harbor to greet Owens aboard the *Queen Mary*. The Cleveland delegation, headed by Herman H. Finckle, was infuriated, as was yet another interested party, Bill Robinson. "Paulson's group is making a cheap political affair of the whole welcome," Finckle ranted to anyone who would listen. Under fire all round, Paulson finally compromised with a line that most surely sounded like a self-serving platitude: "After all," he insisted, "the interest of the boy is what every person in the room has at heart."[12]

Its conflicting interests momentarily reconciled, the greeting party met Jesse on the *Queen Mary* early the next morning. But once again the members almost came to blows, this time literally. As Paulson pushed and shoved his way through the crowd toward Jesse, Bojangles Robinson blurted out, "Listen here. You may be a big shot in Ohio, but you don't amount to much around here. I'll punch you in the eye." While he and Paulson exchanged angry words, a Republican representative seized the opportunity to work his way to Jesse's side. Jesse recognized him as Grant Ward, the former Ohio State assistant coach who was now running as a Republican for the United States House of Representatives. "You're going to join the Landon–Bricker club, aren't you?" Ward asked Owens. Before Jesse could answer, an exasperated Bojangles barged back on the scene yelling, "Never mind the politics."[13]

Yet even the forceful Bojangles could not muzzle reporters on the dock. After their predictable questions about Hitler, Brundage, and the AAU, they wanted to know whom Owens would support—Landon or Roosevelt—in the forthcoming election. His answer was a model of noncommitment: "I'll vote for whichever party will enforce the entire Constitution as it applies to Negroes." Like all the other answers to the questions put to him on his return home, this one was gauged for a pleasant, unabrasive effect; unlike the others, this one would be instrumental in putting money in the bank.[14]

Why all that concern for the political opinion of a mere athlete? The question is ill-worded, for in 1936 Jesse Owens was no mere athlete. With Joe Louis having fallen recently under the fists of Max Schmeling, Owens was *the* black athlete in all of America. He was Mr. Olympics even for people who knew little and cared less about the Olympic Games; he was Mr. Track and Field, even for people to whom only baseball, football, and boxing really mattered. He was All-World, the Champ of his sphere, and his political endorsement would presumably carry weight with black voters. Politicians clamored for his support because of two fundamentally new features of American political life. For the first time ever, in 1936 the black vote promised to be a decisive factor in a presidential election, and for the first time since the Civil War blacks would not be voting *en masse* for "the party of Lincoln."

Largely as a result of the great Negro migration from the South, by 1936 about 2.5 million blacks lived in Northern cities. Clumped in nine industrial states were no fewer than a million newly enfranchised black adults, potential voters. Democrats and Republicans assiduously sought their support. Both parties appointed Negro campaign managers; both committed substantial funds to winning the black vote. "In no election since 1860," *Time* magazine observed, "have politicians been so Negro-minded as in 1936."[15]

Just a few years earlier neither party courted the black vote, because the Republicans held it uncontested. The Democratic Party was the citadel of white supremacy in the South; to vote Democrat was to vote for a continuation of lynchings, black disfranchisement in the South, and segregated labor unions in the North. Although 50 percent of the black population was unemployed in 1932, almost 70 percent voted for Herbert Hoover. "Until recently," *Newsweek* commented in 1936, "Negroes supporting the Democratic ticket would have seemed like Jews backing Hitler." As James Weldon Johnson framed the issue in 1934, blacks had long known that "the party of Lincoln" seldom ever put forward a candidate "who even slightly recalled the qualities of Lincoln," but they still believed it was "the better part of wisdom to stand with lukewarm and apathetic friends than with avowed enemies."[16]

Roosevelt's New Deal changed all that. In the congressional elections of 1934, for the first time in American history black voters went more for Democrats than for Republican candidates. To be sure, Roosevelt did not champion the black cause. As Governor of New York he had ignored blacks in both his legislation and his political appointments. During his first presidential term, he consistently deferred to Southern whites, whose support he needed for his program of economic reconstruction. He even purchased property in Warm Springs, Georgia, openly identifying himself as an adopted son of the Cracker State. Worst of all, he refused to exert leadership in the passage of legislation that would make lynching a federal offense. By the summer of 1936, the nation's black community had suffered no fewer than seventy-two lynchings within the past four years, causing the NAACP to denounce this "irradicable stain" on Roosevelt's prospects for reelection.[17]

Even the early New Deal programs discriminated against blacks, who consistently received far less direct aid and work relief than did whites. At first the black press attacked the New Deal as "the same raw deal," but by 1936 they had to admit that the Democratic program was better than nothing, and altogether better than what the Republicans offered. One of Alf Landon's platform promises was a return to local and state control of pensions, work relief, and unemployment benefits. The very idea struck fear in the black community. "If Governor Landon were older and more experienced in government," warned the *Baltimore Afro-American*, "he'd know that there are fourteen States that can't be trusted to administer relief, old-age pensions or unemployment insurance for colored people."[18]

Like most of the black press, the *Afro-American* had been solidly Republican prior to the New Deal. Despite all of President Roosevelt's shortcomings, his economic measures transformed suspicion into support. The *Amsterdam News* reflected a vast swell of editorial opinion when it observed in the autumn of 1936 that "it would be a calamity, indeed, if the Roosevelt program were stopped where it is today, no matter how earnestly the Republican Party might try to carry on."[19]

The youthful Jesse Owens ran against the tide of the black opinion. "President Roosevelt has done something but not enough to benefit the people of the colored race," Owens announced on September 2, just a week after returning home from Europe. He would support Landon for President. He liked Landon's common sense: his unwillingness to "spend more than he has in his pocket or in his bank account." He trusted his sincerity: "Governor Landon does not promise much, but what promises he makes, I think he will keep." Jesse wanted to meet the candidate in person.[20]

A meeting was arranged, of course, for a deal had already been struck with Republican headquarters for Jesse to stump for Landon. Representative Joseph W. Martin, Landon's campaign manager in the East, made arrangements for Owens to receive a handsome fee for his public support. The money came from the personal bank account of a multimillionaire Republican booster in Ohio, Joseph Newton Pew, Jr., a vice president of Sun Oil Company who resented the New Deal's "antibusiness bias." One of Jesse's closest friends says the fee was $10,000. A black newspaper of the day reported $15,000, crowing that "Dixie dollars" could not buy Jesse's services. Whatever the exact sum, the Republicans won the raffle.[21]

Miffed at Owens's ingratitude for their past patronage, the Democrats took what little revenge they could. Governor Davey quickly dissolved the committee he had appointed to raise money for the purchase of a house in Cleveland. Even more irritated was Jesse's New York agent, Marty Forkins, to whom the political announcement came as a complete surprise. Already having extreme difficulty in finding a solid offer for Jesse's talent, Forkins feared that political involvement would close all the entertainment doors. "He absolutely will not enter into any political campaigning," Forkins declared to the press. He overestimated his own powers of persuasion. Marty Forkins was accustomed to dealing with ambitious, obedient stage and screen personalities in New York, not with a young black athlete who was eager to take whatever lucrative assignment he could find.[22]

While Forkins and the Democrats fumed, Owens boarded a plane for Kansas to meet Alf Landon. In Chicago he stopped over for a night as a guest of the Republican National Headquarters. There he met the Republican vice presidential candidate, Colonel Frank Knox. Early the next morning he flew on to Topeka for a meeting with The Man himself. Photographers gathered around as the candidate and his prize campaigner chatted. Landon asked for details on each of Jesse's Olympic victories, but as one of Landon's aides noted, the session was largely given to "picture-taking and hand-shaking." Jesse remembered it differently. Landon was "the most interesting man" he had ever met, he told an audience three weeks later. Their conversation, he recalled, "covered almost every subject except politics."[23]

Perhaps it was just as well, for a political discussion would have been embarrassingly awkward. "I am too young to know anything about politics," Owens once admitted when asked why he was stumping for Landon rather than Roosevelt. To the

Republicans he sold his name, athletic exploits, and personal charm. That was enough. Years later he proudly recalled that he was "the guy who was the beginning of the celebrity stable in political campaigns."[24] He was just that, no more, no less.

Beginning in Boston on September 29, he appeared in a different Eastern city every night for the next two weeks, calling upon his listeners to support the Republican ticket. Large crowds turned out to hear him and to get his autograph afterward. Mostly they heard a series of anecdotes about the Berlin Olympics—that the Germans were wonderfully efficient, that Hitler was "a man of dignity," that the Olympic officials were "great," and that Ralph Metcalfe was "a fine fellow and a fine American." Toward the end of each speech, he finally got around to his punch line; Alf Landon would protect the American way of freedom against the "planned economy of Europe as offered by the Roosevelt New Deal Democrats."[25]

The high point of his campaigning occurred in mid-October at a massive gathering in Chicago's Eighth Regiment Armory. More than 10,000 black Republicans gathered to enjoy the music of the Olivet Church choir, then to cheer the introductions of old party stalwarts such as Roscoe Conkling Simmons, William E. King, Patrick H. Moynihan, and Oscar DePriest. Owens's inspirational speech that night, on "Americanism," prompted an enthusiastic reporter for the *Chicago Defender* to frame an equation that was soon to become enshrined in the annals of American folklore: Owens was "himself a great American and a typical example of what this land of opportunity affords." In summary, according to the *Defender*, "The day was great for Jesse Owens, great for the Race, and great for the Republican party and America."[26]

From that pinnacle of acclaim, Jesse left for Columbus early the next morning, and there he bumbled so badly that another reporter for the *Chicago Defender* tore him to shreds. He reverted to his Olympic anecdotes, but in such "simple unsteady terms" that he seemed one of the "jokes of the country." How could he do this "for the few small crumbs" he was receiving from the Republican table? Some malicious unseen hand had seemingly "misguided the world's greatest sprinter," the *Defender* commented, "only to wreck the glory he had achieved and to wrest from him his laurels." In a similarly critical vein, just two weeks later the *Amsterdam*

News rhetorically asked, "Why does Jesse Owens destroy his fine reputation by dilly-dallying with politics when sports is his game?" Newspapermen of that day were simply not accustomed to seeing their athletic stars dabble in politics. Nor did they know that Jesse's payoff outweighed his pride. His fee amounted to considerably more than a "few small crumbs."[27]

But nothing Jesse Owens or anyone else could do would have salvaged Alf Landon's candidacy. Landon lost in a landslide, garnering a mere eight electoral votes in the traditionally Republican states of Vermont and Maine. According to a Gallup poll, about 76 percent of all Northern blacks voted for Roosevelt. In Jesse's hometown of Cleveland, where less than one-third of the black population voted Democrat in 1932, fully two-thirds went for Roosevelt over Landon. "Poorest race I ever ran," Owens recalled years later. "But they paid me a *lot*," he added. "No, I won't say how much—but a *lot!*"[28]

☆ ☆ ☆

From other sources, too, he made a lot of money in the fall of 1936. Frequently he was wined and dined at the Cotton Club in Harlem, where sweet deals were made to the accompaniment of music and dance. Marty Forkins arranged endorsements of food, clothing, and service industries "on a local basis" in the black press. He also contracted for Jesse to appear at various banquets and ball games in the fall, always for a fee, and even came through with a contract for a series of radio appearances, reportedly for a total of $26,000. In mid-November Owens announced that he had "given up all ideas of running as an amateur again" but that he had already made "about $50,000" since his return home from the Olympics. His figures were probably inflated, as the black press always tended to overstate the financial success of its public figures. Without doubt, though, Owens made a bundle. Two years later the United States Government filed a tax lien on $20,000 for which he paid no taxes in 1936.[29]

Whatever his precise income, that $20,000 alone would have put him at a princely level for the Depression era. In 1936 four of every five Americans earned less than $2,000, and blacks made much less still. Only 10 percent of all Americans earned more than $3,000, and less than 1 percent made more than $10,000 a year. At the very least, Jesse's spendable income exceeded $300,000 in 1980s terms, for he was required to pay little more than 3 percent in income taxes. Prices, of course, were minuscule by today's standards. In 1936 one could purchase the finest automobile for less than a thousand dollars. Brown sugar cost five cents a pound, Sunnyfield Corn Flakes ten cents a box, a pound jar of peanut butter nineteen cents, and fresh fish only six cents a pound.[30]

For the first time in his life, Owens could spend freely. First he bought a shiny 1936 Buick sedan, his first of many annual new automobiles. He purchased Ruth reams of jewelry and an entirely new wardrobe. For his parents he bought a new, modern eleven-room house in Cleveland then furnished it with about $2,000 worth of new furniture. "Boy, it certainly tickles me to see how happy Mom is now," he beamed to a reporter. Emma Owens was happy, no doubt, but the sudden leap from ghetto poverty to comfortable splendor disoriented her. As a friend recalls the scene, when she was first shown her big new house, she sat on the front porch, surveyed the yard, and muttered aloud, "You got me here, but you're not gonna get my [snuff] plug away from here." All the while, Jesse and Ruth were looking at vacant lots for a new house of their own, built to their specifications. "Ruth has to have a lot of contraptions I don't know much about," Jesse proudly told reporters. "She'll be boss of the job."[31]

In the domestic fashion of the day, Jesse controlled the bank account. He dipped into it often to buy gifts for friends and benefactors. For the children of a Cleveland newspaper reporter who had befriended him, he bought watches and bicycles. For his old junior high mentor, Charles Riley, he had a bigger surprise. Several days before Christmas he took Riley down to the showroom of a local automobile dealer and presented him with the keys to a new dark blue Chevrolet sedan. Riley was overcome with emotion. In recent weeks his old Model T Ford had broken down several times; he had just about run out of bailing wire. He proudly drove the new Chevrolet home, and neighbors came by the house all afternoon to admire the gift.[32]

Like so many aspects of Jesse Owens's life, this cheerful little episode had a dark, sad side. Charles Riley's delight quickly changed to despair. Years later Owens said he paid

$800 cash for the car, but soon after Riley got it home, he learned from the dealer that Jesse had paid only the down payment, not the entire purchase price. Riley had to pay the balance. For the next several years, he struggled to make monthly payments out of his meager teacher's salary, too embarrassed ever to inform his family—much less the world at large—of the arrangement.[33]

While spending freely, Owens entertained hopes of a lucrative movie contract. Various rumors had him working first for Paramount Pictures, then for Twentieth Century–Fox. At Thanksgiving he announced that he and Ruth would soon be driving their new Buick to Hollywood, where he was scheduled to costar with Warner Oland in a Twentieth Century–Fox production, "Charlie Chan Goes to the Olympics." They never made the trip. The movie did get made, but Owens appeared in it only in a brief newsreel from the Berlin games. He was on the screen for a mere ten seconds or so, and never was his name even mentioned. Fortunately, that was the last of his numerous phony offers.[34]

Offsetting that disappointment was an announcement on December 15 that he had been named the Associated Press Athlete of the Year. He received fifty-three first-place votes from sixty-nine sportswriters, reminding the *Chicago Defender* of an ironic comparison with the landslide victory of Roosevelt in the recent presidential election. Owens was the first track athlete ever to win the award since its inception in 1931. He was the second black winner, Joe Louis having received the honor the year before. The finalists, in order after Owens, recall a sterling era of competitive sport: Carl Hubbell, the leading National League pitcher; Larry Kelley, Yale's All-American end; Maximilian Schmeling, the victor over Louis; Glenn Morris, Olympic decathlon champion; Fred Perry, England's world tennis champion; Joe DiMaggio, a young Yankee centerfielder; Joe Louis, tied for eighth place with Forrest "Spec" Towns, Olympic hurdler; and Jerome "Dizzy" Dean, the St. Louis Cardinals' pitching ace.[35]

They were giants of their day, a day far removed from ours. They were all males, and eight of the ten were Americans. Except for Owens and Louis, they were all white. They represent a distinct era of American life. Their athletic stature now seems all the more imposing because of the depression of their terrain.

☆   ☆   ☆

When Owens received word of his award, he modestly replied, "Well, I only tried to do my best in athletics." The past tense pained him, for although he was now barred from amateur athletics, his competitive juices still flowed, whetted by years of intense training and high-level contests. While campaigning for Alf Landon, Jesse once complained to a reporter that what he disliked most about the speaker's circuit was his having to sit and wait too much. He brimmed with nervous energy. "He is anxious to get out and exercise his famous legs," the journalist commented.[36]

Even an exhibition race would do, especially if Jesse could get paid for it. In late November the Cleveland *Gazette* announced that its hometown hero would display his speed in Havana, Cuba, on the day after Christmas. He was to run a 100-yard sprint against Cuba's fastest athlete, Conrado Rodriques. But once again the AAU intervened, threatening to ban Rodriques from all amateur competition in the United States if he competed against the "professional" Owens. Rodriques withdrew, but on December 17 Marty Forkins informed the press that Owens would make his professional track debut by running "against time," by himself, during the halftime of a soccer football game in Havana.[37]

Something better came up—more spectacular and presumably more lucrative. By the time Jesse arrived in Havana on Christmas Day, Forkins had arranged for him to run not against the clock or against some other athletes, but against a thoroughbred horse named Julio McCaw. It was an old gambit of showmanship, introduced by the P. T. Barnum Circus forty years earlier. In 1916 a New York Giants baseball player, Hans Lohert, raced a horse around the bases in a Texas ball park. At a California state fair in 1932, a Brooklyn Dodgers showboat, Frenchy Bordagaray, did the same. More recently, the amateur miler Johnny Fleeson had taken a mile handicap in a race against a horse over a two-mile course. This kind of spectacle especially appealed to audiences during the drab days of the

Great Depression, for it provided both novel entertainment and the opportunity to get rich quick by betting on the event. A contest between a thoroughbred horse and the world's fastest human certainly promised excitement. It was a promoter's dream.[38]

Unfortunately, the weather did not cooperate. Two days of intermittent rain turned into a steady drizzle on the morning of the race, discouraging would-be spectators. By noon the rain stopped, but only 3,000 people showed up for the soccer game and the halftime spectacular. Still, they cheered expectantly as Owens came out of his dressing room and onto the field, and at the end of the race they poured out of the stands to get his autograph. Despite the wet track and a four-month layoff, Jesse ran the 100 yards in the remarkable time of 9.9 seconds, finishing several yards ahead of the hard-charging Julio Mc-Caw and his jockey, J. M. Contino.[39]

The event is steeped in legend. According to Owens's numerous later accounts, he was able to beat the thoroughbred because the starter fired his gun near the horse's ear, causing him to rear up while Jesse sped away too far in the lead for Julio McCaw to overtake him. In truth, promoters of later races between Owens and horses in the United States devised that imaginative technique. Newspaper accounts of the Owens–McCaw contest indicate that Jesse was given a 40-yard handicap at the start.[40]

Of far greater importance than this factual discrepancy is the personal attitude that Owens later read back into the event. He was humiliated, he insisted years later. The whole affair supposedly made him "sick," feeling like "a spectacle, a freak," but he had to do it because he needed the money and could make it no other way. "People said it was degrading for an Olympic champion to run against a horse," Owens told an interviewer in 1971, "but what was I supposed to do? I had four gold medals, but you can't eat four gold medals. There was no television, no big advertising, no endorsements then. Not for a black man, anyway." True, he could not eat gold medals. True, there were no television contracts in 1936, nor could a black man cash in on advertisements in the white man's press. On the matter of endorsements, however, the older Owens conveniently forgot his lucrative involvement in the ill-fated Landon campaign, not to mention various other handsome contracts arranged by Marty Forkins. During the four months prior to his Havana exhibition, he had already made more money than his father and brothers had earned all their working lives. Owens received $2,000 to display his prowess in Havana, enough to buy two new Buicks or to live comfortably for a year. It was extra money in the bank, and he was glad to take it.[41]

What about the supposed humiliation? From the vantage point of the civil rights era in the 1960s, a handsome, world-famous black athlete pitted against an animal seemed the height of insensitive exploitation and personal indignity. It was "a new kind of slavery," the older Owens recalled. But that was not the way he saw it in 1936. At least two black reporters interviewed him at the end of the race, and both recorded essentially the same bubbly words: "Since I haven't competed for a long time, and considering the condition of the track, I am satisfied with my showing. I would be willing to race a horse without a handicap, even from scratch provided the animal selected is not remarkably fast." Most telling of all was Jesse's final line: "It sure feels good to get out on the cinders again."[42]

A black man in a white man's world, he was most assuredly vulnerable to exploitation. But he was also an athlete, addicted to running, competing, winning. There is more than meets the eye in his stumbling explanation, years later, that he raced against horses in order "to survive—no, because I thought I had to do it in order to survive." For the young Owens in 1936, survival had as much to do with his athletic compulsion and physical self-image as it did with his bank account; it was kinetic as well as financial. A race against a horse was no ideal contest by any means, but to a restless young man barred from amateur competition while not yet freed from the athletic impulse, it was better than nothing.[43]

☆　☆　☆

In the final days of 1936 Jesse Owens looked back on a year filled with incredible peaks and valleys. He had begun the year on academic probation at Ohio State, ineligible for inter-collegiate athletic competition. Once he became eligible again in the spring, he breezed from one victory to another, right through the Olympic trials and the Berlin games. His Olympic gold turned to dross, however, when the AAU banned him from all future amateur competition, when numerous job offers failed to materialize, and when he performed poorly in Alf Landon's disastrous campaign effort. Out of all those disappointments, he ascended to the heights of financial success and received the personal satisfaction of winning the Associated Press Athlete of the Year award. That uneven pattern of victory and defeat carried through right to the end of the year. Scarcely had he collected his handsome fee from the Havana exhibition when he learned that he had just lost his very last race in 1936.

He finished second to the Olympic decathlon champion, Glenn Morris, in the balloting for the James E. Sullivan Trophy as the outstanding amateur athlete of the year. "Stop kidding me," Morris reportedly said when informed of his selection. Jesse barely hid his own disappointment. "That's funny," he replied flippantly to the news, then added with a broad smile, "but I'm glad the best man won." Reporters asked him if he thought his turning professional had anything to to with his loss. "I don't see how that could have anything to do with it," he answered. "The things I did were done when I was an amateur."[44]

He was being less than candid. For several months the black press had nervously debated his chances to become the first black athlete ever to win the Sullivan Award. Some editors predicted failure because of racial prejudice; others realistically feared that Jesse's troubles with the AAU and his obvious desire to exploit his amateur fame for financial gain would destroy his chances with the Sullivan committee. Fully two months before the final balloting, Roi Ottley of the *Amsterdam News* posed several hypothetical questions that could well be asked of each candidate. Has he upheld the amateur code? Does his character promise "success as a leader and force for good in the community"? What vocation is he now engaged in? Jesse Owens, in Ottley's estimation, would not do well on the test: "Our feeling is he might flunk."[45]

He did flunk, but by a narrow margin. When the Sullivan committee sent out its final ballots to its six hundred selectors, it instructed them to disregard Owens's recent commercial endeavors as well as his problems with the AAU. The instructions apparently fell on deaf ears. Many respondents left

Jesse's name completely off their final list; several penciled in their obvious explanations. Morris, on the other hand, appeared on every ballot, for second or third place if not first. Still, he barely won with 1,106 points to Jesse's 1,013. Daniel J. Ferris of the AAU presented the award to Morris, lauding him as "the athlete who, by his performance, example and influence as an amateur and a man, has done the most during the past year to advance the cause of sportsmanship." In the Sullivan committee's further praise of Morris, Jesse took a passing shot to the solar plexus: Morris was "one of the real heroes of the Olympic Games; he received many offers to capitalize on his athletic fame, but he turned them all down to retain his amateur standing."[46] Jesse Owens's gold was tarnished.

CHAPTER 9

Chasing Rainbows

IF AN OLYMPIC CHAMPION'S FRENETIC DASH from one moneymaking venture to another upset the American amateur establishment in the 1930s, it disturbed European sportsmen all the more. Jesse's race against a horse in Havana was the last straw. Franz Miller, the eminent German Olympic official and starter of the Berlin sprints, predicted early in 1937 that Owens would "vanish unhonored and unsung" as a result of his erratic behavior. Like most Germans, Miller had only the highest regard for Owens's athletic abilities but was saddened to see a man use his Olympic medals as "stepping-stones to this nonsensical path" of commercial exploitation. In Miller's opinion, such exhibitions were "only possible in such earnestness in the United States."[1]

Germany took care of its star athletes in other ways. In the wake of the Berlin games, German medalists received handsome appointments and promotions in Hitler's armed forces and civil service, and in local government, industry, and schools. Gotthard Handrick, a lieutenant in the Luftwaffe, received immediate promotion to the rank of captain when he won a gold medal in the modern pentathlon and subsequently rose rapidly to the rank of full colonel. The gymnast Konrad Frey enjoyed an even more spectacular access to Olympic booty. He was an unlettered locksmith when he won his gold medal, but the Reich Minister of Education waived the educational requirements and appointed him as a physical instructor for a large school district. Those are but two examples of a common pattern in which an authoritarian government and a compliant social system rewarded their nation's athletic heroes. In Nazi Germany, as in today's Communist bloc countries, a gold medal ensured a gem of a job.[2]

In the democratic West, on the other hand, the connection between amateur athletic achievement and economic security has always been tenuous at best, especially for black American track stars in the 1930s. In that distant era, the President of the United States had not yet begun inviting Olympic champions to the White House for superficial conversations and vote-winning photographs. If President Roosevelt ever considered such a gesture in 1936, he quickly dismissed it from his mind. His posing for a picture beside Jesse Owens, Ralph Metcalfe, Cornelius Johnson, and all the other black medalists would have lost rather than gained him votes in the South. As the journalist Paul Gallico candidly remarked, the black athlete of the 1930s was readily acknowledged as "a full-fledged citizen, and a true American" when he starred in college football or led an Olympic charge to victory. "At other times," Gallico added, "he remains just plain nigger, and we'd rather he weren't around, because he represents a problem."[3]

For all its social dimensions of inferior housing, educational opportunities, and public facilities, the "problem" was primarily economic. Like Irish immigrants of old, even famous, talented blacks in the 1930s need not apply for the better paying jobs in industry, much less for white-collar management positions. Save for the rare exception, such as Paul Robeson, the entertainment industry too was racially segregated. Such gifted black artists as Louis Armstrong, Ethel Waters, Ella Fitzgerald, and Duke Ellington performed mostly for all-black audiences or for chic whites who warmed best to the style of Stepin Fetchit and Jack Benny's Rochester, whose blackface humor pathetically played to white stereotypes.[4]

Black amateur athletes faced a double disadvantage once their athletic careers were finished. Like many white athletes, they were mostly untrained for anything more than running and jumping, and their color barred them from those avenues down which some white athletes made the transition to material comfort—commercial endorsements, public relations work, and movie contracts. To be sure, those were not necessarily dignified roles, whatever the color of the skin. Johnny Weissmuller, the gold medalist swimmer in the 1924 and 1928 Olympics, turned his talents to playing the inarticulate Tarzan and Jungle Jim in the movies. Buster Crabbe, a 1932 Olympic swimming champion, also played Tarzan, Kaspa the Lion Man, Thunda the Jungle Man, Buck Rogers, Flash Gordon, Captain Gallant, Billy the Kid, and numerous other punch-'em-up, shoot-'em-up Hollywood characters. Unfortunately, Crabbe gave up his dream of becoming a lawyer for those mindless, mediocre roles in B movies.[5]

But at least Crabbe's Olympic achievement launched him into a moneymaking career. In sharp contrast, Eddie Tolan, the black track star of the 1932 games, danced for a while on the black nightclub circuit, then almost starved before landing a lowly job as a clerk in a Detroit county records office. Unlike Weissmuller and Crabbe, Tolan was a runner rather than a swimmer. But the difference was most assuredly color rather than specialty. The white runner Glenn Morris also landed a Tarzan role shortly after he beat out Owens for the Sullivan award. Even the sprinter Sam Stoller, rejected at Berlin, rode his track fame to appearances in thirteen movies, including one with Carole Lombard and Mae West. Hollywood welcomed talented Olympic athletes—white ones, that is. It had no place for black Tarzans or black wooers of Mae West.[6]

So what could black Olympic champions do for a living once they hung up their athletic togs? As a general rule, their postathletic careers depended not on their medals or press clippings, but rather on their level of education. College dropouts, such as Tolan, Mack Robinson, and Cornelius Johnson, struggled desperately to survive at various jobs that provided scant psychic or monetary rewards. At the opposite extreme were two California members of the 1936 team. James Lu-Valle, bronze medalist in the 400 meters, returned home to finish his degree at UCLA, then earned a doctorate in chemistry and mathematics at the California Institute of Technology; recently he retired as Professor of Chemistry at Stanford

University. The winner of the 400 meters at Berlin, Archie Williams, returned home to earn his engineering degree at Berkeley, worked for a while as an engineer in the San Francisco Bay area, flew for the Air Force for twenty-two years, and worked until retirement as a teacher of computer science in a Bay Area high school. Of the same vintage, Fritz Pollard, Jr., winner of the bronze medal in the 110-meter hurdles, subsequently took his baccalaureate degree from the University of North Dakota, then studied law and worked in local and Federal government.[7]

Most of the black males from the Olympic class of '36 ended up somewhere between the difficult straits of Robinson and Johnson on the one hand, and the professional careers of LuValle, Williams, and Pollard on the other. Ralph Metcalfe, already having taken his B.A. from Marquette, returned from Berlin to accept an offer to coach track at Xavier, a black college in New Orleans. After World War II Metcalfe became an important political figure in Chicago. David Albritton and Johnny Woodruff, sophomores in 1936 at Ohio State and the University of Pittsburgh, respectively, both completed their undergraduate programs and later earned master's degrees. Albritton worked briefly in the Cleveland YMCA, then went off to coach track for several years at Alabama State College. Returning to Ohio, he served two terms in the state legislature while building a successful insurance business in Dayton. In New Jersey, John Woodruff also achieved comfort and personal satisfaction in several educational and business activities.[8]

What about Jesse Owens? After his moneymaking binge during the last four months of 1936, he still faced the need for long-term security. He had a wife and child to support, with another child on the way. But no permanent job was forthcoming. Years later Jesse dramatically recalled his post-Olympic experience:

> I came back from Berlin and the 1936 Olympics to a welcome few people have ever experienced. The streets of New York were lined with tens of thousands of men and women and children wanting to see me—to touch me—as I moved through on top of a new convertible. It was something else. But it didn't completely fool an Oakville sharecropper's son. Every newspaper had a pic-

ture of my face on its front page, and people I'd never met from society and business were buttonholing me to come to their plush suites for drinks and dinner and yachting trips; but one omission stood out more and more as the months passed.

No one had offered me a job.[9]

With numerous variations in detail, Jesse repeatedly told of his post-Berlin difficulties. Here is a condensed version of the same, almost forty years after the fact:

After I came home from the 1936 Olympics with my four gold medals, it became increasingly apparent that everyone was going to slap me on the back, want to shake my hand or have me up to their suite. But no one was going to offer me a job.[10]

Now embedded in the public memory, Jesse's own view of his post-Olympic troubles is a part of a larger, familiar litany: Hitler might have snubbed him, but the President of the United States didn't invite him to the White House, either. From Nazi Germany he returned to racist America, to be sent again to the back of the bus; his athletic feats were applauded, but no one offered him a job. Unfortunately, this whole scenario is filled with half-truths, none more glaring than the job question. It is true that no one offered him a permanent job. More to the point, no one offered him a job tailored to his limited abilities, and no one came forward with a good job offer unless he would return to finish his college degree. Four years later he returned to Ohio State, but he never obtained the degree. In the meantime, he "sprinted from job to job," as the *Chicago Defender* lamented in 1939. Within three years of his Olympic triumph, he briefly held at least five different jobs and undertook three entrepreneurial ventures of his own. Despite the impermanence, he made incredibly good money for that era.[11]

☆ ☆ ☆

In late January 1937 Owens signed a contract with Consolidated Radio Artists of New York City, reportedly for $100,000, to lead a touring twelve-piece band of black musicians. By now he and Ruth had decided not to build a new house in Cleveland. Instead they bought a fine old home on Westchester Avenue and had it modernized. At his parents' new home on East 87th Street, Jesse had a garage in the rear converted into an apartment for one of his sisters and her husband, and he paid the down payment for yet another house on the same street for another sister. He traded in his 1936 Buick, having driven it less than six months, for a new 1937 Buick sedan.[12]

One month after signing with Consolidated Artists, Owens made his debut at a nightclub in Harrisburg, Pennsylvania, then moved for a week's engagement in Harlem's Savoy Ballroom. Rain fell heavily on the Savoy's opening night, but 3,000 people paid to witness the event. Louis Armstrong and Jimmy Durante sat among the entertainment stars, watching Jesse perform in a dazzling white suit with tails. He looked better than he performed. "Well, I couldn't play an instrument," he later recalled. "I'd just stand up front and announce the numbers. They had me sing a little, but that was a horrible mistake. I can't carry a tune in a bucket." The *Amsterdam News* generously observed that he "acquitted himself like a veteran."[13]

After Harlem, the group moved to Philadelphia for a week's engagement, then went on the road in a series of one-night stands. "We played black theaters and nightclubs all over hell," Jesse remembered years later. "It was rough going; there'd be knife fights right on the dance floor some nights. Promoters'd run off with all the dough after a dance. Whooooee. It was a long way from the Olympic ideal." Owens quickly became weary of the seedy scenes, monotonous repetition, and frantic pace of travel. Frequently he could be found in the company of the black singer Midge Williams, but still he became homesick and eager to quit. "Leading a band is all right financially, and it's a lot of fun," he told a group of Knoxville College students in early April, "but socially, it's no good." Several days later in Richmond, Virginia, he developed a severe case of strep throat. He threw in the towel, announcing that he would "try to go back to school next year, finish my education, and try to do something worth while for my race."[14]

During the summer of 1937 several good things seemed to be happening for his race. On June 22 Joe Louis sent a smashing right fist to the jaw of James J. Braddock in the eighth round, making Louis the first black heavyweight champion since the legendary Jack Johnson. Just a month later four of the Scottsboro Boys, jailed since 1931 on trumped-up charges, were freed from their Alabama prison. In late July Jesse himself went south as a guest of honor at the fiftieth anniversary of the founding of Mound Bayou, an all-black utopian community in Mississippi.[15]

Amid speeches, dances, and the showing of a film of Joe Louis's victory over Braddock, Owens competed in a sprint exhibition against a high schooler named Berkeil Naylor, Mississippi's black interscholastic champion. Jesse gave him a 5-yard head start and beat him easily. Sad to say, though, he found Mound Bayou down at the heels. Founded in 1887 as "a place where a Negro may get inspiration by seeing what other members of his race have accomplished," the little town had languished under mismanagement and Depression economics. By 1937 it was a sleepy, dilapidated colony, declining in population. Scarcely was it an inspiring place any longer.[16] No doubt Owens gladly returned to his home in the North to pursue his dreams of further financial success.

In the autumn of 1937 he considered organizing a professional track-and-field league around the talents of Eddie Tolan, Ben Johnson, and himself. "This market hasn't been tapped," he explained to a reporter. The athlete, competitive and proud, still lurked just beneath the businessman's façade. "Give me 30 days and I'll knock off a 9.7 hundred," he told one journalist. But the businessman won out. Instead of a professional track league, Jesse decided to found and manage a touring all-black basketball squad. He took his cue from the Renaissance Big Five, who operated out of New York City, and the Harlem Globetrotters, a Chicago-based operation. Jesse recruited his team mostly from the Cleveland area and named it the Olympians.[17]

In mid-November 1937 they opened their season in a Cleveland recreation center, and then they hit the road. During the week of Thanksgiving, they played four games in the Pittsburgh area. By New Year's Day they had played twenty games, winning all but one. At the halftime of each game, Owens stepped to a microphone to speak briefly about his Olympic experiences, completing his part of the program with a demonstration of his running techniques. Occasionally he ran exhibition races on the court. On December 30, in the Drake University Field House at Des Moines, Iowa, he beat four Drake sprinters in a 50-yard dash, finishing just two-tenths of a second shy of the world mark.[18]

He still hoped for reinstatement by the Amateur Athletic Union. When the Olympians arrived in Chicago for several games in early January 1938, he stopped by the office of J. Lyman Bingham, an assistant to the president of the AAU, to request that his case be reviewed. Curiously, he argued that the Havana horse, Julio Macaw, had never run professionally before their race, which meant—according to Owens—that the Havana exhibition a year earlier did not constitute a professional event. The logic was shaky and unconvincing. So was Jesse's explanation to the press; "I've made more money than I ever thought I would during the past year, and I did it without capitalizing on my athletic ability. But my heart is still with amateur athletics."[19]

More than his own amateur status was at stake. To the AAU he had to respond to questions about the Olympians basketball club, which was playing regularly against college teams. Were the Olympians receiving money—more than reasonable expenses—for their exhibitions? Were they scheduled to play more than the specified number of games per month allowed by the AAU? On both counts, Owens's answers failed to satisfy AAU officials. By early February 1938 the Olympians were suspended by the AAU, making them ineligible to compete against any more college teams.[20]

Yet they carried on with their tour, playing against various local amateur and semiprofessional clubs. By late January they were moving from one town to another in the Colorado Rockies, battling snowstorms all the way. By mid-February they were in Bellingham, then Yakima, Washington. Two months later they arrived back in Ohio for their final game of the season against the Log Cabin Big Five in the Cleveland 372d Regiment Armory. In the end, although the Olympians reportedly won all but six of their 142 games, their tour was reckoned a financial failure because of poor management, unsatisfactory bookings, and bad weather conditions in the West. Much of the blame fell on Jesse's shoulders. Apparently he made little money on the venture.[21]

But he was not discouraged. For the summer of 1938, he organized a touring softball squad, the Olympics, which played mostly within the state of Ohio. Proximity to Cleveland was important, because Jesse's exhibition sprints and broad jumps were an essential part of the promotion for the games. He drove to each engagement in his Buick in the late afternoon and returned home each night. As of late April 1938, he was regularly employed as a bath-house attendant in Cleveland's recreation department. The starting salary was $1,160, a modest but livable income for that day. In an interview with the local press, Jesse indicated that he was weary of travel and wanted to settle down. He intended to remain at this job for some time. In the autumn he would resume his work toward a baccalaureate degree as a part-time student at nearby Western Reserve.[22]

That dream seemed to vanish two months later, when Owens was dismissed from his job for political reasons. Because he was not a member of the Cleveland Civil Service Commission, a kind of city employees' union, he was replaced by a person from the regular Civil Service ranks. Actually, the dismissal came as a blessing in disguise, for within a week Owens landed a better-paying position as a playground director in the federally funded Work Projects Administration (WPA). Later he recalled that the salary was $130 a month, more than $1,500 a year, for "watching kids on the swings." Yet neither the money nor the low-key activity satisfied the energetic, ambitious young Owens. He wanted more. Every week he put several hundred miles on his car, driving to and from athletic exhibitions with the barnstorming Olympics softball team.[23]

Once Owens drove to an engagement in Brooklyn, New York. For the first night baseball game ever held at Ebbets Field, Larry MacPhail, the Dodgers' owner, spared no expense in promoting the event with a magnificent pregame show. Babe Ruth made a guest appearance. The radio announcer Red Barber and a 300-pound local musician competed in a footrace. Owens displayed his skills in three events. First he ran a 100-yard dash against Ernie Koy of the Dodgers and Lee Gamble of the visiting Cincinnati Reds, giving them a ten-yard handicap. Jesse was clocked at 9.7 seconds but finished a yard or so behind Koy, with Gamble bringing up the rear. Then Owens long-jumped 23 feet, 8 inches. In his final exhibition, he lost by a full ten yards to Dodger Gibby Brack, who sprinted 120 yards while Jesse cleared ten low hurdles. One reporter observed that "Brack should have given Owens a handicap."[24]

McPhail, whom the *New York Times* dubbed "the Barnum of baseball," reportedly paid $4,000 for his pregame carnival on that evening of June 15, 1938. His star attraction, Owens, got a reasonable slice of the total. But Cincinnati Reds pitcher Johnny Vander Meer stole the show. Only five days earlier, Vander Meer had pitched a no-hitter. Once the preliminaries were finished, he promptly turned in another goose-egg performance. To this day, he is still the only pitcher in the history of major league baseball to toss consecutive no-hit games.[25]

Jesse Owens's contribution to that night's memorable athletic feat was well-publicized and well-paid, but it was more carnival showmanship than athletics. He willingly accepted the role of a sideshow artist, a gimmick runner selling his name to attract crowds. Shortly afterward he again stooped to the level of vaudeville in a "race" against Joe Louis. At Yankee Stadium in late June, Louis got sweet revenge against his German nemesis, Max Schmeling, whom he finished off in the first round while 90,000 spectators roared their approval. Just two weeks later Louis and Owens lined up for a 60-yard sprint in Chicago between games of an American Giants and Birmingham Black Barons doubleheader. The race was a farce, of course. At the starter's gun, Owens reportedly "tripped and fell down" while Louis lumbered off. Jesse recovered his balance and closed the gap, but the Brown Bomber "beat" the world's fastest human as the crowd cheered.[26]

☆　☆　☆

From the late summer of 1938 until the end of 1941, Owens suffered a series of disappointments, business reversals, and personal failures that would have destroyed a less resilient individual. Before finishing out the summer as a playground director in Cleveland, in early August he invested a bundle of money and lent his name to a new business, the Jesse Owens Dry Cleaning Company, at East 101 Street and Cedar Avenue on Cleveland's East Side. "Speedy 7 Hour Service by the World's Fastest Runner," read a huge advertisement in the local black press. "Fame is fickle and temporary," the editor of the *Call and Post* commented, with reference to Jesse's earlier "offers" that amounted to nothing. "Jesse must now proceed on his own business ability and not on his fame as a runner."[27]

The advice was disregarded on two counts: Jesse could scarcely make his way by his business ability, because he had little; nor would he cease capitalizing on his athletic fame. His WPA summer job behind him, he left his dry cleaning business in the hands of others as he traveled far and wide racing against horses and local athletes in the autumn of 1938. One week he was in Louisiana; the next he ran in Pennsylvania. Occasionally he returned to Cleveland to check on his business and to perform running stunts for local merchants and charities.[28]

In early October he received the stunning news that the United States Government had placed a lien of $746 against his home for his failure to pay income tax on an estimated $20,000 earned in 1936. Neither the newspaper accounts nor FBI memoranda indicate if the figure represented Jesse's total earnings during those four months after the Berlin games or whether $20,000 was the only portion for which he paid no taxes. Whatever the case, in 1938 he was called on the carpet. As Ruth Owens reportedly said to the press, "Jesse earned the money, so I guess he'll have to pay it."[29] A much more serious and widely publicized evasion of income taxes nearly thirty years later was not Jesse's first scrape with the Internal Revenue Service.

With a lien on his home, he scrambled all the more frantically to make money in the winter of 1938–39. Once again he took his Olympians basketball team on a western tour, but this time with an added incentive. At each stopover he called upon local liquor wholesalers to promote the interests of his latest employer, the Calvert Distillers Corporation. Unfortunately, during his prolonged absences from home his dry cleaning business languished, with creditors knocking on the door. In early May 1939, Owens appeared in Federal Court to file a petition of bankruptcy.[30]

Years later he blamed the collapse of the business on two unscrupulous partners. They fled the scene and were never heard from again, he recalled. Like so many of Jesse's recollections, however, that was merely the way he wanted, or needed, to remember the facts. None of the contemporary newspaper accounts mention any kind of duplicity. What they all indicate, in fact, is that Jesse's later accounts of the case were filled with inaccuracies and exaggerations. According to Owens, the business had made big money and had expanded to more than a dozen branches; the local press indicated that the Jesse Owens Dry Cleaning Company struggled from beginning to end, all at a single site. Much later Jesse recalled a whopping debt of

$114,000; on another occasion he cited a figure of $55,000. In fact, his petition in Federal Court listed assets of $2,050 and liabilities of $8,891. His largest debts were on cash loans from individuals, several bills from clothing stores, city and county taxes, and $400 he still owed on his latest Buick.[31]

As Jesse later recalled the crisis, his father came to his rescue—not with money, for he had none to offer, but rather with solace and practical advice. First they prayed for divine guidance. Then old Henry Owens devised a fifty-year plan for paying off the debt and told Jesse to write it down on paper. With that in hand they went to a local banker, who surprisingly agreed to lend the entire amount. Or so Owens told the story thirty years later, adding transparent piety and sentimental filial devotion to his evasion of responsibility for failure.[32]

In truth, Jesse paid off that bankruptcy debt by doing more of what he had been doing for the past two years: selling his fame to the highest bidder, for whatever exhibition the moguls of showmanship thought the public wanted. That was not quite what the Cleveland *Call and Post* had in mind when it declared:

> Jesse is still young enough, if he is made of the right stuff, to take this defeat, and come back and justify the confidence millions of people have placed in him. It is a far cry from the adulation and cheers of the world to the ignominy of a bankruptcy court, but there is a trail that leads back. We hope Jesse will take this and in a new field establish himself in the good graces of the public.

As if to reassure itself of its confidence in the young Owens, the *Call and Post* insisted a month later that "he's made of the right stuff."[33]

He was certainly made of energetic stuff. During the summer of 1939 he traveled extensively with the Indianapolis Clowns, a barnstorming baseball team that the *Chicago Defender* twenty years later still considered "the best drawing card outside of the major leagues." The all-black Clowns, managed by a white man, Ed Hamman, were a baseball version of the Harlem Globetrotters. They performed stunts and humorous gags throughout each game. At the end of the evening's entertainment, Owens raced a horse for 60 yards. Apparently it was with the Clowns that he devised the technique of having the starting pistol fired near the horse's head to make it rear up, allowing Owens to get a head start. Older blacks in the South, especially, still vividly recall watching Jesse run against horses.[34]

Ed Hamman remembers something else. He usually rode beside Jesse in the front seat of the Buick, following the team bus. When they stopped for food, in the North as well as the South, Owens was frequently refused entrance by the front door, and called a "nigger" in the process. At first Hamman refused to enter restaurants that barred his traveling companion, but Owens persuaded him to ignore the insults and bring out sandwiches for them to eat in the car. "Ed, you can't help it," Jesse calmly explained. That adaptability, so repugnant to a later generation of angry blacks, served Jesse well in the late 1930s. He was constantly on the road, a steady target for racial bigots who often did not know—as Hamman put it—that they were "talking to Jesse Owens, a man who had brought honor to his country." In addition to his travels with the Indianapolis Clowns, Jesse also accompanied another touring squad, the Toledo Crawfords, in the late summer and early autumn of 1939.[35]

Despite the discomforts and embarrassments, travel apparently suited the restless Owens far more than did a steady, settled job. Early in 1940 he accepted employment as a salesman for an East Cleveland branch of the Lyons Tailoring Company. Lyons hired him "because of his popularity among the Negro population," admitted the manager, who exploited his popularity to the hilt. Advertisements in the local black press featured Jesse in a smart three-piece suit, poised in a sprinter's starting position. "Come in and shake hands with the greatest athlete of all time," the caption read. "Jesse will be glad to show you the newest and smartest Spring patterns and colors in fine imported and domestic fashions."[36]

Perhaps he did show the clothing, but he didn't sell much. He was not one to concentrate on customers and sales. His mind wandered. He "spent too much time observing people passing the store, especially pretty women," his employer complained. Jesse did more than look. According to the irritated manager of Lyons, "whenever a pretty girl passed the store he ran down the street after her." Jesse's days as a clothing salesman were numbered. After scarcely six weeks at the job, he was dismissed.[37]

Pretty women on the sidewalk might have been his greatest distraction, but that was not the most serious of his employer's complaints. In mid-March, Jesse's mother died at the age of sixty-four and was given a fine funeral in the Olivet Baptist Church. Years later Jesse recalled that he cried "like a baby, off and on, for three days after the funeral." His Lyons boss wailed too—but in anger, and for years afterward, claiming that he was never repaid the $200 he loaned Owens for the funeral expenses.[38]

☆ ☆ ☆

With the coming of summer in 1940, Owens once again took to the road to exhibit his speed at baseball games, county fairs, and carnivals. For most of June he was scheduled in the Midwest, and for July as far south as Shreveport, Louisiana. He had barely begun his odyssey, when he narrowly escaped serious injury in a violent auto collision in Elgin, Indiana. Another car smashed at full speed into the side of his Buick at an intersection, sending Jesse to the hospital with cuts on his head and arms and nasty bruises on his legs. He was lucky. His car was a total loss. Four days later he bought a new one and was back on the road. He had bills to pay, commitments to keep. But by now the black press, if not its readership, had grown weary of their hero's perpetual motion, his inability to hold a job, his unwillingness to settle down. "He has run against everything from humans to horses and autos for money," Fay Young of the *Chicago Defender* lamented.[39]

Apparently Owens, too, sensed something wrong in his life. He was nearly twenty-seven years of age. Had he been a professional baseball player, he would be at his peak; as a sprinter, he was past his prime and banned from amateur competition to boot. Since the Berlin Olympics, he had held one job after another and scrambled from one failure to the next in businesses of his own making. Through all his ups and downs, he had made more money than any sharecropper's son or urban ghetto migrant could have realistically expected. But he had spent it as fast has he made it and was still without long-term security or direction for the future. Now another Olympic year stared him in the face, even though the games scheduled for Tokyo had been canceled. Had they been held, new stars would have burst on the scene, breaking the records and dimming the memories of Berlin. As in the ancient reckoning of time, another modern Olympiad signaled the inexorable passage of years, the mature athlete's greatest enemy. Even Jesse Owens would not always be the world's fastest human.

One of his minor records, in the 220-yard low hurdles, fell to a Texan, Fred Walcott, in the spring track season of 1940. Just two months later, an unknown black athlete at Alabama State College, Leo Tarrant, ran the 100-yard dash in 9.9 seconds and the 220 in 21.5 seconds, edging him toward Owens's records. All the while a versatile young UCLA athlete was long-jumping more than 25 feet, causing sportswriters to predict that as soon as he learned to leave the take-off board more smoothly, Owens's long-jump mark would surely fall. Jesse recognized the name. He was Mack Robinson's younger brother, Jackie, a phenomenal four-sport star as a sophomore at UCLA.[40]

In early June 1940, Owens once again announced—as he had regularly done for the past three years—that he would be returning to Ohio State in the fall to earn his degree. This time he meant it, but it was no easy feat. He and Ruth now had three lovely daughters: eight-year-old Gloria, wise beyond her years, three-year-old Marlene, and baby Beverly. Jesse loved to buy them the finest clothes made, whatever dolls and toys they wanted, and all the food they needed—all that he had not enjoyed in his own youth. How could he do that as a returning student? Shortly after he moved them to 296 South Oakley Avenue in Columbus, he began operating a dry cleaning business on North High Street. To pay his tuition and incidental expenses, he assisted Larry Snyder with the track team. Officially he was listed in the university directory as an "Assistant Trainer" in the Department of Athletics and Physical Education.[41]

Busy on the track, at the laundry, and in the classroom, he scarcely noticed that a new men's dormitory, Baker Hall, opened in the fall of 1940 just after a new president, Howard Landis Bevis, took office. Nor did he give much attention to yet another losing football season, with head coach Francis A. Schmidt stepping down to be replaced by Paul Brown. But he could scarcely ignore campus activities that were altogether different from what he had known four years earlier. While

Army, Navy, and Marine Corps recruiters did a brisk business in anticipation of war, students openly debated the virtues and faults of Communism, conducted antidraft protests, and organized a "peace strike" for the spring of 1941. One student group, calling itself the Committee on Democracy in Education, regularly held debates on such topics as racial discrimination, conscription, and civil liberties. No doubt those outbursts of student activism made Owens feel old before his time, out of step with the current college generation.[42]

Once again he found himself unable to cope with the demands of class work. Earlier he had struggled even to pass the easy courses into which he was channeled in order to keep him eligible for athletics. Now he had to take the tougher science and mathematics courses required for graduation. He was simply not up to the task. None of his moneymaking endeavors for the past three years had been of an intellectual nature. Always physically restless, now he was mentally rusty, more unable than ever to sit and concentrate at the books.

Distractions outside the classroom hit him from all sides. Just after he began his first quarter of study, his father suffered a heart attack, requiring Jesse, Ruth, and the three girls to go hastily to Cleveland for a deathbed vigil, an open-coffin wake, and the funeral service. When they returned to Columbus, the dry cleaning business demanded every spare minute outside class. Even the coming presidential election proved a distraction, as Jesse once again received a handsome offer from Joseph Pew of Sun Oil Company to campaign for the Republican candidate, Wendell Willkie. This time he refused. Rumors had him supporting Roosevelt and offering to debate Joe Louis, who was campaigning for Willkie. But the rumors were false. In the end, the Brown Bomber stumped for Willkie in a manner as awkward and futile as Jesse's work for Alf Landon had been four years earlier.[43]

Jesse stumbled as a student. At the end of the fall quarter of 1940, he was expelled for low grades, but he was readmitted immediately as "a special case." To Ohio State's credit, it made every effort imaginable to provide its most renowned athlete with a college degree. To the credit of individual professors, they refused to participate in a charade by lowering their standards. Jesse could not meet the academic standards. At the beginning of all four quarters he was enrolled in 1940–41, he was on probation "for low grades." Finally, in December 1941, he gave up, finishing with a cumulative grade point average of 1.07 out of a possible 4. He never came close to the average of 1.5 needed for graduation.[44]

On the eve of World War II, Jesse Owens was tired of chasing rainbows.

CHAPTER 10

Patriotic Games

As Owens prepared for his last unsuccessful attempt to cope with final exams at Ohio State, an unprepared American naval garrison at Pearl Harbor, Hawaii, suffered a surprise attack by hundreds of Japanese warplanes in the early morning of December 7, 1941. Americans gasped at the news of eighteen ships sunk or severely damaged, about 170 planes destroyed, and almost 4,000 lives lost. President Roosevelt denounced Japan's "unprovoked and dastardly attack" and immediately asked Congress to declare war. Within the week America was also officially at war against Hitler and Mussolini in Europe. In the anxious atmosphere of December 1941, Jesse Owens's failure to obtain a university degree seemed of little importance.

The war proved to be supremely important in the black American's struggle for equality. A previous generation of black spokesmen had responded to America's entry into World War I by calling patriotically for their people to close ranks with the rest of the country in defense of democratic principles, only to see blacks suffer more lynchings and renewed discrimination at the war's end. Black Americans would not make that mistake again. Now they would fight for democracy at home as well as abroad. Refusing to accept racial abuse, they sought racial equality in Mississippi and Michigan as well as victory over fascism in Europe and Japanese aggression.

The necessities of a wartime economy worked to their advantage. Several months before Pearl Harbor, a threatened mass march on Washington in protest against the reluctance of defense plants to hire black workers nudged President Roosevelt to issue an executive order prohibiting racial discrimination by unions and industries engaged in government-contracted work. Enforcement of that mandate was spotty, but by 1945 black membership in labor unions had doubled to over a million. Some 2 million blacks found employment in defense plants. The ratio of skilled to unskilled black workers doubled, and black women in industry quadrupled in number.[1]

With mixed success in breaking down racial barriers in training programs, facilities, roles, and recognition, more than a million blacks served in the armed forces during World War II. But black leaders scarcely assumed, as they had in World War I, that American gratitude would produce racial benefits. "We have neither faith in promises, nor a high opinion of the integrity of the American people, where race is involved," the editor of the *Pittsburgh Courier* noted. "Experience has taught us that we must rely primarily upon our own efforts." Several organized protests at Army bases and riots in American cities gave notice of a black presence that was no longer servile. Membership in the NAACP—an aggressive civil rights advocate at that time—grew tenfold during the war, to half a million. In the midst of the war a new organization, the Congress of Racial Equality (CORE), emerged to combat Jim Crow laws and practices in the United States.[2]

No reformer, Jesse Owens belonged to neither the NAACP nor CORE. Instead, during the war he joined the Urban League, whose moderate policies reflected his own perspective. At the outset of the war he was exempt from the draft because he was married with three children. Later he was reclassified to 1-A status but was deferred because he worked in a war industry.[3] Although he was never a spokesman for black rights, he represented an essential ingredient of black progress. The war brought him the first steady employment he had ever known. In January 1942 the new director of a national fitness program in the Office of Civilian Defense, John B. Kelly, announced that Owens would be in charge of the program for blacks.[4]

Rumors had the Owens family moving to Philadelphia, near Civilian Defense headquarters. In fact, Ruth and the girls remained for a time in Columbus, then moved back to Cleveland, while Jesse traveled about the country organizing exercise programs, conducting clinics, and lecturing on health and physical fitness to black audiences. Occasionally he gave exhibitions, little different from what he had done on his own since the Berlin games. The circumstances, however, were altogether different. The government job was more secure in both scheduling and income, and now Jesse's public addresses and athletic exhibitions carried patriotic significance.[5]

Owens did not remain a government employee for long. In the autumn of 1942 he was in Detroit, holding clinics in the black community of Inkster. He stayed for a week or so in the old St. Antoine YMCA at 63 East Elizabeth Street, rooming with Russell Brown, a Cleveland native whose father had served on the Cleveland City Council while Jesse was in high school. The Browns had moved to Colorado, where Russell starred in high school track and field, but for college he had returned to Ohio State largely because Jesse was there. Now he had an opportunity to befriend his boyhood idol.[6]

He informed Jesse of a lower management job, at good pay, in the Ford Motor Company. The war had transformed the entire automotive industry into an "arsenal of democracy" for the production of planes, ships, tanks, jeeps, and artillery. Within only six months of Pearl Harbor, Ford, Chrysler, General Motors, and Packard had turned out $1.4 million worth of war machines. In addition to its Dearborn operations, Ford had a huge new plant built in 1942 at government expense 30 miles west of Detroit for the construction of B-24 Liberator bombers. Between June 1942 and June 1943, about 30,000 migrants flooded into the area to fill openings created by those wartime measures. Jesse Owens was only one—albeit the most famous one—of 50,000 blacks newly arrived in Detroit. By coincidence, already resident in the city was the man with whom Owens's fame was linked. Years earlier, the family of Joe Louis had moved from Alabama to Detroit.

Another of Jesse's earlier acquaintances, Willis Ward, headed the division of Negro Personnel at Ford Motor Company. Ward was a graduate of the University of Michigan, where he had starred in football and track, beating Jesse several times in head-to-head competition. Now he worked for the powerful, unscrupulous head of Labor Relations at Ford, Harry Bennett. A former sailor and prize fighter, Bennett had for several years fought vainly to prevent unions from gaining a foothold in the company. Just before the war he hired hordes of informers and bullies to break up the organizing efforts of the United Auto Workers (UAW). Once he bribed 1,000 blacks to assault picket lines. Those strongarm methods backfired, as Ford employees voted overwhelmingly for the UAW as their bargaining agent, but Bennett would not give up. Late in 1941 he ordered Ward and his "investigator," Russell Brown, to fire more than a hundred blacks who seemed to be "troublemakers." When the UAW successfully protected its members, Bennett angrily fired both Ward and Brown.[8]

Once he calmed down, however, Bennett reinstated Ward and Brown, and into that troubled situation he hired Jesse Owens in April 1943 as assistant personnel director of black workers at Ford. Jesse quickly rose to the top. Just four months after he began work, Ward was called from the Naval Reserve into active duty, and Jesse took his place at Ford. As Director of Negro Personnel, he screened black applicants, enforced worker discipline, and fired incompetent or uncooperative workers at the River Rouge plant. He constantly found himself caught in the squeeze between Harry Bennett's authoritarian policies and the UAW's determination to protect workers' rights. The quick-triggered Bennett fired him four times for failing to protect company interests, only to rehire him immediately. Still, Jesse's allegiance was clear. "I was working for the company, for the interest of the company," he told an interviewer years later. He toed the Ford line, he insisted, because "we had a war going on" and the building of Pratt-Whitney motors, tanks, and B-24 bombers "was a mighty important job."[9]

Three months after Owens arrived in Detroit, a massive interracial riot erupted in the early summer of 1943. Beginning with racial taunts and minor scrapes in a public park, blacks and whites lashed into each other with rocks, sticks, knives, and guns, overwhelming Detroit's police force. Hostile crowds smashed and burned cars, looted and destroyed shops, and indiscriminately attacked anyone of a different color. The savagery continued for the better part of a week. Finally federal troops had to be called in to restore order. At the riot's end, investigators estimated $2 million in property loss, twenty-five blacks and nine whites killed, and more than four hundred injuries requiring hospital treatment.[10]

After the riot, the main thrust of Owens's job changed. For the next two years he attended more to public relations than to internal labor relations. He worked closely with the Urban League to improve housing for Ford workers, with the local YMCA to provide wholesome recreation, and with the NAACP to air the problems facing black families who had recently moved to Detroit to work for Ford. In all those measures, Jesse projected a benign corporate image that had been sadly lacking under the domineering rule of Harry Bennett.[11]

Unfortunately, Owens's association with Bennett brought an end to his work at Ford. In a managerial shakeup following Henry Edsel Ford's death in 1943, his son, Henry Ford II—the grandson of the aged founder—returned home from the Navy to take over a family business that was reeling from mismanagement, harsh labor policies, and poor public relations. In the ensuing power struggle, the abrasive Bennett and more than a thousand of his appointees were ousted. For Jesse, the hatchet fell in October 1945, when he was out of town on a speaking engagement. Upon returning to Detroit, he was offered a reassignment that was, in fact, a demotion. He refused it. Once again he was cut loose from a secure, traditional job, leaving him to scramble independently. Once again the choice, to some degree, was his own.[12]

He never looked back. To friends, he seemed relieved to be out of the snakepit of corporate politics. Russell Brown remembers him responding "cheerfully" to the news of his dismissal. Perhaps that apparent cheerfulness was a cover for hurt: Jesse had long since mastered the art of smiling in the face of adversity. He and Brown immediately launched a wholesale sporting goods business in Detroit, selling athletic equipment to local clubs, shops, and black colleges. They attempted to obtain a franchise from Wilson, Spaulding, and several other national manufacturers, but all their applications were rejected. Brown still blames their failure on racial discrimination. Whatever the reason, the Jesse Owens and Russell Brown Sporting Goods Company died shortly after birth.[13]

☆ ☆ ☆

While America's aging Olympic superstar darted from one job to another, several younger black athletes finally broke the color barrier in professional sports. Not since the early 1930s had a black played in the National Football League, but in 1945 both Kenny Washington and Woody Strode signed with the Los Angeles Rams. The next year fullback Marion Motley and guard Bill Willis won all-star honors with the Cleveland Browns, champions of the new All-America Conference. Also in 1946, William "Pop" Gates and William "Dolly" King became the first blacks to play on previously all-white professional basketball teams.[14]

Most important of all was the black breakthrough in major league baseball. For more than half a century, a most ironically phrased "gentleman's agreement" among major league owners had barred blacks from participation in the national pastime, relegating them to the poorly organized, ill-paid, and virtually invisible Negro Leagues. At the end of World War II, however, a mixture of opportunistic shrewdness and courageous principles prompted Branch Rickey of the Brooklyn Dodgers to sign Jackie Robinson to a Dodgers contract. A year of minor league seasoning with the Montreal Royals prepared Robinson for his debut with the Dodgers in 1947. Destined for a difficult but brilliant career, he was soon joined in the major leagues by notable blacks such as Larry Doby, Don Newcombe, Roy Campanella, and Satchel Paige. That trickle would soon become a flood at the forefront of a new era of black–white relations in the United States.[15]

But if the future belonged to aggressive, outspoken black athletes like Jackie Robinson, Bill Russell, and Muhammad Ali—not to mention social activists as disparate as Martin Luther King and Stokeley Carmichael—the mood of postwar America was best represented by the moderate personalities of Jesse Owens and Joe Louis. It was a quiet, conservative mood, a time of material progress, an era of social consensus rather than conflict. During the war black militancy had been stifled for the sake of military victory; after the war, several factors conspired to keep blacks content with their chronic separate-and-unequal status. An unprecedented peacetime economic boom provided numerous new jobs, leaving only 5.2 percent of black male workers unemployed in 1948. Even the South underwent rapid industrialization, raising hopes of a "New South" that would be more concerned with commercial profit than with its traditional bigotry. Token signs of racial toleration appeared everywhere: in the highly publicized case of Jackie Robinson, in complete racial integration of the armed forces, and in several Supreme Court decisions culminating in the landmark *Brown* vs. *Board of Education of Topeka* pronouncement that the segregation of children in public schools solely on the basis of race was unconstitutional. For a decade after World War II, black civil rights groups were given to hoping, not fighting, for further progress.[16]

Joe Louis was still their fighter, but only in the ring. Even there, the Brown Bomber was on the downside of an illustrious career. In 1946 he knocked out Billy Conn and Tami Mauriello, then twice defeated Jersey Joe Walcott, before retiring unbeaten in 1948. Unfortunately he returned to the ring to exemplify the futility of a champion past his prime. To the end of his career, however, he remained mild-mannered, soft-spoken, and apolitical. White Americans happily recognized him as "a credit to his race," which simply meant that he kept his mouth shut and his girlfriends black.[17]

Meanwhile, the Owens family lived comfortably in a middle-class Negro neighborhood in Detroit, but to pay the bills after his sporting goods venture folded, Jesse once again hit the road running. At several baseball games during the war, he had raced Helen Stephens, the female gold medalist from the Berlin Olympics. Now his exhibitions took on a more predictable pattern under the patronage of Abe Saperstein, owner of the Harlem Globetrotters and a less famous but similarly clownish baseball team, the Cincinnati Crescents. As he had done during the prewar era with the Indianapolis Clowns, Jesse provided an added attraction for the Globetrotters' and Crescents' barnstorming efforts. Saperstein, however, never required him to run against horses. Instead, he had Jesse demonstrate his quick starts, reminisce about his Olympic experiences, mingle with the crowd, and give autographs. For the better part of four years, Owens stayed on the road. In 1948–49 he accompanied the Globetrotters on a six-month tour of Europe.[18]

Back in Chicago for a Globetrotter exhibition in the spring of 1949, he received an offer from Leo Rose, owner of a chain of clothing stores, to serve as promotional executive of the company. Tired of living out of a suitcase, Jesse gladly took the job. He found an apartment in Chicago, began work immediately, and moved his family from Detroit several months later.[19]

During his first five years in Chicago, Owens served in executive capacities with the Leo Rose Clothing Company, the Hotel Wedgwood, the Mutual of Omaha Insurance Company, the Triad Insurance Company, the South Side Boys Club, and the Illinois State Athletic Commission, all the while receiving a retainer fee of fifty dollars a week for promotional activities on behalf of Leader Cleaners. In his spare time he launched a public relations agency, appeared often on local radio and television shows, spoke at least once a week to school or civic groups, and played golf regularly in a foursome that included his old track opponent and friend, Ralph Metcalfe, who was now the Democratic Committeeman for Chicago's Third Ward. Another Chicago friend observed the obvious: Jesse was "continually on the go."[20]

In the midst of all his commercial and civic activities, Owens clung to his self-image as an athlete and refused to admit the loss of his physical powers. As he explained to a *Chicago Defender* journalist, Fay Young, he took up golf to prove that he "hadn't gone back any" in athletic skill. Young teasingly suggested that golf was an old man's game. "A long way from it," Jesse shot back. In the early 1950s he had a few last flings at displaying his old Olympic speed. At Milwaukee in September, 1950, he ran the 100-yard dash in 9.7 seconds, an incredible feat for a man pushing forty years of age. He had put on several pounds, but his form seemed little diminished by the years. "The slender Owens was out of the holes like a flash," one reporter commented, "floating over the terrain like a feather. He was breathing easy at the finish." At Yankee Stadium in 1952, in his last serious public exhibition, he attempted unsuccessfully to break the base-circling record of 13.3 seconds. The New York Yankees, still an all-white team, were out of town. Jesse performed before a sparse, mostly all-black crowd of spectators, between games of a Negro League doubleheader.[21]

While Jackie Robinson vented his anger and exercised his skills against white opponents, Owens's final athletic performance brought him full circle, back to the confinement of a racially segregated constituency. It was a fitting end to his athletic endeavors. Since the Berlin Olympics, he had made his way on the black night club circuit, endorsed products solely in the black press, taken government appointments that catered to blacks, dealt with Ford Motor Company's black workers, and sold his athletic skills to farcical black barnstorming teams. For all his fame, ambition, and personal charm, Jesse Owens seemed unable to break out of the racial ghetto in which the great majority of less successful blacks languished.

☆   ☆   ☆

Yet a fundamental change was already under way, for in the early 1950s Owens catapulted to eminence in the American mainstream. Arguably, his move to Chicago, putting him in touch with economic opportunities, racially liberal attitudes, and media attention that neither Detroit nor Cleveland afforded, made his biracial acceptance possible. Of far greater importance, however, was the climate of American opinion in the 1950s. Owens suddenly found himself accepted, even wooed, by Americans of all colors, because he provided something they needed.

The cold war did the trick. In the wake of World War II, the United States and the Soviet Union harbored mutual contempt and suspicion of each other's intentions. By 1950 the red flag flew over all of Eastern Europe and China, convincing President Harry Truman, Secretary of State Dean Acheson, and like-minded Americans everywhere that the greedy Communist bear had an insatiable appetite for world domination. The invasion of South Korea in June 1950 merely confirmed their fears. Joseph R. McCarthy, Republican Senator from Wisconsin, played upon those fears with his Communist witch hunt in American governmental, academic, and entertainment circles.

Behind all the bombast, a "cold war consensus" of American opinion, largely manipulated by government officials and information agencies, held that the United States had to take an active role in preventing democratic values from being swamped by conspiratorial Communists. Americans deemed military strength essential to the task. They also believed it necessary to counter Communist propaganda with the "truth" about democracy and the "free world." The allegiance of unaligned emerging nations in Asia and Africa seemed to be at stake.[22]

Democracy, in American rhetoric, meant freedom and equality of opportunity. But there was the rub. The abysmal past treatment and present condition of the American Negro stood as a stumbling block to effective propaganda. In 1949 the actor Paul Robeson, a former All-American football player at Rutgers University, announced to an audience in Paris that American blacks had no reason to bear arms in the event of war against the Soviet Union. Robeson's assertion received worldwide attention, prompting the House Un-American Activities Committee to urge none other than Jackie Robinson to refute it. Robinson complied, insisting that he "and other Americans of many races and faiths" had "too much invested" in the nation's welfare to refuse to stand firm in its time of need.[23]

American cold warriors needed more than black statements of support and national unity. They needed black examples to show the world, examples of success, of social acceptance, of patriotism. They needed Jesse Owens, whose story illustrated the cherished American belief that democracy allowed even a poor black boy to rise from rags to riches.

Jesse's breakthrough began in 1950, when the Associated Press selected him as the greatest track athlete of the past half-century. The balloting was not even close. Owens received 291 votes to Jim Thorpe's 74, with Paavo Nurmi of Finland finishing a distant third. A huge testimonial banquet was held in honor of Jesse's selection in October 1950 at the Sheraton Hotel in Chicago. More than six hundred Chicago businessmen and civic leaders, Olympic officials and athletes, and track coaches and administrators gathered to pay tribute. Few blacks dotted the sea of white faces as Kenneth L. "Tug" Wilson, head of the Big Ten Conference, delivered some opening remarks. Larry Snyder then introduced Ruth Owens and daughters Marlene and Beverly, lauding Ruth for always being "there behind Jesse, giving him encouragement."[24]

Reminiscences, the stuff of myth-making, were in order.

Several speakers vividly recalled Jesse's matchless performance at Ann Arbor in 1935, others his Olympic feats in 1936.
The intervening years went unnoticed. The present outweighed
the past, editing it accordingly. Ralph Metcalfe, once a foe, now
a friend, presented Owens with a plaque. Avery Brundage, a native Chicagoan, joined in the festivities, his part in the AAU's
earlier ban of Jesse buried from view. Just a year earlier Brundage had been elected president of the International Olympic
Committee. From then on he would look to Owens as his most
ardent propagandist and fundraiser for Olympism.[25]

Several years earlier, the Swedish sociologist Gunnar
Myrdal had observed that "the American Negro problem is a
problem in the heart of America. It is there that interracial tension has its focus. It is there that the decisive struggle goes on."
Now, as one speaker put it, Owens had "won the heart of America." Thus began the love affair between Jesse Owens and the
American public, an affair based on mutual needs. Jesse understandably needed respect and acclaim, not to mention financial recompense for his services. America needed a black hero,
especially one from another era who could no longer challenge
the prowess of white athletes, a patriotic, mild-mannered
Negro who would affirm the values of Main Street, U.S.A.[26]

Whether the American hero of the moment is Abe Lincoln
or John F. Kennedy, Babe Ruth or Jesse Owens, he is required
to display a love of children. Jesse Owens passed that test with
flying colors. Shortly after arriving in Chicago, he became a
member of the Board of Directors of the South Side Boys Club,
and from 1951 to July 1952 he served as executive director of
that organization's programs involving some 1,500 black
youths on Chicago's South Side. In truth, he was not a good administrator. He kept records carelessly and botched several
fundraising drives. But it scarcely mattered. Whenever he was
honored at a special gathering or introduced for a public address, some reference was inevitably made to his love of children as exemplified in his work with the South Side Boys
Club.[27]

Journalists made much of his youth work. Reportedly he
spent many hours each week with juvenile delinquents, helping them sort out their problems. Occasionally he was called to
the police station to take some miscreant home in his personal
custody. Tales of his concern for American youths blended

with charming patriotic gestures. According to one report, Owens once organized an all-day amateur boxing program at a ghetto school in Chicago; he showed up early and found to his dismay that no American flag was flying on the pole out front. He scrounged around until he found a flag, then climbed up the pole to attach it to the top. The feat was dangerous and wonderfully daring for a middle-aged man, athletic though he was. "He could have been killed," an admirer recalled years later, "but Jesse Owens wanted that American flag flying."[28]

In yarn and in deed, he kept the flag flying and his image intact as a hero always ready to attend to youth. At Berlin's Olympic Stadium in 1951, he summoned West Germans to join with the United States in opposition to Communism. Three years later he told a story that effectively wrapped his Olympic past and the cold war present into a single bundle, cradled in an encounter with a young German boy. As Owens described the scene, he was returning to his dressing room after his much-applauded Berlin speech when a boy asked him for his autograph. As he signed his name in a worn scrapbook placed before him, Jesse was startled to find a picture of Lutz Long, his opponent and friend at the Berlin Games of 1936. "My father, sir," the boy explained. Then—as Owens told the story in 1954—he first learned that Long had been killed in the war. "We have to talk, son," he said as he put his arm around the boy's shoulders. "You and me have to talk and get to know each other."[29]

It is a touching story, and probably true in its essentials. Certainly it was repeated often enough in subsequent years. In the 1950s, however, it served the particularly useful purpose of portraying Owens as a modern American hero with a human touch and interracial appeal. To youths and adults alike, for whites as well as blacks, he represented the intoxicating dream that economic and racial differences would become inconsequential when people took the time to "talk and get to know each other." For blacks especially, he counseled moderation: "You don't get yourself ahead crying 'Foul!' all your life," he insisted for the public record. That was the closest he ever came to acknowledging the infant civil rights movement. Years later he would publicly applaud the principles of Martin Luther King, but in the 1950s he distanced himself from protest speeches and mass demonstrations. "We all know what's wrong with this world," he told one reporter. "You know it. I know it. I can't change it with wild words. But I *can* bring two people, the other fellow and me, a little bit closer if I am a gentleman. . . . I will listen to him; he will listen to me. Maybe—no guarantee, remember that, my friend—but maybe we will part not so far removed in outlook as when we came together."[30]

This simple, optimistic prescription for racial conflict was peculiarly suited to the conservative tone of the Eisenhower years. During the electoral campaign that first brought Dwight D. Eisenhower to the presidency in 1952, Owens campaigned for Republican William G. Stratton for Governor of Illinois. Stratton held out a vague promise to create an Illinois Youth Commission with Owens as its head. After the election that plan was momentarily shelved. Instead, in January 1953 Stratton appointed Owens as Secretary of the Illinois State Athletic Commission.[31]

The pay was good. Jesse's annual salary of $6,000 made him the highest paid member of the Athletic Commission. His duties largely involved the supervision of amateur and professional boxing bouts in the state, especially the establishment of appropriate safety standards. A chairman, two commissioners, and four "athletic inspectors"—all appointed by Governor Stratton—assisted in the program under Owens's direction. Three clerical secretaries ran the office in the State Office Building at 160 North LaSalle Street in Chicago.[32]

Jesse relished the status that went with the appointment, his first position of recognized authority since his difficult days at Ford. He liked the flexibility of the job even more. The chairman and commissioners made most of the hard decisions, while secretaries attended to routine details, leaving Jesse free to bounce in and out of the office to meetings with important political and athletic officials and to give frequent addresses to local civic and school groups. In the late spring of 1954 he delivered the graduation speech at the school to which he owed the most, East Tech High School in Cleveland. As always, he used athletics as a metaphor for life that is best lived when people strive to excel and take the time to "walk together and talk together" in mutual respect.[33]

Still unwilling to confine himself to a single enterprise, Owens regularly conducted his own radio and television shows on local Chicago stations. Nor did his tasks as Secretary of the Illinois Athletic Commission prevent him from attending to the business of his own public relations agency. "He's the busiest man I ever saw," one of his secretaries told a visitor. On the day of a major boxing or wrestling program, he was kept busy dispensing favors to friends and influential Chicagoans. He seemed always to have free tickets at his disposal; on those infrequent occasions when the tickets ran out, he personally met his cronies at the gate to let them in. To an observer awed by the ringing phone and heads popping constantly into the office on the day of a big wrestling match, Owens shrewdly explained, "It makes them important not to have paid the price of the ticket, which is inconsequential. They are interested in saying they got it because they knew so-and-so."[34]

☆　☆　☆

Jesse, too, got things from friends in high places. In late July 1955 he was summoned to Washington, D.C., for a day's briefing in preparation for an extended goodwill tour of India, Malaya, and the Philippines, sponsored by the International Educational Exchange Service, an arm of the U.S. Department of State. Like no other event, his visit to the Far East under the auspices of the State Department typified his political usefulness as a symbol of American democracy during the cold war era.[35]

The fall of China to Communism, the Korean War, and the collapse of the French garrison at Dien Bien Phu (1954) had turned American attention eastward. In Malaya and the Philippines, Communist insurgents threatened; India, strategically situated near China and the Soviet Union, seemed an important testing place for democracy in the non-Western world. The American government eagerly offered India support in the form of economic aid and technological expertise. Goodwill emissaries, including Jesse, supplied a kind of icing on the cake of diplomatic attentions.[36]

Arriving in India in early October, for three weeks Owens conducted two track clinics a day and spoke often to school groups in New Delhi, Bombay, Madras, and outlying villages. He represented America as a land of opportunity where even a black man like himself could succeed; he called upon his Indian audiences to join in the democratic crusade against modern tyrants (Communists), whom he deemed no less evil than the Nazi regime he had "defeated" in 1936. Attracted by his athletic fame, audiences warmed to his personal charm, especially when photographs of him wearing a turban appeared in the Indian press. Local dignitaries, athletic officials, and curious children dogged his heels. Newspapermen clamored for interviews. As a New Delhi columnist put it, he became "the darling of many a heart" during his tour of India.[37]

Whatever impact he made on behalf of better Indo-American relations, he most certainly won the plaudits of the press back home. "There is something pleasant happening to United States public relations in New Delhi these days," a correspondent for the *New York Times* wrote. "Jesse Owens is in town." An official for the Danforth Foundation also happened to be in town—New Delhi and Madras—at the same time Owens was there. He wrote to the *New York Times* praising Jesse's "splendid work" for the United States, "a job of international relations superbly done." Glossy *Life* magazine, dedicated to the principle that a hundred pictures are worth a single word, carried photographs of Owens in a turban displaying his athletic form, conversing with Indian officials, and addressing attentive schoolchildren. *Life*'s few words said it all: Jesse Owens was "a practically perfect envoy in a country which has violently exaggerated ideas about the treatment of Negroes in the United States."[38]

During October and November 1955, Owens appeared in twenty cities of India, Malaya, and the Philippines. When he returned home in early December, a pleasant surprise awaited him in Chicago: Governor Stratton had finally decided to proceed with his earlier plans to create an Illinois Youth Commission, with Jesse as the executive director. He would serve under another black, Joseph Bibb, who directed the Illinois Department of Public Safety. Bibb's office oversaw the state police and penetentiary system. The youth commission would deal with youthful offenders, but more importantly it would promote camping, supervise park programs, and organize playground activities for the purpose of preventing juvenile delinquency.[39]

Like his prior work with the Illinois Athletic Commission, Jesse's job was loosely defined. He traveled frequently, all over the state, supervising programs and making the new Youth

Commission visible by his presence. Even when he was in Chicago, he could scarcely ever be found in the office. "Jesse is racing about the city with the same speed that carried him to world marks on the track, back in the mid-thirties," the *Chicago Defender* commented in the spring of 1956. He met regularly with youth clubs, park directors, and juvenile delinquency officers. At nights he was often seen at ball games surrounded by boys whom he had brought with him—basketball games in the winter, baseball games in the summer. By all accounts, he well deserved the award presented him at the seventh statewide conference on Human Relations at the University of Illinois.[40]

In the summer of 1956 Owens threw the weight of his Youth Commission into a cooperative endeavor with the Chicago Park District, the *Chicago Defender*, and several other organizations to produce a "Junior Sports Jamboree" for Chicago youths. The year 1956 was an Olympic year, exactly two decades after Owens himself had starred at Berlin. Now he was promoting a kind of junior Olympics. On August 10 a torch relay led a parade at the outset of the two-day event. The United States Olympic swim team gave an exhibition. Then about 1,800 youngsters, mostly blacks, girls as well as boys, ages twelve to seventeen, competed for prizes in swimming and track-and-field contests. Owens hoped the local gathering would grow into a statewide program and eventually into a nationwide Junior Olympics.[41]

At face value, that hope seemed unrealistic. With the exception of 1936, when a boycott controversy called attention to the Berlin games, Americans had traditionally been uninterested in the Olympics. According to a Gallup Poll in 1956, four out of five Americans did not even know that the games were to be held that year in Melbourne, Australia. Not until the Olympics began to be televised in the 1960s did the American public become attentive. Fully a decade earlier, however, the press and political leaders became intensely concerned about the performances of American Olympians. The new presence of Soviet athletes caused the change.[42]

Excluded from the Olympic movement ever since the Bolshevik revolution of 1917, Russian athletes were finally invited to participate at Helsinki in 1952. In view of their inexperience in international competition, they did surprisingly well. Their narrow second-place finish behind the traditionally dominant American team raised anxieties in athletic and political circles—if not yet in the wider public consciousness—in the United States. Early in 1956 Owens himself predicted that future Olympic gatherings might well become "a dual meet between the United States and the Soviet Union." The Melbourne Olympics, it seemed, would be a supreme test of strength, a symbolic confrontation between East and West in which contrasting governments, economies, and societies would be on trial—"war minus the shooting," the English novelist George Orwell called it.[43]

The emergent importance of the quadrennial Olympic Games worked miracles for the popularity of Jesse Owens in the United States. Of all past Olympians, he was undoubtedly the most accomplished and most acclaimed. Only two more recent Olympic champions rivaled Owens in reputation: Bob Mathias, a handsome Californian, decathlon gold medalist in 1948 and 1952, and Bob Richards, a preacher and pole-vaulter, victor at the 1952 and 1956 games. But both Mathias and Richards lacked several of the elements that made Owens famous. They were single-event champions, not versatile holders of *four* gold medals in a single Olympics. Being white, they were without black appeal in an age when blacks like Harrison Dillard and Mal Whitfield were dominating the track-and-field events. On the eve of the Melbourne Olympics, the *Chicago Defender* pointed proudly to "the exploits of tawny-hued performers" in recent years: Their "string of stirring accomplishments" had served "to make America proud." Yet none now seemed so brilliant as "the incomparable Jesse Owens," whose victories "years ago at Berlin" remained the yardstick of excellence.[44]

Much of the appeal of Jesse Owens lay precisely in the phrase "years ago at Berlin." For all their sterling qualities, the achievements of Bob Mathias and Bob Richards—and of Harrison Dillard and Mal Whitfield—were too recent, unseasoned by years of myth-making. Time and circumstance had not intervened to give extraordinary meaning to their feats. No tall tales identified any of them, in morality-drama fashion, as a virtuous victor over the evil Hitler. In short, they lacked romance; they lacked propaganda value.

In recognition of Owens's value, White House officials

asked him (and several other sports figures, including Mathias) to attend the Melbourne games as a personal representative of the President of the United States. Owens readily accepted the assignment, of course. A *New York Times* reporter described him dressed in a champagne-colored tropical suit, "striking a sartorial note of elegance" as he cheerfully endured a bumpy plane ride between Honolulu and Melbourne. Upon landing, he was met by the United States Consul General to Australia, followed by newspaper and radio reporters. After a lively, impromptu interview, Owens was placed at the disposal of the Commissioner of Police for New South Wales, who escorted him to several schools, hospitals, and boys' clubs for speeches. According to all reports, he "was 'absolutely fantastic' in his ability to size up an audience and make the appropriate remarks in a most acceptable manner."[45]

The Australians, akin to Americans in their love of sport, were gracious, efficient hosts for the 1956 Olympics. Unfortunately, the Suez crisis and the Hungarian revolt against Soviet rule, both occurring within a month prior to the games, cast a pall over Melbourne. The Suez episode caused a minor boycott; the Hungarian disaster created an atmosphere of rancor between Soviet and Hungarian athletes. Several nasty incidents—a Soviet flag trampled by Hungarian patriots, a Hungarian water polo player bashed in the head by a Russian opponent, unsportsmanlike political gestures after several contests—marked the Melbourne games as unmistakably representative of the Cold War era.[46]

For Owens, though, two other events marred the pleasure of being lionized everywhere he went. First, he saw his own 400-meter relay team record broken by an American aggregate composed of Ira Murchison, Leamon King, Thane Baker, and Bobby Morrow, whose time of 39.5 seconds lopped three-tenths of a second off the standard established by Owens, Metcalfe, Draper, and Wykoff at Berlin. Worse still for the patriotic Owens, an early American lead in the unofficial team point totals faded, finally to be surpassed by the Russians. At Melbourne it became painfully obvious that the versatility of both male and female Soviet athletes made the Soviet Union the premier Olympic nation.[47]

Official praise for Owens's work as "a worthy representative of the President of the United States" flowed freely from

Sydney to Washington in the form of letters from Colin Delaney, the New South Wales Commissioner of Police; K. F. Coles, president of the New South Wales Society for Crippled Children; and Orray Taft, the American Consul-General in Sydney. Jesse's "warm and spontaneous" manner and "keen appreciation of the problems of youth" made him "an excellent ambassador for his country," his Australian hosts said.[48]

Duly impressed, Eisenhower Administration officials immediately tapped Owens for yet another assignment. Two months after the Melbourne Olympics, they asked him to serve in a program that the President considered "of the greatest importance": the People-to-People Program, a cooperative endeavor between government and private agencies for the enhancement of "understanding and agreement between Americans and other peoples" throughout the world. The "Sports Committee" of which Owens was a part numbered sixty-four prominent Americans, including such unlikely "sports" figures as Bob Hope, Bernard Gimbel of New York, and Dr. Joyce Brothers. In the patriotic game, Jesse Owens had made the big leagues.[49]

CHAPTER 11

The Back Side of Success

WHEN AT HOME, OWENS ENERGETICALLY PROMOTED athletic programs through the Illinois Youth Commission. He saw sport as an antidote to juvenile delinquency. The athletic "code of ethics," he told one audience, "stresses respect for the rights and property of others, playing the game according to rules and regulations." Owens expected athletes to stand tall as role models of sportsmanship and clean living. In the fall of 1956, just prior to his departure for Australia, he organized eighteen sports clinics in Chicago, with big-name athletes leading each group. "The top athletes," he explained, "can keep the kids interested and out of trouble. They inspire kids, just as I was inspired when I was younger."[1]

He carefully groomed his own image for inspirational purposes. His motive, in part, was to do good. Yet he also knew that his various political appointments and commercial endorsements depended, as one of his employers put it, on his being publicly "idolized" as an exemplar of "success in American life."[2] Keenly aware of the fickleness of public opinion, he dressed, spoke, and acted always with an eye to the impression he was making. "The public will not tolerate nonsense from anyone it has taken to its bosom," he explained candidly to an interviewer.

> You have to keep that in the forefront of your thinking at all times. The public has made you, even though you have won something on your own. It is the public which seeks you out. The public will not stand for prima donnas for long. There are many times now when I don't feel like doing something—signing autographs or speaking for an audience or having dinner with people I have never seen—but the public is not interested in explanations. You got to smile. You must. The moment you begin to think you are an ordinary human being with ordinary human being rights, then the public does not want you any longer. If you are ordinary then the public can no longer look up to you. I can get teed off. I am just as fallible as the next man, as you, but I cannot show that I am teed off.[3]

Jesse's admission that he was "just as fallible as the next man" carried more meaning than most people suspected. Ordinary foibles existed on the back side of extraordinary virtues. Generous with his own money, Owens sometimes avoided creditors. A law-abiding, patriotic citizen, he nevertheless was remiss with his income tax payments. Usually candid, he occasionally slanted the truth to his own advantage in the reconstruction of his rags-to-riches saga. A devoted family man, he engaged in numerous extramarital affairs. Of all those "ordinary" contradictions, his sexual exploits were the first to cause a family crisis. Shortly after the move to Chicago, at the very apex of his public acclaim in the 1950s, the Owenses' marriage suffered intolerable strain.

There is nothing novel, of course, in private sexual escapades carried on behind highly respectable public images. In this century American presidents such as Franklin D. Roosevelt and John F. Kennedy have led the parade, as have inspirational leaders like Martin Luther King. Certainly Owens was not the first, or the last, popular athlete who romped frequently to bed as well as on the field. The inimitable Babe Ruth set the style; sexually active athletes in Jim Bouton's *Ball Four* followed in his train. Nor was Jesse the only traveling businessman to find female companionship away from home. Arthur Miller's fictitious salesman, Willy Loman, was not merely an authentic 1950s character; he was a man timelessly on the road.

Never had Owens been a model of marital fidelity, but in the 1950s his sexual energies were released with an urgency associated with what researchers now call a "midlife crisis."[4] Just after his fortieth birthday he became internally disoriented: unhappy with his past, uncertain of his future, unsure of his worth. External acclaim brought no sense of personal satisfaction. Several years after the crisis, Owens recalled that he was "over forty years old, the age when a man is supposed to have built something, and instead all I really had was something that happened nearly twenty years before." Despite his prominence, his future seemed murky, his past a millstone around his neck. "Suddenly it wasn't nice having everyone and his brother ask what it was like in 1936. . . . It was a reproach now. I was getting to be just another old jockstrap. . . . Maybe I was fur-lined, but I was still a jockstrap."[5]

For all his fears of being a mere jockstrap, however, Owens was still an aging athlete—proud of his youthful skills and achievements, struggling with the loss of physical powers. When his Olympic records first began to fall in the late 1940s, he scarcely seemed to mind. Records were "made to be broken," he calmly observed. But several years later his few remaining marks became jealously cherished. In 1956 he provided radio commentary for Bobby Morrow's assault on his record in the 100-yard dash. Outwardly he faced the prospect calmly; inwardly he ached with anxiety. "It was that my 100-yard dash mark seemed connected to all kinds of other things—I didn't know what exactly—and if this boy wiped one of them from the books, he'd wipe them all away somehow."[6]

Confronting his own mortality, Owens simultaneously clung to his past and sought deliverance from it. He winced with pain when one official recorded Morrow's time at 9.2 seconds, one-tenth of a second off the record. Other officials registered slower times, leaving the record momentarily intact, but Owens left the stadium profoundly shaken by his own vulnerability to the ravages of time and youthful usurpers of his crown. As he later related the event, he rushed home to spend more time with his wife and daughters and to rearrange his business affairs and speaking engagements in order to attend to "things that really matter." A wise friend advised him "to build on what you know, what you love." The track career of the "child prodigy" was now behind him, but surely there was "something larger, something related to that part of your life, which you can use as an anchor for the new."[7]

No doubt Owens turned to family and friends to find safe passage through his crisis. He also turned all the more actively to sexual liaisons with women in Chicago and places afar. For the aging but still handsome Owens, sexual prowess apparently compensated for the loss of athletic prowess. With women other than his wife, he could remain youthful, competent, extraordinary. "Women to him was like running the hundred yard dash," says one friend. "He picked them up at every yard. Jesse was an Olympic champion at sex." Certainly in sex he could be more than a mere "living legend."[8]

In his secret affairs, Jesse also found some release from the burden of respectability that sat heavily upon his shoulders. "Sometimes people forget you're a human being, and that you're no different than any other mortal man," he complained to an interviewer. More candidly than he intended, he admitted that he "would like to do some things the same as anyone else would do it and nothing would be said about it. But you're not supposed to do certain things." He did his "certain things" privately, discreetly. Only his close friends knew. Allusions to women—white as well as black, blondes and brunettes, shapely and homely types—flit in and out of their reminiscences. Most refuse to elaborate in detail. Says one, "What do you want me to do, ruin Jesse's reputation?"[9]

Arguably, Owens's appetite for sex derived from a source altogether different from the better-known activities of Babe Ruth. The Babe's fabled antics arose from an infantile egotism. A product of a broken, indigent home, he ate, drank, hit home runs, and made love outrageously, greedily, like a child who could never get enough of anything. For Owens, on the other hand, frequent amorous flings served as escape hatches, releasing the pressures of respectability. "People won't let you do it . . . you're not supposed to do certain things," but only if people knew. One way Jesse Owens coped with the demands of an All-American image was "to do some things the same as anyone else would like to do." His thing was sexual conquest.[10]

☆ ☆ ☆

During Jesse's frequent absences from home, Ruth kept herself busy with Brownies, Girl Scouts, and the local

Parent–Teachers Association. She singlehandedly steered her three daughters through their difficult teenage years. To the eldest, Gloria, she turned for physical assistance and companionship. Often they talked intimately late into the night in Gloria's room, more like friend-to-friend than mother-to-daughter. Not surprisingly, Gloria became the high achiever of the family. She captained her high school debate and basketball teams, was president of her senior class, and delivered the honorary student address at her graduation from John J. Pershing High School in Detroit. The middle daughter, Marlene, glided through school on her dazzling good looks and charm. The youngest, Beverly, became the rebel of the family. She spoke her mind freely, took school work lightly, secretly dyed her hair, and wore outlandish outfits. When Jesse was home, she toned down her unorthodox ways in order to avoid his disfavor. In his absence she began seriously dating her future husband, Donald Prather, when she was only fourteen.[11]

When Jesse returned home for one of his brief visits, he always brought gifts for the girls, mostly rings, bracelets, and earrings. For all his generosity, however, he was not a physically demonstrative father. Never did he playfully touch or hug his daughters, even in the privacy of the home. They all remember him as a "Victorian-type" father who shyly held himself aloof, demanding of them proper dress and speech, respectable behavior, and obedience to paternal commands. Wanting them to be "ladies," he discouraged competitive sports and forbade their taking jobs to earn extra money. When on the roost, he was the cock rooster, expecting to be served. After a round of golf on a rainy day, he always left his muddy shoes on the back steps of the house for the girls to clean. Only Beverly complained openly.[12]

Ruth never complained. Jesse was her first and only love. His word was law, his desires paramount. He believed woman's place to be in the home, and after they moved to Detroit in 1943, she never again held a paying job. He assumed his male freedom of movement to be sacrosanct; she never questioned where he went or what he did. He provided generously for his family's comfort. She paid with loneliness in his absence and total attention in his presence. Whenever he returned home from his rambles, she had his favorite food steaming hot, his children scrubbed and prettily dressed, his every whim supplied. On one day of the year, she could always expect him home, for on September 12 she annually arranged a grand birthday celebration. It was Jesse's birthday, of course. By every traditional standard, Ruth Owens was the compleat wife and mother.[13]

Her roles of wife and mother came into conflict in 1949, when Jesse decided that the family should move from Detroit to Chicago. For the family, it meant leaving a comfortable house and neighborhood, the girls' friends and schools, and Ruth's support system of civic clubs, bridge partners, and potluck-supper friends. Gloria, in her senior year in high school, refused to move. She remained in Detroit with a friend of the family while Ruth and the younger girls joined Jesse in Chicago. The dutiful wife won out over the devoted mother in Ruth Owens, but she could find no solace for the abandonment of the teenage child of her own teenage years.[14]

A more devastating heartbreak awaited Ruth in Chicago. By the time she arrived, Jesse had already established a circle of friends, to whom he introduced her at parties and dances. Never had Ruth seen such parties. In Detroit she had enjoyed, in her own words, "a nice clean life," a "square" social pattern composed of potluck suppers and bridge parties in her middle-class neighborhood, with friends who neither drank nor smoked. She left Detroit utterly unprepared for the kind of "forward women" she met in Chicago. They shamelessly flirted with Jesse right before her eyes, and were then astonished to learn that he was married. Ruth was astonished that he had not told them earlier. Crushed and frightened, she sulked in the corner with her arms defensively folded while Jesse danced and spread his charm in the manner to which he was accustomed. Ever afterward she looked back on those first few weeks in Chicago as the time when she, at thirty-four years of age, came to know "the facts of life."[15]

Those facts were not pleasant. Earlier, Ruth had heard rumors of Jesse's amorous flings but had ignored them. Her father had been unquestionably faithful to her mother; surely Jesse was the same to her. After all, she reasoned, Jesse was a handsome, attractive man, often gone from home, causing gossip that seemed mere malicious prattle. In Chicago she learned differently. No longer could she avoid the truth. She learned for the first time about Jesse's disastrous affair with a nurse several years earlier. Shortly after his dismissal from Ford Motor Company and his failure in a sporting goods business in Detroit, he had accepted a government-sponsored assignment to travel from one city ghetto to another, showing films of childbirth to indigent pregnant women. His assistant, a black female nurse, became pregnant several weeks into the tour. Future engagements were immediately canceled, and the scandal was hushed up.[16]

Always the faithful, submissive wife, Ruth blamed herself even for the pregnancy. As she recalled several years later, she was the one who had suggested that a nurse accompany Jesse on that ill-fated tour to provide medical expertise and commentary on the childbirth films. She had been too naïve, too careless, she admitted, "too calm and cool about things instead of looking things straight in the face." Impractically she decided, but too late, that she should have "packed up the children and everything else and gone along with him" on his barnstorming jaunts. Yet for all her newfound realism, Ruth simply could not believe all the tales making the rounds of the Chicago rumor mill. "I've always maintained," she insisted, "that the poor boy would have to be a super human to do all the things that people say he does."[17]

Her "poor boy" was, in fact, a man in his forties, by no means finished with his boyish exploits. Chicago neighbors saw the Owenses as "quiet and conservative people," but behind closed doors Jesse and Ruth wrangled over his errant ways. In public the tension showed on her deeply lined face; friends feared a nervous breakdown or alcoholism. She often paraded to the office of Jesse's public relations business in new dresses, jewelry, and furs, only to be secretly derided as a vain wife bought off. Several of the office girls were themselves Jesse's clandestine lovers. He kept a private apartment in Chicago for his rendezvous.[18]

Profoundly hurt, Ruth dealt with her wounded pride and shattered confidence by turning all the more to her daughters' needs. Gloria, upon graduation from high school, briefly entertained the idea of enrolling at the University of Michigan. Instead, she entered Ohio State to pursue a Bachelor of Science degree in education, while her sisters attended Chicago schools. In December 1953 Gloria became the first member of her family ever to receive a college degree. Proud parents and sisters attended the graduation exercise, accompanied by Ruth's mother, Mrs. Solomon, who had helped raise Gloria. They seemed a happy, eminently successful family, headed by a Buckeye immortal.[19]

In 1956 the second daughter, Marlene, followed in her father's and sister's footsteps to Ohio State. Several months later the youngest, Beverly, eloped before finishing high school. Suddenly the Owens nest was empty. With no grandchildren yet on the scene to claim her attention, Ruth suffered seizures of panic. Despite Jesse's wayward behavior, she increasingly sought to serve him. "You're not a wife; you're a mother," he had complained earlier. Now she would be a wife, totally, but within a confined, homebound definition of the role. "I ask him if he's going to be home for dinner. If he is, then I prepare dinner for him," Ruth poignantly explained to another woman. "Any time he feels that he wants to, he can always bring somebody home for dinner and there are no questions asked, whether it be man or woman." In exchange for material comfort and continuation of the marriage, she placed minimal emotional demands on her man: "He can always bring somebody home, but all I ask is, above everything, respect me. Do what you want to do, but respect me."[20]

For her own self-respect, Ruth needed desperately to get out of the house and join Jesse in his glamorous life of travel and public meetings. But old patterns were difficult to change. "Now I would like to be a part of his life," she lamented shortly after all the children left home, "but he's so accustomed to going without me that I think sometimes he forgets to even ask me, 'Would you like to go?'" She could scarcely make her own needs heard. "I don't know how to do it, you know. I try, of course. I'm a woman. I mean, I'll ask so often, but after that the hell with it." Ruth Owens's predicament cut across all class and color lines. She could well have served as the perfect exemplar for Betty Friedan's "feminine mistique," for she was the consummate devoted mother and dutiful wife, taken for granted, suffering "the sickness that has no name": the powerlessness and psychological depression caused by the customary inequality of the sexes.[21] She paid a high price for her husband's success.

Only close friends knew about the impasse. For them, surely, it came as no surprise. Long had Jesse been sexually wayward. His prolonged absences from home combined with Ruth's utter domesticity had merely confirmed the traditional patriarchal assumptions that both parties brought years earlier to their teenage marriage. When Ruth learned of Jesse's infidelities just as she was struggling with a physical move to an alien environment and the loss of her motherly role, a crisis was inevitable.

☆ ☆ ☆

Not so predictable, and even less widely known, was yet another dark spot on the back side of stardom. Unlike his marital problems, this one was not of Jesse's doing. Ridiculous as it now sounds, just as he was traveling most and speaking out the loudest on the virtues of the American way of life, he fell under the censorious eye of the Federal Bureau of Investigation, which suspected his being tainted by association with various groups that the Director of the FBI, J. Edgar Hoover, deemed "un-American." The anti-Communist crusade in cold war America threatened to chew up and spit out one of its most ardent patriots.

Much of the psychology of that crusade now seems beyond the bounds of reason. At its forefront was a bigoted, narrow-minded little man, J. Edgar Hoover. Having established his credibility in the gangbusters era of the 1930s, he became arrogantly authoritarian on behalf of Americanism during the cold war era. Except for physical size and longevity in office, he differed little from the witch-hunting Senator from Wisconsin, Joseph R. McCarthy. They thought along strikingly similar lines. They entertained morbid fears of Communism and of Communist infiltration into all aspects of American life. They saw any hint of criticism of anything American as Communist-inspired. Reform groups, even the most moderate civil rights organizations, were suspect.[22]

High on Hoover's list of dangerous individuals was the "Communist dupe," a well-meaning but gullible person who unknowingly aided the Communist cause by lending his name to "subversive" organizations. The more famous the person, the more potentially dangerous his influence. Prominent blacks especially required surveillance because, as Hoover saw it, the Communist Party was determined to use equal rights spokesmen "to hoodwink the Negro, to exploit him and use him as a tool to build a communist America." The specter of Paul Robeson loomed large; the emergence of Martin Luther King loomed on the horizon. The warped mind of J. Edgar Hoover held Jesse Owens suspect because of his color, despite his conservative ideology.[23]

The FBI's earliest "evidence" on Owens chillingly reflects the cold war mode of operation: indiscriminantly mixing rumor, gossip, and innuendo with documented facts to build a case of suspicion. Shortly after the Berlin Olympics, Owens's name appeared in the *Daily Worker,* a Communist Party newspaper. In 1937 he allegedly "sent greetings" to the National Negro Congress; a minor Michigan newspaper listed him as a member of the Committee to Seek Unity of Racial Groups; and he was said to have attended a rally sponsored by the American Youth for Democracy. J. Edgar Hoover considered all three groups even more subversive than the Communist Party, for they were supposedly "front organizations," veiling their real intentions. Spurred by unsubstantiated reports of Owens's associations with them, the FBI developed his file under the heading of "Foreign Inspired Agitation Among the American Negroes."[24]

In 1953 an old Olympic teammate, Donald Lash, was caught in the crossfire. Having joined the FBI as an agent attached to the Indianapolis office, Lash was invited to a youth seminar sponsored by the local YMCA, where Owens would be the featured speaker. Lash, assuming that he would be asked to introduce Owens, feared for his own job if he publicly endorsed a man held suspect by the FBI. He sought advice from his superiors and received a file of "derogatory data" on his former friend. Finally he declined the invitation "because of official commitments."[25]

Three years later the FBI embarked upon a more systematic, comprehensive investigation of Owens. The prod came in the form of a letter from the head administrator of the Bureau of Security and Consular Affairs, Scott McLeod, informing J. Edgar Hoover that President Eisenhower was "considering the appointment of Mr. Jesse Owens to a top level position in the Department of State." On the President's behalf, McLeod requested "a full field investigation" of Owens.[26] Hoover complied with a vengeance.

At their Director's command, FBI agents swung into action. In more than a dozen American cities—from New York to Los Angeles, from Chicago to Birmingham, Alabama—they collected birth, educational, marriage, tax, and police records; they checked work and credit ratings; they interviewed numerous friends, teachers, coaches, employers, and business associates. Even Owens's parents, siblings, wife, and daughters came under scrutiny. Much of the information was of a factual nature—place and date of birth, schools attended, athletic records, employment, income, travel, and the like—but even many of these simple facts were wrong. Investigators recorded everything they saw and heard in its raw form, exercising little critical judgment on the context or source of information. If the 126-page report on Jesse Owens is in any way representative, an FBI file is much more a body of opinion than a compilation of verified facts.

In various forms, the investigators put two subjective questions to their informants: What was Jesse Owens's character, good or bad? Was he a loyal American? To the first query they got mixed responses. Privacy statutes have caused several negative judgments to be blacked out of the file released under the Freedom of Information Act, but numerous characterizations of Owens as "a ladies' man," an undependable employee, and a poor credit risk remain unaltered. According to one witness, Jesse was "a man who cannot assume responsibility"; there was "something lacking in his character because of his failure to pay his debt." One of his former employers refused to recommend him for a government position but quickly added that his loyalty to "the American form of government" was beyond dispute.[27]

On the loyalty issue, Owens received nothing but praise. He was "not radical in any of his views," one Chicagoan insisted, nor was he "apt to fall into the trap of allowing his name to be used in any front type of Communist organization," added another. Whatever his personal failings, he was "a true American, and a definite credit to his race," a member of the Illinois Athletic Commission said. He was "both a credit to the United States, and to his own race," an employee of the Saperstein Sports Enterprises offered. He was "not only a credit to his own race but to the nation as a whole," a Chicago YMCA official chimed in. Jesse's personal credit rating might have been shaky; his credit rating as a patriot was altogether firm.

So was his reputation as a propagandist for American interests in the world. A former colleague on the Illinois Athletic Commission doubted that Owens would be "capable of handling a desk and the ensuing responsibility that goes with it." Still, he enthusiastically recommended him for a government appointment in "public relations" abroad. Others refused to qualify their endorsements. According to one businessman, Owens was "an extremely patriotic American who has the ability to sell his love of country to other peoples." A sports official lauded his "continually selling Americanism." Most unreserved of all was the recommendation of a Chicago journalist: Owens would be an "ideal choice" as a goodwill ambassador "because he possesses considerable diplomatic qualities and would be an excellent choice to refute allegations of racial discrimination in the United States."

Despite the accolades, nothing ever came of the President's reported interest in appointing Owens to a position in the State Department. Perhaps the flimsy allegations of his connections to subversive groups and the negative assessments of his character and administrative abilities nipped his prospects in the bud. Yet the FBI's report did not deter President Eisenhower from selecting him as one of his personal representatives to the Melbourne Olympics. J. Edgar Hoover's office submitted the results of its investigation to the Office of Security during the first week in October 1956; just a week later the Department of State recommended Owens to the President for the Melbourne junket. Moreover, four months later Eisenhower invited Jesse to participate in his People-to-People Program. Suspicious as one might be about the secret workings of Washington bureaucracies, it is simply impossible to ascertain how much the FBI's investigation of Owens worked to his immediate detriment.[28]

It could scarcely have helped him in the long run. Over the next few years his file made the rounds of Washington: to the CIA in 1958, to the State Department in 1962, and even to the White House in 1968 and again in 1972, when Johnson and Nixon administration officials requested information on individuals who might be invited to the White House for special occasions. In spheres other than athletics, Jesse Owens was a man of many records. Ironically, his sterling public record of patriotic service in the 1950s provoked another kind of record, secret and potentially harmful, in the files of the FBI.

☆   ☆   ☆

Back on the surface of life, Owens waltzed happily into the decade of the 1960s. In April 1960 he was enticed to Los Angeles on bogus Olympic business, to be surprised as the guest of honor on Ralph Edwards's popular television show, "This Is Your Life." Friends, coaches, and former Olympic teammates showered him with praise. Even the feeble Charles Riley, now eighty-two years of age, made the trip to California from his retirement home in Florida. In the summer of that year, Jesse attended the Olympic Games in Rome and daily struggled through the hordes of admiring autograph-seekers to watch his old Ohio State mentor, Larry Snyder, coach the American track-and-field squad. Two months later the two men enjoyed a more relaxed time together as Owens proudly returned to Ohio State to crown his daughter, Marlene, as Homecoming Queen. To the delight of 83,000 spectators, he reminded Marlene that this "could only happen in America." Finally, in December he closed out the year receiving a trophy of his own: the Sportsmanship Brotherhood Award for outstanding public service.[29]

Along with the delights of the year, however, two sobering episodes intruded. At the Rome Olympics Jesse saw his last Olympic record, the long jump, decisively broken. A twenty-one-year-old black American, Ralph Boston, shattered Jesse's twenty-four-year-old mark in both a preliminary jump and the finals. Even the silver medalist, Irvin "Bo" Roberson, topped the record that Owens had set in 1936. No longer vulnerable to spasms of despair over the loss of his athletic prowess, Jesse still betrayed his age in referring to the fall of his final record in terms of death and dying. "It's like having a pet dog for a long time," he told a reporter. "You get attached to it, and when it dies you miss it." For the public record, though, he felt "happy over Boston's wonderful achievement."[30]

Within the same week he received the sad news of Charles Riley's death in Sarasota, Florida. Since his retirement from Fairmount Junior High in 1943, Riley had struggled against heavy financial and physical odds. Toward the end of his long life he became virtually deaf and blind. His Christian Science faith could not bring him "back to normal." Worst of all, he harbored a grudge against Owens, who had not kept in touch since their last visit in 1946. In the mid-1950s he scrawled a letter to Jesse, recalling the goals they "worked for and accomplished" years earlier; now the protégé had emerged as a world-renowned figure while the mentor lived out his barren life in Florida retirement, feeling unappreciated. Nursing his bitterness, the aged Riley never posted the letter. His mind wandered. Once he boarded a bus and traveled aimlessly until his son retrieved him from a Tallahassee hospital.[31]

His appearance on the "This Is Your Life" show was undoubtedly the crowning moment of his declining years. His plane ride, hotel, hosts, and the Owens family were all "wonderful," Riley wrote to a friend. When the show was aired in Sarasota, friends in the trailer park gathered to watch and cheer. Not until his death, though, did Riley receive the recognition he deserved. All the Cleveland newspapers carried long obituary features on the man who "first discovered the possibilities as an athlete of the spindly Negro boy who was a pupil in the eighth grade of his school." Two days later Owens announced to a group of Boy Scouts that "Charles Riley was the source of what I do and what I say today." In subsequent years that line became greatly embellished, but from the Riley family's point of view, the appreciation came a bit late.[32]

Unaware of those feelings, Owens plunged zealously into the presidential campaign of 1960, supporting the Nixon–Lodge ticket. The Republicans lost the election, but it was soon rumored that Jesse was being considered for a position in a national physical fitness program envisaged by the new Democratic President, John F. Kennedy. Owens himself fed the rumors. In one of his weekly columns for the *Chicago Defender*, he informed his readers that he was scheduled to go to Washington soon to accept an award. While in the capital he would be talking to one of the President's assistants. "So watch out," he jokingly warned, "I may be pounding on your door asking you to do a few pushups next week!" But no firm offer ever materialized. Perhaps his FBI file surfaced once again. It is more likely that his well-known political affiliations outweighed his athletic fame. To his great advantage, he had been widely recognized as "100% Republican" during the

Eisenhower years, a reputation that worked to his disadvantage under the Kennedy and Johnson Democratic administrations.[33]

Closer to home, politics also played a large part in Owens's loss of the directorship of the Illinois Youth Commission. When a Democrat, Otto Kerner, took office as the Governor of Illinois in January 1961, Jesse's politically appointed position became tenuous at best. His widespread popularity prevented immediate ouster; presumably he could have held on to his job by avoiding controversy and ingratiating himself with Chicago's Democratic bosses. As events proved, he could do neither.[34]

In July 1961 Owens unwisely took sides in a local Chicago cab drivers' election for a Teamsters Union boss. On the eve of the election, he appeared on a platform beside James R. Hoffa in support of the reelection of Joseph P. "Joey" Glimco. Backed by the Chicago underworld, Glimco had ruthlessly pressured the city's cab companies into illegally requiring Teamsters membership of all their job applicants. Owens was out of his element. To a crowd of five hundred members of Local 777, he admitted ignorance about "the inner workings" of the union but praised Glimco for having "improved the conditions of the people." In the end he urged his listeners to "keep the people you have"—Glimco and his friends.[35]

Owens may well have been paid for his effort. No records were kept, of course. His friends, however, argue to the contrary, insisting that his involvement with the Teamsters was peripheral, simply a matter of poor judgment. Whatever the motive, his blunder gave the Democrats the chance for which they had been waiting to dismiss him as head of the Illinois Youth Commission. Supposedly a model for youth, he had publicly supported a man whom a U.S. Senate committee had recently described as "a common thug and criminal." On the day after Glimco lost his election, Owens lost his job. He officially resigned, which was merely a means of avoiding the public humiliation of being fired.[36]

Years later Owens grumbled about losing his official position as a benefactor of Illinois youths because of "political reasons," implying that the Democrats replaced him because he was not of their party. Obviously the truth was more complex than that. As usual, Jesse had contributed to his own undoing. According to one report, Jimmy Hoffa immediately offered to put him in charge of public relations for the Teamsters. If such an offer was ever made, Jesse refused it.[37]

He had much else to do. In 1960 he and Ted West, a former advertising adviser for the *Chicago Defender,* started a sales and promotional partnership, Owens–West & Associates. In 1963 they began inviting black housewives to the Tiki Room, just behind the office of the *Defender,* for weekly luncheons, at which they introduced the women to products and moneymaking opportunities. All the while, Owens frequently sold his name to the Quaker Oats Company, a local grocery store, a real estate firm, and Meister Brausing Beer Company for endorsements in the *Defender.* The beer advertisements ran regularly for about a year, causing a stir. By his own count, Owens received 4,000 letters of protest, forcing him to cancel the contract. The public had spoken; his image was at stake.[38]

Capitalizing on the magic of his name, Owens–West & Associates sponsored a Jesse Owens Track, Field, and Picnic Day at South Chicago's Washington Park in July 1963. Out of that event came Owens's lucrative long-term association with Atlantic Richfield Company (ARCO). Black friends brought the Chicago gathering to the attention of the former professional football player Eddie Bell, an ARCO employee. Bell examined a brochure and persuaded his superiors to purchase the event—especially Owens's name—outright for publicity purposes. In 1964 Jesse signed a contract for $2,500, and in the following year the first ARCO Jesse Owens Games for boys and girls ages ten to fifteen were held in Chicago. It became an annual event, soon to involve more than a million youngsters each year in hundreds of towns and cities throughout the United States. Not surprisingly, Owens's commitment to ARCO enlarged over the years. Today his widow annually receives an ARCO check for $40,000 for the exclusive commercial use of his name.[39]

By the mid-1960s Jesse no longer had to scramble for lucrative opportunities. His problem was just the reverse: deciding on the best of many offers to endorse products, provide information for ghost writers, and address sports banquets, civic clubs, and businessmen's groups. He had to winnow out the proposals that held least appeal. Highly attractive was an invitation from the office of a struggling young Major League baseball club, the New York Mets, who asked Owens to join them—for a goodly sum, of course—as an exercise and running coach at their 1965 spring training camp in St. Petersburg, Florida. Jesse leaped at the chance. Weary of the speaker's circuit, he welcomed a physically active assignment. It would get him out of icebound Chicago to a sunny clime; it was a short-term commitment, ideally suited to a man whose attention span was short.[40]

The Mets were an incompetent team, the laughingstock of the baseball world, but Owens took his job seriously. Beginning in late February 1965, for several weeks he appeared daily on the field at 10 A.M. to lead the Mets in a warmup lap, body bends, pushups, "bicycle" leg exercises, and sprints. As if he needed identification, his white sneakers and gray sweatshirt with "Ohio State University Athletic Department" emblazoned in maroon letters set him apart from the crowd. Unfortunately, whatever good he did for the Mets was not readily apparent. In 1965, their fifth season, they once again provided more laughs than sporting thrills.[41]

☆　☆　☆

Shortly before he went off to Florida for his working holiday, Owens was interviewed by the *New York Times*. As background for his readers, the reporter briefly chronicled the usual athletic records and civic activities. Then he let Jesse put his own early fame in perspective. "I came along at a time when the Negro in America needed an image," Owens said. "I got more than my share of adulation. Joe Louis was another figure from that era. I think we fulfilled a need." Apparently Owens, if not Louis, still fulfilled some needs. "He remains one of the most magnetic of all sports heroes," his interviewer commented. "People who have never met him idolize him. He has accepted this as part of his life, and he does not want to rock the boat."[42]

The boat seemed steady, the captain at ease and in full control. "Now, 28 years after his Olympic glory, Jesse Owens is a happy man," his interviewer happily reported. "He is successful in business, he is a renowned speaker, he is a grandfather four times and he is a man at peace with himself." For an American public frightened by the rising tide of protest from dissatisfied blacks, the successful, satisfied Owens had consoling words. "If I had to do it all over again," he claimed, "I probably would. More people have been kind to me than not, and they have looked upon my accomplishments more than the color of my skin." In summary: "I have led a happy life, and I am a happy man."

He protested too much. Some would say he forgot too much and covered too much. Whatever the truth, Owens's external circumstances meshed with certain internal mechanisms to allow him to profess unalloyed contentment in the late autumn of 1964. That combination soon became disengaged, casting him into a slough of despond. True to an old pattern, his difficulties resulted from an intricate mixture of personal failings and factors beyond his control.

First, a medical problem laid him low. Several days after he returned to Chicago from the Mets' spring training camp, he took to the golf links with his old friend Ralph Metcalfe. As Owens teed off to start the game, a severe pain shot down his spine into a leg. He felt paralyzed and had to be removed on a stretcher. Doctors, diagnosing a ruptured disc, recommended surgery. Jesse refused, fearing complications. After a few days of rest he checked out of the hospital but crumbled under excruciating, immobilizing pain before he could get home. Finally he submitted to the neurosurgeon's knife. He recovered so quickly from the operation that he was back on the golf course playing well enough to win a local tournament by the end of the summer.[43]

Just two days after that golfing victory, however, he received word of a problem from which he would not recover so easily. He was under investigation by the Internal Revenue Service for not having filed income tax returns during the four-year period of 1959–1962. According to Owens's business partner, Ted West, when the IRS first began looking into the case it could hardly ever find Jesse at home or in the office. Instead, the investigators leaned heavily on West, putting pressure on him by pulling out his own tax returns in an unsubtle threat to find him in arrears if he did not cooperate in the investigation. West's wife had been chronically ill, requiring large medical expenses. Those deductions gave IRS agents leverage to obtain the business records they wanted.[44]

Jesse later claimed that he "never tried anything dishonest," that he "was tied up in a lot of business deals" and let someone else take care of his records, and that his failure to file his taxes was a mere "blunder," not a deliberate crime. In truth, he knew all along that he was courting disaster. The Illinois Youth Commission and Owens–West & Associates regularly deducted the proper amount of withholding tax from his earnings, but Owens neglected even to file returns, much less to pay the taxes due on the money he made in speaking engagements, radio and television appearances, and commercial endorsements. Close friends knew of his cavalier attitude. Bud Greenspan, for one, recalls that he repeatedly urged Owens to conform to the law. "Oh, I'll pay it sometime," Jesse shrugged. "But Jesse," retorted Greenspan, "it's a criminal offense." Owens avoided the issue. "All they want is the money," he reasoned.[45]

Like many prosperous Americans, Owens thought the federal government wanted too much money in taxes from high-bracket citizens. He adamantly opposed a progressive tax scheme. In 1961, in two articles he wrote on boxer Floyd Patterson for the *Chicago Defender*, he complained that Patterson was being taxed much too heavily on his championship purses. "Why," Owens rhetorically asked, "should we take away 90 per cent of what he earns, and just 5 per cent from a preliminary fighter who hasn't worked as hard and doesn't have the same talent—the kind that makes this country great and makes our race proud we've got the man who owns it!" In the mind of Jesse Owens, a raw form of free enterprise and a simple form of patriotism complemented each other. "Let's let a man who earns some money be able to keep it. Believe me, it'll benefit the guy at the bottom, too. They don't have any 'rich men' in Russia, you know." Little wonder that he was a favorite spokesman for conservative America; little wonder also that he was taken to court by the Internal Revenue Service.[46]

On November 19, 1965, the government filed its indictment in the Federal District Court in Chicago. U.S. Attorney Edward V. Hanrahan announced that Owens would be summoned to appear for a hearing before Judge Joseph Sam Perry on December 6. "We have nothing to hide," Bernard Kleinman, Owens's lawyer, told the press, "and this charge will not mar his excellent reputation as a citizen and sportsman."[47] For all the public optimism, however, the Thanskgiving and Christmas holiday season turned out to be a nightmare in the Owens household.

After the hearing, Owens went to trial on December 21, pleading *nolo contendere* (no contest). Early in the trial, a government witness revealed that the defendant had not, in fact, filed tax returns for eight years, 1954–62. At the demand of Jesse's lawyer, Judge Perry threw out that sensational bit of information, because the statute of limitations on criminal proceedings limited evidence to the previous six years. Yet even for the period from 1959 to 1962, government investigators showed that Owens's unpaid taxes amounted to $68,166 on a gross income estimated at $142,000. His attorneys did their best to deflect the issue, arguing that Jesse's deductions should be reckoned extraordinarily high because of his frequent travel. When that argument failed, they insisted that many of their client's speaking engagements were for charity and that much of his "income" was actually expense money. They were grasping at straws. Owens was found guilty as charged.[48]

At his lawyers' request, Judge Perry scheduled a final hearing in late December to hear character witnesses on Owens's behalf. Witnesses included Kenneth L. "Tug" Wilson, the former commissioner of the Big Ten Conference and now head of the United States Olympic Committee; Sidney A. Jones, Jr., an associate judge of the Circuit Court of Cook County; Leo Fischer, sports editor of the *Chicago American;* and Jonathan A. Janes, a local clergyman. All claimed to have known Owens for many years and lauded both his patriotism and his tireless activities for sports organizations, charities, and youth groups. The session lasted only forty-five minutes. Judge Perry then delayed sentencing until February 1, 1966, repeating his earlier promise to treat this case "the same as any other."[49]

The month of January 1966 was undoubtedly the bleakest period of Owens's entire life. Liable to a maximum penalty of four years in prison and a fine of $40,000 (in addition to the delinquent taxes), he feared the worst. Nervously he paced around the house, alternately snapping out at whoever was present and retreating into a quiet, depressed shell. Some of his "friends" deserted him in his time of need. What Owens later remembered most vividly was that his golf foursome was suddenly reduced to two, as the other two found silly excuses not to be seen in public with such a pariah. Yet a Chicago doctor came through handsomely, paying the first installment of $9,000 required immediately by the court on the unpaid taxes.[50]

At the sentencing on February 1, Judge Perry raised a flicker of hope in the distressed Owens when he announced early in the session that he would not be imposing the maximum penalties. After a long oration on the nature and means of taxation, Perry chided Owens for his willful mistake but acknowledged that he had been "subject to tremendous pressure" in his busy schedule, devoting himself to good causes. Jesse's record of public service was "good, very good," so the judge saw no reason why this "one error" should prevent him from "going right ahead" with his activities. No jail sentence seemed appropriate, nor would Jesse even be put on probation. He would merely be fined $750 for each of the four years no income taxes were filed, a total of $3,000.[51]

Chastened but free, Owens walked out of the courtroom a deliriously happy man. He had been found guilty of a crime, yet in one sense he stood vindicated. In the end, he was rescued by the public service he had rendered and the public image he had so carefully maintained.

CHAPTER 12

An Athlete
Growing Old

IN THE COLD LIGHT OF GROUNDHOG DAY, February 2, 1966, the literal price of Owens's freedom amounted to something more than $100,000 in delinquent taxes, fines, and lawyers' fees. Reportedly, he had only $1,500 in his savings account. To his distress, his invitations to speak to church and youth groups dried up "like puddles in a sandstorm." Before too long he would be back on the road captivating audiences, as a reporter in Bangor, Maine, colorfully noted, "to a point where you could have heard a biscuit land on the floor." But 1966—the thirtieth anniversary of the Berlin Olympics—was not a happy year for the fifty-three-year-old Owens.[1]

National events made him feel all the older, for in the mid-1960s the established civil rights movement merged with an infant anti–Vietnam War movement to produce campus demonstrations, ghetto riots, and protest marches alien to Jesse's generation. Martin Luther King urged passive resistance on a mass scale—first against racial discrimination, then against the war. Militants like Malcolm X, Stokeley Carmichael, and H. Rap Brown combined "black is beautiful" slogans with chants of "Hell no, we won't go [to Vietnam]!"

America's newest black athletic superstar, the boxer Muhammad Ali, embodied the brash mood of the day. As Cassius Clay, he won an Olympic gold medal at Rome in 1960; bantering with reporters all the way, in 1964 he defeated Sonny Liston for the heavyweight crown, then promptly adopted his Black Muslim name. Shortly after Owens's tax trial, Ali declared that he had "nothin' against them Viet Cong." Less than a year later he refused military induction.[2]

Ironically, while Owens deplored the aggressive, activist spirit of the 1960s, it worked to his advantage at the tax trial. Just before Judge J. Sam Perry announced a lenient penalty, he contrasted Jesse to the dissidents. "Now, while you have been going around . . . supporting our country and our way of life and our democracy," said the Judge, "there are other people running around over this country offering their blood and going out to other countries and aiding and abetting the enemy openly ." Judge Perry and Jesse Owens had more in common than their Alabama background. They were of the same age and ilk: socially inclined to law and order, and patriotically inclined to detest antiwar demonstrators. "It would be a travesty, to my way of thinking," the judge concluded, "if I under these circumstances exercise my discretion improperly or excessively here against a good citizen for one mistake."[3]

The good citizen was out of step with the younger generation. He kept his shoes shined; they wore sandals. He purchased expensive, smart suits; they donned dashikis and jeans. He kept his hair and mustache closely trimmed; they let their manes grow long, their beards shaggy. He liked jazz; they preferred rock and "soul" music. He met strangers and friends alike with a traditional handshake; they offered varieties of the "black" handshake. Greeted in that fashion at a party in the home of one of their daughters, Ruth once froze in her tracks, saying, "I don't know anything about *that.*" Jesse didn't either. He chided his middle-aged business partner, Ted West, for letting his hair grow modishly long; he recoiled in horror at the sight of his son-in-law, Malcolm "Hemp" Hemphill, in a dashiki.[4]

Differences in style represented different views of the world. The 1960s were a liberal Democratic decade of debate and change; Owens was a conservative Republican. He held only contempt for the social welfare programs begun under

Kennedy and accelerated under Johnson. "No man ever reached greatness—in athletics or anything else," he declared, "with a society and a government that taught him you can get something for nothing." He rightly considered himself as charitable as the next man: for needy friends and dire poverty cases he dug deep into his pocket, and to charitable organizations he gave freely of his time. "But I'm always trying to get them to help themselves," he insisted. In Owens's view, welfare checks, subsidized housing, and food stamps weakened "the fiber" of mind and will.[5]

Although Owens spoke his mind freely against the government's domestic policies, he had little sympathy for active protests against social injustice and the nation's foreign policy. He admired Martin Luther King's principles, he said, but he rejected his tactics. He thought Muhammad Ali (whom he insisted on calling Cassius Clay) received "some terribly bad advice" and made "a terrible mistake" in refusing induction. The problem, for Jesse, manifested itself close to home when his eldest daughter Gloria and her husband joined protest demonstrations in Chicago and Washington. It was not easy to avoid taking sides in the turbulent sixties—for social change or the *status quo*, for or against the war, for radical or moderate measures of redress. Least of all could Jesse Owens avoid the fray.[6]

To his credit, he tried to come to terms with the concerns of the younger generation, but late-night dialogues with hostile activists often ended in frustration. "Look," Jesse once exclaimed in the wee hours of the morning, "sometimes I'm so concerned just getting my *own* self together that I don't feel up to changing the whole damn world!" In that outburst he unintentionally bared his soul. A survivor from another age, he saw the world in personal, individualistic focus, not in broad social terms. Economic and political structures of poverty, racial bigotry, and militarism escaped him. "Hell, I can't forget my upbringing," he told one journalist. "I started at the bottom—and look at me now. I've got two homes, and I'm free to travel, and I know where my next meals are coming from." He was not ready to attack "the Establishment that gave that to me."[7]

Any emphasis on racial differences made him uneasy. Talk about black history, black life-styles, and black pride left him cold. Black Power advocates revulsed him. "The black fist is a meaningless symbol," he insisted. "When you open it, you have nothing but fingers—weak empty fingers. The only time the black fist has significance is when there's money inside. There's where the power lies." Jesse Owens was a pragmatist. "I'm looking at what's going to work," he repeatedly insisted.[8]

What had worked for him was a patient personality, a conservative ideology, and an unwavering patriotism. His patriotism, especially, was a composite of pragmatic realism and self-interest. "I know no other country in the world. Let me make it here," he said. "All that I have and all that I expect to get is under this flag." For all his ups and downs, he had "made it"; he had much, and expected more, of America's bounty. Africa held little appeal. Even less was he moved by activist complaints that young black men were being sent off to fight other non-Caucasians on behalf of white America. As he boldly announced to a black college audience, he considered himself "an American first and a black man second."[9]

He was on a collision course with angry young black athletes of a different outlook.

☆ ☆ ☆

A revolt of black athletes against racial discrimination spun off the protest rallies and street demonstrations of the early 1960s. First came ineffectual boycotts against inferior housing and social activities provided for black athletes at several track meets and football games. Then the movement shifted to the college campus, the demands expanding to include numerous academic, social, employment, and athletic interests of black student athletes. At the center of the storm stood the imposing figure of Harry Edwards, a black sociology instructor at San Jose State College in California. Himself a former athlete, Edwards in 1967 organized a disruptive boycott of San Jose's opening football game against the University of Texas at El Paso, a school notoriously abusive of black athletes. The game was canceled. Success encouraged Edwards and his friends to set their sights on a much larger, more visible arena for protest, the Mexico City Olympics in 1968.[10]

They were stepping on Jesse Owens's turf. Since the Melbourne Games of 1956, Owens had constantly talked up the

Olympics to American audiences, depicting them as quadrennial tests of America's free enterprise system. To his mind, the Olympics meant much more than "a temporary battle for gold medals"; they were a part of "the permanent battle for men's minds" between the United States and the Soviet Union. At innumerable fundraising dinners he insisted that the United States should have "the best dressed, best coached and best team of all those competing in the games."[11]

The best team in track and field required the full participation of black athletes. When Owens first got wind of the boycott scheme in October 1967, he responded cautiously. "We have been conscious of racial problems for many years," he told reporters. "But it is no good dropping out of the Olympics. We have to be there, we have to be everywhere it counts." Ralph Metcalfe agreed, as did Rafer Johnson, the black decathlon champion from the 1960 games. All three expressed sympathy for the motives behind the rebellion but rejected the method of protest. Owens took most of the heat. He was horribly "gullible and misinformed," Harry Edwards declared. "I'm sure," Edwards added, "Jesse Owens grasps the whole Olympic picture, agrees deeply with us and would move to our support but for the bonds forged long ago."[12]

An announcement by the International Olympic Committee in February 1968 added fuel to the boycott movement. According to the IOC, South Africa, whose apartheid policies had caused it to be banned from the previous Olympics in Tokyo, had now altered its ways sufficiently to deserve an invitation to Mexico City. Black African nations reacted furiously. No fewer than thirty-two African teams threatened to stay home if South Africa competed. Black American athletes, sensitive to their African heritage, now had double cause to disrupt the Olympics in a show of black solidarity.[13]

In public lectures, in the press, and on radio and television, Owens took the offensive. He largely ignored the African question, seeing it as peripheral to American concerns. He knew that militant blacks now considered him "a member of the old school," but he insisted that they had no monopoly on suffering "a lot of injustices in our nation." Pragmatically he denounced the proposed boycott because blacks could "bridge the gap of misunderstanding more in athletics than anywhere else." In mid-March 1968 Jesse aired his message for thirty minutes over a West Coast regional television network, inspiring the President of the IOC, Avery Brundage, to write him a note lauding his "enlightened remarks on the Olympic Games." Harry Edwards's group was causing Brundage headaches. In an unsubtle reference to Edwards, Brundage noted to Owens that it was "easy for those who have no chance of participating to talk of boycotts."[14]

Television made it easier for Olympic enthusiasts to oppose the boycott, for by 1968 televised sport had come of age—in "living color" in most American living rooms. Just a dozen years earlier the Olympic Games were unavailable to American viewers. Brief segments of the Olympics were first aired in 1960, and the volume was increased in 1964. Then the ABC network, desperate to improve its low ratings behind NBC and CBS, purchased exclusive rights to the Mexico City games. By the spring of 1968 ABC executives were sparing no expenses to heat up viewers' interest in the forthcoming event.[15]

Not by coincidence, America's most famous Olympic hero, Owens, and the newest, most aggressive of the media, television, found each other in 1968, to the advantage of both. Yet a strange thing happened on the way to Mexico City: All three major networks rejected an attractive hour-long documentary entitled "Jesse Owens Returns to Berlin." Written and independently produced by Bud Greenspan in 1966, the film went begging for buyers. Finally an independent sports network, founded only seven years earlier for sports specials, aired it on March 30, 1968.

Executives of the three networks said they rejected the film because they used only prime-time specials produced by their own staffs. Privately, however, Greenspan was informed that his subject matter was simply unacceptable. In the racially overheated atmosphere of 1968, the script seemed too laudatory of blacks. Despite his widespread interracial popularity, Owens was too prominent before the camera, too dominant in old film clips, for white America to stomach. Not normally given to perverse wit, Jesse rose to the occasion, suggesting to Greenspan, "Why don't we show negatives and I will be white and the Nazis will be black." But timid executives feared that white Americans had had their fill of blacks marching, shouting, burning, and looting on the evening news. Presumably the public could not discriminate sufficiently to stay by their sets for an hour-long presentation by even the friendly Owens, or so the network moguls thought.[16]

They misjudged the public. No fewer than 180 local television stations carried the film in the United States, and it was aired simultaneously in fifteen foreign countries. Today, as clips from Leni Riefenstahl's film of the Berlin games are shown frequently on television, it is difficult to imagine the first public response to footage featuring the fleet-footed Owens gracefully pulling away from the pack, sailing high and far through the air, and breaking into a broad smile for the camera. The effect was stunning, and all the more so because Americans had never before been exposed to those visual images. Just five months later the premiere television presentation of Riefenstahl's entire *Olympia* was the first major program on sport ever produced by the National Educational Television Network.[17]

In the meantime, Owens's spring prime-time special provided a new handle for his assault on the boycott movement. The Berlin games having been brought sensationally alive in the public consciousness, Jesse pulled out all his old stories to draw comparisons between Berlin and Mexico City. "Then we had the Jewish problem and now we have the civil rights question," he repeatedly told his audiences. "The parallel is real because the social problem is a vital one to the Negro." Actually, the parallel was about as real as a four-dollar bill. The boycott controversy in 1936 centered on Hitler's persecution of German Jews. For all its authoritarian policies, the Mexican government was of no concern to American blacks in 1968. Their complaints were with their own society, not with foreigners.[18]

But for Owens's purposes, it hardly mattered. His comparisons quickly gave way, always, to entertaining references to Hitler, to Lutz Long, and to the ticker-tape parade when he returned home from Berlin. Those stories in turn supplied openings for his central homily: that the lot of the American black might still be less than wonderful, but it had vastly improved since Jesse's youth. Opportunities for black Americans were now growing by "leaps and bounds." Black athletes would therefore do "an injustice to both themselves and to their country" by boycotting the Olympics. In summary, "the

Olympics should not be used as a battleground for civil rights."[19]

The prospect of all-out battle diminished over the summer of 1968. Once the International Olympic Committee reversed its decision on the South Africans, banning them from Mexico City, black African nations dropped their boycott threats. All the while, American militants were divided over tactics. A few, such as All-American basketball player Lew Alcindor (later Kareem Abdul-Jabbar), stuck by the original plan to boycott. Most finally decided against it. They searched instead for alternate forms of protest, possibly some public demonstrative act at the games.

In the early summer, Owens stayed busy conducting athletic clinics in Panama, El Salvador, Nicaragua, Honduras, and Costa Rica for the Middle American Sports Federation, a nonprofit group founded to develop athletics in Central America. In July he accepted an appointment to the public relations staff of baseball's American League, working out of a special office in Chicago, but he was often away from the office on speaking engagements. Whatever the occasion, whatever the topic of his speech, he invariably came around to the subject of the forthcoming Olympic Games.[20]

Many American fans read his "preview" of the Olympics in the widely circulated *TV Guide*. For the first three-quarters of the essay, Owens introduced the leading American athletes who would be going for gold. Then he turned to "an unhappier aspect of the games this year": the specter of black athletes using the Olympics as a forum of protest against America's treatment of its black citizens. Holding out the hope that racial and national pride would prevent his fellow countrymen from doing "anything to embarrass the United States in so conspicuous a world arena," he once again drew parallels with the Berlin Olympics:

> There were no more angry people than black Olympic competitors in Berlin in 1936. We had insults thrown at us by our host nation; Hitler didn't accord Negroes and Jews the same courtesies he did others who came to Berlin. That made us more determined to prove that, in the eyes of God, we were every bit as good as any man.

A rousing passage, this. Unfortunately, it was largely fictitious. More on the mark was Jesse's prediction that the Mexico City Games would be "one of the most exciting Olympic meets ever."[21]

☆   ☆   ☆

Owens wore several hats to Mexico City. He went as a guest of the Mexican government, who invited several former Olympic stars to attend official receptions and to sit in a special box at the stadium. He also served as a consultant for the United States Olympic Committee, working as a liaison between athletes and the committee, primarily to keep black athletes happy and "out of trouble," without public incident. Finally, the Mutual Broadcasting Company paid him to provide radio commentary on the games. In what had by now become a quadrennial ritual, adoring fans mobbed him everywhere he went.[22]

In arenas scattered near and far, nearly 8,000 athletes from more than a hundred nations competed fiercely despite the debilitating thin oxygen at Mexico City's high elevation. African runners, having trained arduously in similar atmospheric conditions, shocked the world by dominating the long-distance events. The light air assisted American long jumper Bob Beamon, whose astounding leap of 29 feet, $2\frac{1}{2}$ inches dropped Owens into a distant fourth on the record books. The most intense excitement, however, was generated by precisely the thing that Owens feared most: a dramatic political demonstration.[23]

The incident featured sprinters Tommie Smith and John Carlos, angry blacks from San Jose State who had been heavily involved in the abortive boycott campaign. When Smith finished first and Carlos third in the 200 meters, they mounted the victory stand shoeless, displaying black socks. Smith wore a black scarf around his neck. While the "Star-Spangled Banner" was played, they lowered their heads, each raising a clenched, black-gloved fist in silent defiance of American prestige and Olympic protocol. That scene, emblazoned in photographs on the front pages of newspapers around the world, remains one of the most memorable of all the moments in Olympic history.

The distressed Owens attempted to retrieve the situation.

American and international Olympic officials convened immediately, determined to punish the offenders. Out of that heated session, Jesse was assigned to meet with Smith, Carlos, and the other black athletes to hear their case, to elicit apologies if possible, and definitely to demand promises of no further embarrassing gestures. That night he met with about twenty-five athletes. Surprised to find several whites in the group, he asked them to leave. "It's nothing against you other men personally," he explained, "but these are my black brothers, and I want to talk to them. I think you can understand."[24]

He thought wrongly. "Why should we ask them to leave?" one of the black athletes asked. "These guys have supported us all along." The whites stayed. As Owens later told the story, Harold Connolly, a white hammer-thrower whose Olympic experience stretched all the way back to 1956, let out whoops of support for his unrepentant black teammates. By Jesse's account, John Carlos's "explanation" of his actions was pathetic: "It don't make no difference what I say or do. I'm lower than dirt, man. I'm black."

Owens quickly reached the end of his patience. "You know, Carlos," he yelled, "you talk about Whitey this and Whitey that. Everything's 'get Whitey out of my hair!' But when it comes to the most private kind of meeting of all, here you are with good old Whitey! He goes everywhere you go. Man, I can get along without him. How come *you* can't?" The meeting degenerated into angry accusations and raucous baiting. A vast ideological chasm separated Owens from the younger athletes. He left the room frustrated and saddened. Early the next morning Olympic officials banned Smith and Carlos from the team and expelled them from their quarters.

Owens feared that "sick headlines in every town in America" would leave the impression that most blacks sympathized with the Smith–Carlos demonstration of racial anger and disrespect for the flag. Shortly after he returned home from Mexico City, he set himself the task of countering that impression. Soon he and ghostwriter Paul Neimark were working together on a book, *Blackthink,* to put the record straight. In the early spring of 1970 a columnist for the *Chicago Defender* warned that the forthcoming fruit of their efforts would "set many mouths flapping."[25]

Never was a truer prophecy spoken. Prior to publication, excerpts of *Blackthink* reached a wide audience in *Reader's Digest*, whetting the public's appetite for Owens's full assessment of the black militants. He pulled no punches. The "fire-fanning blackthinkers" were "pro-Negro bigots" worse than the anti-Negro bigots he encountered in his youth. They were "professional haters," he insisted. As likely as not, they lived in high-rise apartments, dined in fine restaurants, and sequestered themselves on university campuses. The radical campus crowd especially raised Jesse's ire: "It isn't enough for them to attend the finest universities in the world. They want to run them, appoint the teachers, tell the president what courses to have taught. When they don't get their way, many of them bomb the campuses or burn the libraries."[26]

According to Owens, the vast majority of American blacks disagreed with "the rantings of a few soapboxing blackthinkers." The "new Negro" was eminently respectable and respected, striving to succeed with never a sympathetic thought for racial riots, and all the less for revolution. They were "*the silent black majority* that has neither spoken nor been spoken for." Certainly Tommie Smith and John Carlos had not spoken for them at Mexico City. That was an isolated incident, Owens claimed. Other black athletes "wouldn't have dreamed of copying the Smith–Carlos stuff."[27]

As usual, Owens wove tales from his own experience around contemporary examples of black success in sport and business to demonstrate the "tremendous progress" that blacks had made within the past few decades. He had a simple prescription for blacks who had not "made it" in America: they needed to "fight harder to make equality work." His most unguarded statement was this: "If the Negro doesn't succeed in today's America, it is because he has chosen to fail." Owens and his ghostwriter quoted approvingly from Gunnar Myrdal, the Swedish sociologist who observed, years earlier, that "the Negro middle class is more puritan than the white middle class." Jesse's puritanism was something more than an upright image; it was a view of the world, of success by means of the work ethic, and of the failure that reflects a flawed character.[28]

By special invitation, about thirty of the Elect attended a reception in Chicago to honor Owens on the publication of

Blackthink. His longtime admirer and friend Herb Douglas, a Schieffelin & Company executive, arranged for Schieffelin to foot the bill. The negative publicity surrounding Jesse's tax problems were now buried in the past; corporations eagerly sought his endorsement of their products. By 1970, in addition to the long-term contract with Atlantic Richfield Company, he regularly represented Schieffelin, Sears, United Fruit, U.S. Rubber, Johnson & Johnson, and the Ford Motor Company. By his own conservative estimate, his income amounted to about $75,000 a year.[29]

With the Republicans once again in the White House, Owens returned to political favor. In the spring of 1971 President Nixon sent him as a goodwill ambassador to West Africa on a ten-day visit to Abidjan, the capital of the Ivory Coast. The American government was seeking firmer diplomatic and commercial ties with the moderate government of Félix Houphouet-Boigny and to that end contributed an entire library to the city of Abidjan. Ivory Coast officials in turn named a street in their capital city in honor of Owens. Even a teenager's innocent question about Eldridge Cleaver and Angela Davis—scarcely Jesse's kind of people—failed to diminish his pleasure at the country's enthusiastic reception.[30]

In the late spring of 1971 American viewers warmly received a television documentary on "The Black Athlete," narrated by Owens. Prior to its airing, he went on tour to promote the film in thirty cities, yet again under the sponsorship of Schieffelin & Company. Predictably, the script touched lightly on past prejudices in order to dwell upon racial progress and present opportunities for blacks in sport. By now the networks welcomed Owens before the camera. As a part of their advertisement for the forthcoming Munich Olympics, ABC featured "Jesse Owens Returns to Berlin," the same film Roone Arledge had rejected four years earlier.[31]

Behind the scenes, however, Jesse Owens was a troubled man. As he told it, from the day he and his ghostwriter sent the typescript of *Blackthink* to the publisher, he had second thoughts about his fiery rhetoric, his broad-brush denunciation of the motives of all black militants, and his insistence that any black American could succeed by trying hard enough. The reception of *Blackthink* had been curious. Virtually without exception, reviewers praised the book; its reception in the "white" press was extravagantly positive. But the response of the black community had been mixed. Letters flooded Jesse's mailbox. A few lauded his courage; hundreds damned his insensitivity to the racism and intolerable social conditions suffered by millions of blacks. Even his barber, a moderate, older man, suspected him of not liking blacks. *Blackthink* needed some rethinking.[32]

Once again Owens collaborated on a book with Paul Neimark. They produced *I Have Changed* for publication in the summer of 1972. As the title suggests, it is an attempt to reverse fields, to tone down the offensive passages in *Blackthink*. Jesse tried valiantly to identify with his critics. He defended the legitimacy of protest against racial prejudice and poverty. He admitted that inferior education, housing, and job opportunities still faced most blacks. He pointed out the woeful absence of blacks in the upper echelons of business, politics, and sports. "Probably I haven't changed enough," he noted. "But at least I can say, even while writing this, that *I'm still changing.*"[33]

For all his concessions to the heroes and ideas of the younger generation, however, he retained the mind-set of another era, another ideology. His public addresses and responses to interviewers remained essentially the same. "It's not racial awareness, it's achievement," he still believed. "The opportunities are here for everyone," he still said with unqualified optimism. In addition to his fervent patriotism, he clung to his emphasis on individual effort and a simple insistence that blacks needed to "think positively in order to achieve anything." As always, he gauged achievement primarily in terms of the money one could make in an America he still considered a land of abundant opportunity. "You can make as much money as you want to make in this country or as little," he announced even before *I Have Changed* went out of print. "It all depends on you and how much you want to put into it."[34]

When *I Have Changed* first appeared in the bookstores, Owens was away in Germany attending the Munich Olympics. Predictably, reporters pumped him for memories of the last time the games were held in Germany—at Berlin in 1936. All the old yarns about Hitler's sinister snub and Lutz Long's generosity surfaced anew. Unfortunately, both the drama of 1936 and the new stars of 1972 (such as the swimmer Mark

Spitz, the winner of a record seven gold medals) were eclipsed by tragedy: the brutal kidnapping and murder of eleven Israeli Olympians at the hands of Palestinian terrorists.[35]

That horrid episode, followed by a heated debate over whether or not the games should continue after the memorial service for the fallen Israelis, cast yet another of Owens's involvements into the background. In a little-publicized, uncanny replay of the Mexico City scene four years earlier, two black athletes used Munich's victory podium for political protest. Once again Jesse was cast in the role of mediator, a role for which he was ill-equipped.

The Munich culprits were Vincent Matthews and Wayne Collett, gold and silver medalists in the 400-meter run. While the National Anthem played, they turned their back to the American flag, stood casually chatting with hands on hips, and conspicuously shifted from one foot to the other. The crowd booed; press and television reporters rushed forward for interviews. Infuriated American officials gathered immediately to determine their means of punishment.[36]

Early the next morning Owens met with Matthews, Collett, and several other athletes in the room of Hoover Wright, a black assistant track coach. Matthews and Collett were scheduled to run on the relay team; now their places were in jeopardy. Owens urged them to apologize. When they refused, he asked their permission for him to represent their case before the IOC. Refused again, he shifted tactics, informing Matthews and Collett that he had been working for several large corporations that were only too willing to hire black athletes. As Matthews later related the story, Owens implied strongly that this act of political protest could well close the door on good jobs. "You don't have to say you're sorry," he pleaded. "You could just say that you weren't aware of what you were doing." He still felt certain that he could "get these companies to come to the forefront after the Olympics are over."

Matthews would have none of it. "That all sounds nice," he retorted, "but how come you never came to us before? None of your so-called large companies stepped forward for all the other black athletes after other Olympic Games." At the end of his tether, Jesse murmured, "Yeh, yeh, I know. But these things are changing." With that, he gave up. "Well, that's it," he shrugged to Coach Wright, and walked out.

Several hours later American Olympic officials summoned Matthews and Collett for a brief lecture on their violation of the Olympic spirit. As if on cue, a messenger entered the room with a letter from IOC President Avery Brundage, informing both athletes that they were disqualified from any further Olympic competition. Matthews's later account of the incident had little to say about Brundage and the others, however. He reserved his bitterness for Jesse Owens, "a sports legend in the United States" who could "do no wrong in the eyes of the American public," but whose age, experience, and status prevented him from understanding, much less encouraging, the young with whose principles he disagreed.[37]

☆　☆　☆

Throughout the 1970s Owens played the role of senior Olympic statesman. Appointed to the Board of Directors of the United States Olympic Committee in 1973, he regularly campaigned for funds to equip and train athletes. Numerous small gifts and some large corporate grants were essential, he believed, to protect "the American free enterprise system" of Olympic sponsorship. He feared the alternative. Government subsidies would produce a "factory" system on the Russian model, he warned repeatedly. Under government support, politicians would "run the show" to the detriment of the nation's athletes. "We are the only nation that is not subsidized," he told a New York audience, "and I hope to heaven we never will be."[38]

On the eve of the Montreal games in 1976, a reporter for the *Chicago Defender* noted that Owens was "getting around more than crabgrass" promoting the Olympics. Also promoting his own financial interests, he traveled constantly to deliver addresses to athletic and business groups at a minimum fee of $500 for each speech. His repertoire included four topics—motivation and values, religion, patriotism, and marketing—but as he never spoke from a written text, he freely interchanged the parts according to the impulse of the moment. "He emphasized God, mother, country, hard work and clean living, and he got it across very well," an old Ohio State teammate, Charlie Beetham, recalls. For some of his old Olympic teammates, however, Owens's predictable "sermon" became something of a joke. Says one, "Jesse should have been one of those jackleg preachers."[39]

Audiences seemed not to mind. They invariably warmed to Owens, and he to them. "When he enters a room" observed one reporter, "he doesn't so much take it over as envelop it; he is friendly to all, outgoing and gracious." At age fifty Jesse had candidly admitted that he was "very much like an actor" whose greatest reward was applause: "I live on the warmth and enthusiasm people show when I come to the end of a speech." Beyond age sixty, he needed and sought the approval of his audiences all the more.[40]

Of the few journalists willing to cast a critical eye on the message and manner of the legendary Owens, none was so outspoken as William O. Johnson, Jr., a staff writer for *Sports Illustrated*. In Binghamton, New York, Johnson closely observed Owens at a teenage track meet and banquet. Jesse's oratory seemed filled with clichés and platitudes, "grandiose and soaring, perhaps more notable for its delivery than its content." His public manner, too, appeared stylized, gauged for pleasant effect. "He is a kind of all-round super combination of 19th-century spellbinder and 20th-century P.R. man, glad-hander, evangelistic small-talker. Muted bombast is his stock-in-trade. Jesse Owens is what you might call a professional good example." Under Johnson's perceptive gaze, "Jesse Owens and the Jesse Owens image were working nicely in tandem."[41]

That tandem pulled in numerous honors to brighten Jesse's twilight years. In 1972 he received an honorary Doctor of Athletic Arts degree from Ohio State, a satisfying if late compensation for the baccalaureate degree he never got. In 1974 the National Collegiate Athletic Association presented him with its highest accolade, the Theodore Roosevelt Award for distinguished achievement since leaving competitive athletics. In that same year he was inducted into the Track and Field Hall of Fame. Two years later he received the nation's highest civilian honor, the Medal of Freedom Award, from President Gerald Ford in recognition of his serving as "a source of inspiration" for all Americans. By now, political affiliation mattered little: Democratic President Jimmy Carter bestowed on him the Living Legends Award in 1979 for his "dedicated but modest" endeavors "to inspire others to reach for greatness."[42]

Yet none of those nationally publicized awards meant so much sentimentally as did two local honors. One pertained to his recent activities, the other to his distant past. In the early 1970s Jesse and Ruth left the bitter cold and ice of Chicago for the sunny clime of Arizona and a fine new home in Scottsdale, near Phoenix. In early March 1976, the state of Arizona celebrated a "Jesse Owens Day" with a large, formal luncheon in Phoenix in honor of the fortieth anniversary of his Berlin triumphs. In 1979 the city of Decatur, Alabama, invited him to appear as guest of honor at its annual festival, to receive the Audie Murphy Patriotism Award. A white mayor made the presentation just a few miles from Owens's birthplace. The famous son of a poor farm laborer had come full circle, victoriously back to his roots.[43]

In the mid-1970s he came full circle in a less happy sense: back to zero on the record books. Years earlier all his important track records had fallen, leaving only an obscure record of 6.6 seconds in the indoor 60-meter dash, which he set at Madison Square Garden in 1935. Now, in 1975—precisely forty years later—that final standard fell to a 6.4-second dash by Cliff Outlin in a dual meet between the United States and the Soviet Union. Owens found little consolation in Outlin's being a fellow Alabama native from Birmingham. The news made him "a little sad," he admitted to reporters: "It's like losing a member of the family."[44]

Even the "immortal" Jesse Owens was not exempt from the physical losses that come with the passage of years. He still walked briskly on his toes in a style reminiscent of the youthful gait in old newsreels, but now he tired quickly. He continued playing golf regularly but struggled to hold his form on the back nine. Now he wore glasses to read fine print. He still dashed madly from one speaking engagement to another, only to find himself fatigued and susceptible to the pneumonia that had plagued him from youth. A severe attack in 1971 almost killed him. As a precautionary measure, he took to puffing a pipe in a vain attempt to cut down on the pack of cigarettes he had smoked daily for thirty years or so.[45]

He indulged fully in one of life's compensations to the aged: dispensing words of wisdom to the young regardless of their inability, or unwillingness, to hear. In 1973 at a track meet at Franklin Field in Philadelphia, he met an ambitious twelve-year-old sprinter and long-jumper whose ears perked up at the magic name of Jesse Owens. Lauding him as "a spunky little guy to be jumping against all these big guys," Jesse advised him to "have fun running and jumping, but never overburden yourself with what you're trying to do." The boy's name was Carl Lewis.[46]

In an article for *Today's Health*, Owens cautioned American youths against being "too athletic," too intense in their win-or-die commitment to spectator sports. "Athletics should not mean an isolated hour when we work at doing knee bends or running the mile," the man whose entire youth was given to athletic training and competition insisted. "It should be part of the pattern of our lives—a long walk when we might have driven, a day in the country instead of the stadium," a man wedded to the automobile and the city prescribed.[47]

Yet his age and eminence gave him license for advice. In 1976 he produced a little book for track and field athletes, offering practical pointers on how best to warm up, run, and jump. His name alone sold the book.[48] Although he was an athlete growing old, Jesse Owens suffered not the fate of A. E. Housman's memorable "lads who wore their honour out"—ex-athletes "whom renown outran," whose names "died before the man."[49]

CHAPTER 13

A Legend Memorialized

No longer able to run, Owens reminisced more than ever. Occasionally he dreamed of an irretrievable youth. "Now and then," he noted in 1972, "when I drift off to sleep, time dissolves, 1936 somehow becomes 1956 or even 1972, and I see myself out there, but not *then*, now—*now*—putting it all together somehow for just one more brief slice of time." As he sensed his time running out, he became philosophical. Life now seemed not a sprint, but a marathon, "a long, long, long-distance race over hills and through valleys, sometimes even with stops along the way." Sheer speed of movement no longer mattered, for no decisive "finish line" beckoned. "As long as you live, there's another hill, another valley," the aged Owens reflected.[1]

For years he had referred perfunctorily in public speeches to God, faith, and religion to support his emphasis on ethical values, hard work, and patriotism. Behind that agreeable formula, however, friends saw no signs of religious sensibility, much less of zeal, until late in his life. By some accounts, Owens claimed to be a "born-again believer" at the end. His

last cooperative effort with his ghostwriter, Paul Neimark, resulted in a thin little "spiritual autobiography" recalling the
many valleys of physical, emotional, and financial crisis
through which prayer and the presence of the Almighty had
brought him. For the public record—and presumably in private—America's greatest aging athlete made his peace with
what he characteristically called "the Great Referee."[2]

With his wife, too, Owens made his peace. Their midlife
marital storms having subsided, he and Ruth stuck together.
Some friends thought the love had long since died, that she
would have divorced him years earlier had she not been determined "to hold the family together." But she was determined
in more ways than they knew. According to Jesse, they moved
from Chicago to the sun, clean air, and simpler life of Arizona
largely at Ruth's insistence. Having learned, finally, to voice
her own needs, she got her compensations. She remained happily in her comfortable Scottsdale home or visited her
daughters in Chicago while he traveled; proudly she stood at
his side in the reflected glory of his numerous awards.[3]

Regularly on Jesse's birthday and at Thanksgiving and
Christmas holidays, they joined their daughters, sons-in-law,
and grandchildren in Chicago for sociable celebrations. The
divisive political arguments of the 1960s behind them, their
family gatherings took on a comfortably warm glow. Only
Jesse's inability to sit still for long lent an abrasive edge to the
occasion. His energy was better suited to the golf links and
cookouts at Union Pier on Lake Michigan, where the family
periodically gathered in the summer at a cottage Jesse had
bought just before the move to Arizona.[4]

Owens's closest circle of friends received a jolt in the
autumn of 1978, when Ralph Metcalfe dropped dead of an apparent heart attack in his Chicago apartment. At Metcalfe's
funeral, old athletic chums confronted their own tenuous hold
on life. They decided that it was "getting late" for them, so late
that they "oughta start getting together" regularly. They
agreed to meet each year around Jesse's birthday, September
13, at Union Pier. In 1979 more than a dozen black athletes enjoyed a reunion playing golf, swimming, eating, drinking, and
talking over a long weekend.[5]

Their first meeting turned out to be their last. It was later than they thought.

☆   ☆   ☆

The sixty-six-year-old Owens was not well. He worked at his usual whirlwind pace in the autumn of 1979 but felt sluggish and short of breath. In early November he flew to Dallas to address an Olympic fundraising group; afterward Helen Stephens, an old friend and teammate from 1936, heard him complain of fatigue. Within the week he was at the Plaza Hotel in New York, taping a commercial for American Express. For several hours he repeated his routine for the cameras. "Do you know me?" he asked as he walked from a curb, addressing the viewer. "My name is Jesse Owens." Finally, when asked to do yet another take, he abruptly refused. "Look! I'm tired now. That's it."[6]

Rest over the Thanksgiving holidays failed to renew his strength. In early December he addressed a religious group in Dayton, Ohio, but in the middle of the speech he began coughing uncontrollably. He nevertheless went on to St. Louis for another engagement the next night, only to become faint on the podium. Scheduled to present some athletic awards at a New Jersey school two days later, he rang Herb Douglas asking him to handle the duties. "I don't know what's wrong," he told Douglas. For John Woodruff, who had booked him for the school, Owens left a message that he was sick and on his way to Chicago for a complete physical examination.[7]

He entered Michael Reese Hospital, and on December 12 received the horrid verdict of adenocarcinoma, lung cancer. The news devastated his family and friends. The Chicagoan Mel Walker remembers his phone ringing and Ruth asking him to come down to the hospital to "cheer Jesse up." When he arrived, Ruth met him in the waiting room.

"How is Jesse?" asked Walker.

"Mel, he's not going to make it," Ruth replied, holding up three fingers to indicate a life expectancy of three months.

Walker recalls feeling as if he had been hit in the chest by a sledgehammer. Ruth asked him to go in and talk to Jesse, but Walker could not compose himself for the task. He went home to bed for three days. Finally pulling himself together, he returned to the hospital. Upon entering Jesse's room, he was met by a cheerful voice: "Mel, I've contacted Mr. Cook at Wendy's. You can contact him now." The reference was to Walker's earlier request for an introduction to the Chicago manager of the Wendy's hamburger chain, a potential source of jobs for local black youths.[8]

The cancer, probably caused by long years of heavy cigarette smoking, had spread throughout the left lung. An operation was out of the question, as was radium treatment. Instead, Owens was put on chemotherapy, a physically exhausting, nausea-inducing drug treatment. Yet he remained optimistic, determined to beat the odds. Speaking engagements had to be canceled; otherwise, he insisted on business as usual. When Herb Douglas visited him at the hospital, he found him in the solarium sneaking a cigarette. Leaving Chicago in mid-January for his home in Arizona, Owens refused a wheelchair at O'Hare Airport.[9]

Two daughters walked him to the plane. For them, this was anything but business as usual; they knew their father was dying. Both were irritated when a flustered Paul Neimark caught them halfway down the terminal ramp with a gift for the man with whom he had co-authored four books and several articles. It was a package of golf balls. "Can you believe that? Golf balls for a dying man!" says Gloria Hemphill, still angry at the incident.[10]

Owens checked into the University of Arizona Hospital in Tucson for a week of further tests and treatment. The head oncologist, Dr. Stephen E. Jones, informed reporters that the cancer had spread further since its detection but insisted that he was "very hopeful" of a full recovery. Avoiding reporters and photographers, Jesse and Ruth slipped quietly out of the hospital to drive in a drizzling rain to their home near Phoenix for treatment on an outpatient basis.[11]

Despite the ravages of cancer and chemotherapy, Owens attended to Olympic matters to the end. Just as he left Chicago for Arizona, President Carter first broached the possibility of a U.S. boycott of the forthcoming summer Games in Moscow as a demonstration of American outrage over the Red Army's invasion and occupation of Afghanistan. Owens initially backed the

President "100 percent." Through his Chicago attorney, Bernard Kleinman, he released a statement to the press explaining that although he firmly believed in athletics as an invaluable means of communication, he remained "first, last, and always an American." If the President decided on a boycott, he would support that decision.[12]

Two weeks later, however, his athleticism won out over his deference to authority. In an interview with a reporter for the Phoenix *Gazette,* he announced his opposition to the boycott because it would be a cruel blow to athletes who had trained for years. Still eager to hold onto his patriotism and his Olympism too, he provided the material for a long newspaper article to be published under his name, arguing that athletes should go to Moscow as individuals rather than as representatives of the United States. Under those terms, he insisted, the American government would not be sanctioning the Moscow games, but athletes would still get to compete in the contests on which they had set their hearts. "The road to the Olympics doesn't lead to Moscow," Owens finished with a typical flourish. "It leads to no city, no country. It goes far beyond Lake Placid or Moscow, ancient Greece or Nazi Germany. The road to the Olympics leads, in the end, to the best within us."[13]

Still strong with words, Owens progressively weakened in physical strength. On March 21 he was flown by helicopter back to the university hospital in Tucson. Doctors announced that he had "taken a turn for the worse" and was now in critical condition. A battery of new experimental drugs failed to arrest infection, irregular breathing, and constant coughing. On Saturday night, March 29, he slipped into a coma. In the early morning of March 31, 1980, his struggle ceased.[14]

Two days later, flags flew at half-mast throughout the state of Arizona, the Governor having declared a day of mourning for the state's most famous resident. The body lay in state all day in the rotunda of the State Capitol in Phoenix, as thousands of mourners paid their respects. Then the body was placed aboard a jet for Chicago, where the family received friends and well-wishers at the Griffin Funeral Home on Martin Luther King Drive.[15]

For the funeral on Friday morning, April 4, about 2,000 people braved the chilling wind and snow flurries to make their way to the Rockefeller Chapel of the University of Chicago. At the front of the chapel sat a glistening gray casket draped with a white, five-ringed Olympic flag of silk. In attendance were several aged comrades from the 1936 Olympic team, all black except Marty Glickman; Robert Kane, president of the United States Olympic Committee; and Larry Snyder and Woody Hayes from Ohio State. Darryl Stingley, a former professional football player paralyzed from a brutal blow two years earlier, sat strapped in a wheelchair near the casket.[16]

The tempo of the service was upbeat. Gloria Hemphill set the tone with her opening remarks. "This is one of the proudest moments of my life," she began with a faint smile, without tears, "to stand here and tell of my father, Jesse Owens." Subsequent speakers displayed wit. Dick Gregory lauded the man for whom a city—Cleveland—was named before he was born. Robert Kane suggested that Saint Peter had already welcomed Jesse and "signed him up to speak at the Apostles' brunch" and that Ralph Metcalfe no doubt greeted his friend at the pearly gates saying, "I beat you this time. I got here first." Dr. Archibald Carey, Jr., a circuit judge and minister emeritus of the African Methodist Episcopal Church, delivered the formal eulogy.[17]

Snow fell gently as former athletes carried the casket out of the chapel for a brief ride to Oak Woods Cemetery. The hearse, overflowing with wreaths of red roses and yellow and white chrysanthemums, dropped a few flowers along the way. A young black man picked up one of the roses and kissed it.[18]

☆ ☆ ☆

Older men, too, eagerly associated themselves with the legendary Owens. Numerous schemes for honorary streets, plaques, statues, athletic buildings, track meets, and awards surfaced immediately after his death. In living memory, only John F. Kennedy and Martin Luther King had been honored so extensively. Memorials for the famous dead reflect the values and dreams of the living, ensuring favorable publicity and lending credibility to claims of excellence. In life Jesse Owens had sold or freely given his support to various institutions, groups, and individuals; in death he continued to serve the interests of others.

Chicago journalists invoked his memory in their campaign against the American boycott of the 1980 Moscow Olympics. David Condon of the *Chicago Tribune* opposed the boycott because, he argued, it would prevent black athletes from electrifying the world "as Jesse Owens did in the 1936 Nazi games." The black journalist A. S. "Doc" Young of the *Chicago Defender* joined the chorus, calling upon President Carter to drop the boycott and dedicate America's participation to Owens. Failing that, Young proposed a "Jesse Owens Freedom Festival and Amateur Athletic Competition" as an alternative to Moscow and as a testimony "to human rights, to human dignity, to human equality, to brotherhood."[19]

Ohio State officials claimed Owens as their own, of course. At his death, President Harold Enarson lauded him as one who "exemplified the foundation on which The Ohio State University has been built—opportunity and excellence." Perennially faced with a fiscally conservative legislature, the university needed every shred of good publicity it could find. In Jesse Owens, it found a gem. On the very day of the funeral, President Enarson and the Board of Trustees announced that the track in Ohio Stadium and three campus recreation buildings would all be named in honor of the man who "carried the name of this university and this country to new heights of world acclaim."[20]

On a less grand scale, parties interested in improving the track at Ohio Stadium seized the opportunity to use Owens's honor as an arguing point. A journalist for the *Columbus Dispatch* observed that the present "deplorable condition" of the track "only demeans the memory of this great alumnus' achievements." The cinder track on which Jesse himself ran had become miserably outdated; other Big Ten teams, accustomed to new synthetic surfaces, avoided Ohio Stadium. "Jesse Owens was a quality individual," noted the women's track coach, "and if you're going to name a facility after him, it should be a quality facility." Apparently the argument carried weight. Money was quickly found for a new synthetic track.[21]

The Jesse Owens Track and the Jesse Owens Recreation Centers were formally dedicated on October 4, 1980, at a spectacular halftime show during a regionally televised football game between Ohio State and UCLA. By then the Board of Trustees had devised yet another means of displaying the name of "one of our most illustrious sons" on the campus of the university. They announced plans for the Jesse Owens Memorial Plaza, a 450-foot-long garden and tree-lined sidewalk leading from Stadium Drive into the rotunda of the stadium. A "statue or other work of art" honoring Owens would be set in the center of the plaza. The total cost of the project, including a new track, was estimated at $1.4 million.[22] Surely no university has ever expended so much energy and financial resources to memorialize one of its failed students.

Ohio State had no monopoly on the use of Owens's name. On March 31, 1981, the first anniversary of his death, plans for an annual "Jesse Owens International Amateur Athletic Award" were made public in the Mercury Room of the New York Hilton. At the head of the press conference stood Ruth Owens; William Simon, president of the United States Olympic Committee; Herbert Douglas, vice president of special markets for Schieffelin & Company; and William J. Schieffelin III, chairman of the company, which served as the primary sponsor of the project.[23]

As the scheme developed, other large corporations participated by buying program advertisements and books of tickets to annual banquets. The proceeds went to the American Cancer Society and the Jesse Owens Memorial Foundation for the provision of college scholarships to "needy but deserving youths." The winner of the first award was Eric Heiden, speedskating champion from the 1980 Olympics. In subsequent years, track stars Sebastian Coe, Mary Decker, and Edwin Moses took the honors at glossy banquets amid much television and newspaper coverage.[24]

Not surprisingly, several memorial track meets were begun shortly after Owens's death. The Jesse Owens International Invitational Indoor Track and Field Meet originated in New York City in January 1982 in conjunction with the Schieffelin-sponsored amateur athletic award. Also in 1982, an annual Jesse Owens Memorial Run of 10 kilometers was organized by the local parks and recreation department and the county chapter of the American Lung Association in Moulton, Alabama. Ohio State joined the act in May 1983 with its inaugural Jesse Owens Track and Field Classic. All the while the annual ARCO–Jesse Owens Games continued, but scarcely with exclusive rights to the use of Owens's name.[25]

Other posthumous recognitions included a street named for Owens in Berlin, leading to the Olympic Stadium; a marble marker set near his birthplace in Oakville, Alabama; and a plaque affixed to the Los Angeles Coliseum a year prior to the 1984 Olympics. Two of those three memorials contained minor factual errors, a curious coincidence for a public reputation steeped in legend. The Oakville inscription placed Owens's birth in 1914 rather than 1913. To the embarrassment of the patrons of the unveiling ceremonies in Los Angeles, their inscription gave him the name *John* Cleveland Owens.[26]

☆ ☆ ☆

In 1983 two other memorial projects provoked bitter arguments. One had to do with artistic taste, the other with local politics and racial attitudes. In the end, both controversies produced stirring affirmations of the legendary significance of Jesse Owens, the interpretations differing in accordance with the distinct interests of the hero-worshipers.

The first involved the "statue or other work of art" to be placed in the Jesse Owens Memorial Plaza at Ohio State. The selection committee, composed of two art professors, a college dean, and a local art museum curator, chose an abstract bronze sculpture by Curtis R. Patterson of Atlanta, Georgia. Ohio artists howled in protest, complaining that the committee ignored local talent. Louder still was the complaint that Patterson's sculpture was an unsightly monstrosity and an inappropriate monument to Owens.[27]

It was certainly unique. More a piece of modern sculpture than a traditional athletic statue, it featured four bronze triangles arranged to form a crosslike passage for viewers. According to Patterson, the four pyramids represented Owens's athletic achievements, the upward angles his "pinnacles of performance" as both an athlete and humanitarian, and the stolidity of the entire structure his strength of life and character. Local sports enthusiasts saw the matter differently. Sculpture honoring an athlete "should look like the athlete and should look like him doing his thing," a Columbus newspaper editor reasoned. Ultimately the debate hinged not so much on the conflict between traditional and modern art as on the essence of Owens's fame. "Jesse Owens was a man of many parts," the Columbus editor shrewdly observed, "but he is being honored at Ohio State because he won four Olympic medals in track events. Don't let anybody tell you otherwise."[28]

The new president of Ohio State, Edward H. Jennings, told everyone otherwise. Scarcely could he and his trustees justify spending $1.4 million on the track, plaza, and sculpture in honor of a mere athlete. Jesse Owens was more than an athletic star; he was "an American hero," Jennings declared in his dedication of the memorial. Referring briefly to the track records, Jennings dwelt on Owens's "beliefs and ideals," his "commitment to human understanding and betterment," his "tireless efforts in behalf of youth," and his "enduring inspiration" for all Americans. The Jesse Owens legend was alive and well in Columbus, Ohio.[29]

In Moulton, Alabama, the legend met with ugly resistance. During the summer of 1983 a white legislator, Roger Dutton, approached Alabama's Governor George C. Wallace for state funds to erect a monument to Owens on the courthouse lawn in Moulton, the Lawrence County seat, 7 miles northwest of Owens's birthplace, Oakville. Wallace, whose former racist policies had become muted by time and political necessity, promised the money. Dutton then submitted his proposal to the four-member Lawrence County Commission, only to have it rejected by a vote of 3–0 with one abstention.[30]

The commissioners, all white, claimed that the courthouse lawn was already too crowded with monuments. One spokesman insisted that a marker to Owens would start a "chain reaction" of local families demanding public memorials for their forefathers. The old Southern states-rights argument was tailored for local use. Opponents complained that Representative Dutton "went at it wrong," presenting the commission with an ultimatum without consultation. "No one wants to be told what they have to do," said one. The local branch of the American Legion unanimously agreed, upset that public taxes should be used for the project.[31]

The whole episode stank of thinly veiled racial bigotry. "If it was a Paul 'Bear' Bryant monument [to the recently deceased head coach of the University of Alabama], would you hear these excuses?" Owens's cousin, Marvin Fitzgerald, asked. "There's only two famous people ever to come out of this county—Jesse Owens and Joe Wheeler, a Confederate general," declared Representative Dutton. "We've got a Wheeler Dam, a Wheeler highway, and a Wheeler Forest, but we don't have anything for Jesse Owens." Apparently that arrangement suited most of Moulton's white citizens just fine. To the press and television reporters who rushed to the scene, the mayor of the town announced that nationwide adverse publicity would not change his mind. "If somebody way off in California or somewhere gives us a bad name, what difference is it going to make?" he asked. "How's it going to affect us here?"[32]

A few more reasonable whites, eager to avoid a racist image for Moulton, persuaded the County Commission to appoint a biracial committee to decide on a site for the monument. Just a week later, however, the committee was dissolved when sixty-four Oakville residents submitted a petition for the Owens memorial to be placed in Oakville. Visibly relieved, the County Commission unanimously accepted the request, happy to be rid of "this Jesse Owens mess." Finally, in early November 1983, a 4-foot-tall granite monument topped with a bronze plaque was erected in Oakville.[33]

Unfortunately, the mean spirit emerging in the dispute had not yet run its course. Just a few hours after the monument was set in place, vandals drove up at night in a pickup truck, tied a log chain around the marker, and attempted to pull it off its pedestal. As the truck's engine roared and its tires spun, the chain broke, arousing nearby blacks from sleep. One stepped outside his house to fire a shotgun into the air, scaring the hooligans away. Early the next morning Oakville citizens gathered round the monument to find a corner of the granite chipped off.[34]

The inscription in praise of Owens glistened ironically in the sun: "He inspired a world enslaved in tyranny and brought hope to his fellow man. From the cotton fields of Oakville to the acclaim of the whole world he made us proud to be Lawrence Countians."

CHAPTER 14

Durable Dreams

THE LEGENDARY APPEAL OF JESSE OWENS rode the crest of the conservative landslide that brought Ronald Reagan to the White House just a few months after Owens's death. President Reagan reaffirmed much of what the late Owens represented. Both exuded optimism, making Americans believe in themselves and in their nation's virtues. Both extolled traditional values in times of upheaval. In 1983 the President addressed a fundraising luncheon for the United States Olympic Committee and took the occasion to praise Owens and Ralph Metcalfe as men "very special to my generation." They were "much more than great athletes, they were great Americans," Reagan reminded an audience of seven hundred, each of whom had paid $500 to attend the luncheon.

The presence of the President ensured a good turnout at the luncheon, of course, but a larger concern for the coming Los Angeles Olympics inspired handsome individual and corporate financial contributions to the cause. That concern was best voiced by the executive director of the United States Olympic Committee, F. Don Miller. As the Soviet Union had not yet announced its intention to boycott the games, Miller warned that "it would be tragic if the Eastern bloc countries were highly successful on our soil and dominated the games."

The President wholeheartedly agreed. He emphasized the need to make the Los Angeles Olympics the most spectacular of all the modern Olympics, a showpiece of American enterprise, and to equip and train American athletes for a decisive victory over the Communist bloc countries. At the end of his speech he paraphrased the patriotic Owens's account of his first appearance on the victory stand at Berlin: "It's a tremendous feeling when you stand there and watch your flag above all the others. For me, it was the fulfillment of a nine-year dream, and I couldn't forget the country that brought me here." Then the President delivered his punch line: "Today, let's not forget the country that brought us here."[1]

Certainly the wider implications of the American dream, as represented in the story of Jesse Owens, stood in no danger of being forgotten. Owens figured prominently in the 1984 Los Angeles Olympics. A four-hour television drama, "The Jesse Owens Story," preceded the games. Jesse's granddaughter, Gina Hemphill, carried the Olympic torch into the Coliseum. Old film clips featuring the youthful Owens in action at the Berlin Games half a century earlier were shown repeatedly. Several on-camera interviews with his family and friends renewed his athletic achievements and personal charm in the public consciousness. Not by coincidence, one of the prime sponsors of the Los Angeles Olympics was Atlantic Richfield Company, which owned exclusive rights for the commercial use of the name of Jesse Owens.

The focus of all the media hype was a widely publicized attempt by Carl Lewis to win gold medals in the same four events that Owens dominated in 1936. Lewis brilliantly met the challenge, far surpassing all of Owens's records. Journalists frequently compared their differences in style, character, and impact. In one sense the comparisons were altogether out of order, for Jesse Owens and Carl Lewis lived in different epochs, by different rules, with different expectations. Owens won world acclaim at a time when black athletes enjoyed little visibility. He burst dramatically on the scene, uniquely placed as well as uniquely skilled. Lewis, on the other hand, represented a culmination of many years of black dominance in American sport, especially in track and field. His exploits lacked shock value.

They also lacked political drama. Whereas Owens's destiny cast him in Berlin, in the presence of Hitler and a gathering storm of total war, Lewis was deprived of a political stage for the strutting of his stuff. Even the Russians and most of their Communist bloc friends refused to compete at Los Angeles. All the showmanship of Hollywood could not impart a sense of moral drama to the sterling athleticism of Carl Lewis; all the chauvinism of American commentators failed to give political meaning to the event.

Beyond the historical and political contrasts, comparisons inevitably centered on differences in style and character. At that level, the achievements of Carl Lewis added immeasurably to the lustre of Owens's name, for Lewis lacked several of the personal traits that contributed to Owens's heroic status. The success of Jesse Owens made a perfect rags-to-riches story; Lewis's suburban, middle-class origins did not. He even made bundles of money in athletics, lived and dressed opulently, and drove a flashy sports car for several years before his Olympic triumph. Moreover, whereas the young Owens was modest and self-effacing, Lewis was outspoken and self-assured, projecting an image of arrogance. By all accounts, Owens made himself accessible to teammates, spectators and the press; Lewis came across as a loner, refusing even to subject himself to the distractions of the Olympic Village. *Newsweek's* Pete Axthelm dismissed him as "a master self-promoter," a "fabled loner" with a "sometimes whining attitude" who confirmed the rule "that mere records do not make legends." The image of the legendary Jesse Owens weighed heavily in that indictment.[2]

Owens's ghost continued to plague the young Lewis as he appeared in New York City six months after the Los Angeles Olympics to receive the Vitalis Award for Sports Excellence. Rich and famous, relaxed and splendidly dressed, Lewis still admitted to twinges of pain at the rough treatment he had received from journalists at Los Angeles. Why had he failed to "become the national hero that moved people the way Jesse Owens did?" a reporter asked. "Maybe that will come," Lewis replied, wisely reminding his interviewer that Owens himself did not become "a major, major personality" until years after the Berlin games.[3]

It remains to be seen if time and circumstance will do the same for Carl Lewis, but the odds are against it. An athlete becomes a national hero only when his personality, achievements, and image fulfill a cultural need beyond the athletic arena. Jesse Owens was a rare individual whose importance transcended athleticism.

☆ ☆ ☆

Heroes inspire others to pursue visions of greatness, and Owens certainly did that. For blacks of his generation, especially, he was an inspirational model of success. Today several survivors of the 1930s testify eloquently to the importance of his example. He was "a role model, and led the way for so many of us to reach our goals," says Herb Douglas, a bronze medalist in the 1948 London Olympics. As a schoolboy in Pittsburgh, Douglas met Owens shortly after the Berlin games and decided to follow in his illustrious footsteps. "I'm sitting here," Douglas says today in his executive suite at Schieffelin & Company in New York, "because I had someone to try to emulate."[4]

In Cleveland, Harrison Dillard says essentially the same thing. An impressionable adolescent in 1936, he eagerly watched the parade welcoming Owens back to Cleveland from Berlin. Jesse personally encouraged his young admirer, giving him confidence to set his goals high. Dillard won two gold medals at the London Olympics in 1948 and two more at Helsinki in 1952. Today he works in the Cleveland school system, enthusiastically tracing the roots of his success to the inspiration of his hero.[5]

Dillard and Douglas are but two examples among the many older blacks who recall Jesse Owens as their guiding star in citizenship as well as athletics. Even for unathletic, unaccomplished blacks, Owens is still important in a vicarious way. "It makes me feel good on the inside what Jesse did," says his unemployed cousin in Oakville, Alabama. "Even if I never made nothing of myself, I feel good that some of my people did."[6]

But some blacks are not so sure about the positive effects

of the Jesse Owens model as a focus for black youths. Almost two decades ago, the black sociologist Harry Edwards complained that Owens had too long been extolled as "the prime illustration of how pride and hope of a minority can be uplifted through the feats of a blood brother." What bothered Edwards was the belief that any poor but athletically gifted young black could achieve social mobility through sports, as Owens did. Jesse was the exception, not the rule, declared Edwards, who still regularly insists in television and newspaper interviews that sport is a dead-end street for black aspirations.[7]

Hard facts support those assertions. An appallingly high percentage of black scholarship athletes never obtain a college degree; pitifully few make the professional ranks. The goal of becoming a high-salaried professional athlete is doomed to nightmarish failure for the great majority of black youths. While a handful gain fame and material success through athletics, most stumble from lack of top-flight ability or untimely injuries to find themselves without an education, without job skills, and without hope. Even those intangible qualities supposedly fostered in competitive sport—determination, courage, and discipline—come to little for blacks who sell their educational birthright for a mess of athletic pottage.[8]

The "radical" Harry Edwards is by no means the only black spokesman to call the athletic mania into question. Moderate, mild-mannered Arthur Ashe, a Wimbledon champion and coach of the American Davis Cup team, also laments the tendency of black youths to waste their educational and career opportunities in blind pursuit of sport. "We have been on the same roads—sports and entertainment—too long," Ashe told an interviewer for the *New York Times* in 1977. "We need to pull over, fill up at the library, and speed away to Congress and the Supreme Court, the unions and the business world."[9] On the road envisioned by Arthur Ashe and Harry Edwards, the life of Jesse Owens—a brilliant athlete but failed student and lifelong "entertainer" on the lecture circuit—provides a poor model for black success in today's world.

Yet his inspirational value remains firm. Despite all his limitations of vision and accomplishment, Owens carved out for himself a life that was fundamentally decent. As a journalist for the *Chicago Defender* put it several days after his death, he taught his people "what it means to excel against the odds."[10]

☆　☆　☆

In his best moments, Owens recognized his own flaws and limitations. "The lives of most men are patchwork quilts," he once observed. "Or at best one matching outfit with a closet and laundry bag full of incongruous accumulations." Hanging in his own closet were some outfits ill-fitted to his heroic image. He was a man, not a god. Most heroes are.[11]

But heroes make something good not only of their external obstacles but also of their own worst traits. Born economically and racially disadvantaged, Owens vaulted to athletic fame, then to material comfort and social acceptance by making a virtue of onerous necessities. Poorly educated, he lauded education and happily saw two of his three daughters receive college degrees. Untrained for a profession, he became a polished speaker and promoter. Unable to sit still and tend to office business, he stayed on the road. Unequipped to think critically or originally, he made a career of embellishing his own story in the affirmation of traditional American values. His youthful optimism undiminished by the years, he voiced an age-old American belief. "In America, anyone can become somebody," he insisted to the end of his days. "Does that sound corny in this day and age? Well, it happened to me, and I believe it can happen to anybody in one way or another."[12]

In Jesse Owens, as in Ronald Reagan, the American dream and American patriotism received a fresh breath of life. Like the President's, Jesse's message appealed most to Rotarians, Chambers of Commerce, corporate boardrooms, and conservative religious groups. But in the larger mainstream of American life his story made people feel good about themselves, their own powers to overcome limitations, and their own potential for fairness. So "we embrace it," noted an admirer, "for it reaffirms the human spirit and makes us believe we are still good, good enough to permit people to grow out of deprivation and make it to the top."[13] So long as people suffer deprivation and strive to make it to the top, the story of Jesse Owens will be embraced.

Notes

JESSE OWENS'S COLLABORATIONS with Paul Neimark are designated with short titles, as follows:

Blackthink   *Blackthink: My Life as Black Man and White Man* (New York: William Morrow, 1970)

Jesse Owens Story   *The Jesse Owens Story* (New York: Putnam's, 1970)

I Have Changed   *I Have Changed* (New York: William Morrow, 1972)

Jesse   *Jesse: A Spiritual Autobiography* (Plainfield, N.J.: Logos International, 1978)

Barbara Moro's interviews (1961) with Jesse Owens and Ruth Owens are in typescript from the Illinois State Historical Library, Springfield, Illinois. ARCO interviews are in typescript from the archives of Atlantic Richfield Company, Los Angeles, California. David Dore's interview (1972) with

Owens is on tape, in the author's possession. The author's interviews are all on tape or in notes.

Prologue (pp. 1–4)

1. *Chicago Defender*, May 5, 1951.
2. For the best source in English on the Berlin Olympics, see Richard D. Mandell, *The Nazi Olympics* (New York: Macmillan, 1971).
3. Quoted from the *Cleveland Plain Dealer* in "The Saga of Jesse Owens," *The Crisis*, 43 (September 1936): 267.

Chapter 1. Southern Grit (pp. 5–16)

1. Kathleen Paul Jones and Pauline Jones Gandred, eds., "Alabama Records" (1931), XXII: 20,27 and LXVI: 97; *1820 State Census of Lawrence County, Alabama* (Huntsville: Tennessee Valley Genealogical Society, 1977), pp. 9, 33.
2. Thomas J. Edwards, "The Tenant System and Some Changes Since Emancipation," in Emory R. Johnson, ed., *The Negro's Progress in Fifty Years* (Philadelphia: American Academy of Political and Social Science, 1913), pp. 38–46; Roy Wilkins with Tom Mathews, *Standing Fast: The Autobiography of Roy Wilkins* (New York: Viking Press, 1982), p. 13; author's interview with John Wiley. Owens erroneously thought his father first began working for a Mr. Clannon. *Jesse*, p. 5.
3. Author's interviews with Spencer Griffin and Elsie Fitzgerald.
4. James Baldwin, *Notes of a Native Son* (New York: Bantam, 1964), p. 1; "Thirteenth Census of the United States: 1910—Population for Lawrence County, Alabama" (Department of Commerce and Labor, Bureau of Statistics, May 12, 1910); *Jesse*, p. 5.
5. *I Have Changed*, pp. 28–29, 142; *Jesse*, pp. 3–10; Larry Snyder, "My Boy Jesse," *Saturday Evening Post*, November 7, 1937, p. 14.
6. *Decatur Daily*, September 4, 12, 13, and 19, 1913.
7. "Thirteenth Census: 1910."
8. *Jesse*, p. 6.
9. Baldwin, *Notes of a Native Son*, p. 137; "Don Newcombe and Jesse Owens Featured in 'Sport'," *The Negro History Bulletin*, 17 (April 1954): 150; Barbara Moro's interview with Jesse Owens.
10. Moro's interview with Owens.

11. ARCO interview with Bud Greenspan.

12. William O. Johnson, Jr., *All That Glitters Is Not Gold: The Olympic Game* (New York; Putnam, 1972), p. 50; Moro's interview with Owens.

13. Author's interview with John Wiley; Moro's interview with Owens; ARCO interview with David Albritton.

14. Moro's interview with Owens; *Decatur Daily*, April 1, 1980.

15. *Decatur Daily*, April 1, 1980; *Jesse*, p. 18.

16. *Jesse*, pp. 15–16, 88; author's interviews with Spencer Griffin, Snora Griffin, Ernestine Fitzgerald, and Elsie Fitzgerald.

17. Wilkins with Mathews, *Standing Fast*, p. 20; *Jesse*, p. 110.

18. *Colorado Springs Sun*, April 1, 1980; *New York Times*, April 1, 1980.

19. Moro's interview with Owens; author's interview with Spencer Griffin.

20. Author's interview with Eulace Peacock.

21. Author's interview with John Wiley.

22. Author's interviews with Spencer Griffin and John Wiley.

23. *Blackthink*, pp. 31, 48. For a contemporary of Henry Owens who was "scared of everything," see Audrey Olsen Faulkner, Marcel A. Heisel, Wendell Holbrook, and Shirley Geismar, eds., *When I Was Comin' Up: An Oral History of Aged Blacks* (Hamden, Conn.: Archon Books, 1982), pp. 22–24.

24. Author's interview with John Wiley; *Jesse*, p. 109.

25. *Jesse*, p. 20.

26. *I Have Changed*, p. 26; Cleveland *Call and Post*, August 27, 1936.

27. *Blackthink*, p. 33; *Jesse*, p. 21; "This is Your Life, Jesse Owens" (1960), film in ARCO archives; *Call and Post*, May 30, 1935, and March 14, 1940.

28. *Blackthink*, pp. 32–35; *Jesse*, pp. 13–23.

29. Author's interviews with Ernest Griffin and John Wiley.

30. *Negro Migration in 1916–17* (Washington, D.C.: Government Printing Office, 1919), pp. 58–65; Louis Venable Kennedy, *The Negro Peasant Turns Cityward: Effects of Recent Migrations to Northern Cities* (New York: Columbia University Press, 1930), pp. 41–57; Harvard Sitkoff, *A New Deal for Blacks: The Emergence of Civil Rights as a National Issue*, Vol. I, *The Depression Decade* (New York: Oxford University Press, 1978), pp. 15–21, 31.

31. Kennedy, *Negro Peasant Turns Cityward*, pp. 25–31.

32. Kenneth L. Kusmer, *A Ghetto Takes Shape: Black Cleveland, 1870–1930* (Urbana: University of Illinois Press, 1976), pp. 1–10;

Emmett J. Scott, *Negro Migration During the War* (New York: Oxford University Press, 1920), pp. 126–27; "This Is Your Life, Jesse Owens"; Moro's interview with Owens.

33. Moro's interview with Owens; *Jesse*, p. 19.

34. Moro's interview with Owens; Johnson, *All That Glitters*, p. 50; *Jesse*, pp. 19–22.

35. Author's interview with John Wiley.

36. *Jesse*, p. 23.

Chapter 2. Friends, Mentors, and Heroes (pp. 17–32)

1. Kenneth L. Kusmer, *A Ghetto Takes Shape: Black Cleveland, 1870–1930* (Urbana: University of Illinois Press, 1976), pp. 10, 178–79; Russell D. Davis, *Black Americans in Cleveland from George Peake to Carl B. Stokes, 1796–1969* (Washington, D.C.: Associated Publishers, 1972), pp. 221, 270.

2. Davis, *Black Americans in Cleveland*, p. 226.

3. Barbara Moro's interview with Jesse Owens; Josef J. Barton, *Peasants and Strangers: Italians, Rumanians, and Slovaks in an American City, 1890–1950* (Cambridge: Harvard University Press, 1975).

4. Moro's interview with Owens; Davis, *Black Americans in Cleveland*, p. 223; Kusmer, *Ghetto Takes Shape*, p. 221.

5. Harvard Sitkoff, *A New Deal for Blacks: The Emergence of Civil Rights as a National Issue*, Vol. I, *The Depression Decade* (New York: Oxford University Press, 1978), pp. 24–25; Kusmer, *Ghetto Takes Shape*, pp. 204–5; Moro's interview with Owens.

6. Larry Snyder, "My Boy Jesse," *Saturday Evening Post*, November 7, 1937, p. 14; *Jesse*, pp. 32–33.

7. Moro's interview with Owens.

8. *Ibid.*

9. Barbara Moro's interview with Ruth Owens; *Blackthink*, pp. 133–34; *I Have Changed*, p. 147.

10. ARCO interview with David Albritton.

11. Daniel J. Levinson, with Charlotte N. Darrow, Edward B. Klein, Maria H. Levinson, and Braxton McKee, *The Seasons of a Man's Life* (New York: Ballantine Books, 1978), pp. 97–101.

12. Harry Edwards, *The Struggle That Must Be: An Autobiography* (New York: Macmillan, 1980), p. 83; Moro's interview with Owens.

13. *Jesse*, pp. 30–32; *Blackthink*, p. 125; *I Have Changed*, pp. 28–29;

author's interview with Harriet Mae Bottorff; Moro's interview with Owens.

14. Author's interview with Harriet Mae Bottorff.

15. *Ibid.; Blackthink*, p. 96.

16. Jesse Owens, *Track and Field*, edited by Dick O'Connor (New York: Atheneum, 1976), p. 18; *Blackthink*, p. 126; *Jesse*, pp. 38–39, 40–41.

17. Cleveland *Call and Post*, May 30, 1935; *Chicago Defender*, December 21–27, 1963; *Blackthink*, p. 160.

18. *I Have Changed*, pp. 31, 81; Owens, *Track and Field*, p. 18.

19. *Blackthink*, pp. 96, 125; Owens, *Track and Field*, p. 115.

20. Dean B. Cromwell, *Championship Technique in Track and Field: A Book for Athletes, Coaches, and Spectators* (New York: McGraw-Hill, 1941), pp. 35–37.

21. Lawson Robertson, *Modern Athletics: How to Train for the Various Events of the Track and Field Programme* (New York: Charles Scribner's Sons, 1932), p. 17; J. Kenneth Doherty, *Modern Track and Field: Promotion, History, Methods* (New York: Prentice-Hall, 1953), pp. 54, 70; Cromwell, *Championship Technique*, pp. 30, 52; Owens, *Track and Field*, pp. 115–16; "This Is Your Life, Jesse Owens" (1960), ARCO film; *Chicago Defender*, October 11, 1983; David Dore's interview with Jesse Owens.

22. Benjamin Brawley, *Negro Builders and Heroes* (Chapel Hill: University of North Carolina Press, 1937), p. 257; *New York Amsterdam News*, August 29, 1936; A. S. "Doc" Young, *Negro Firsts in Sports* (Chicago: Johnson, 1963), pp. 82–87.

23. Davis, *Black Americans in Cleveland*, p. 267.

24. Edwards, *The Struggle That Must Be*, p. 86.

25. *New York Amsterdam News*, September 5, 1936; cf. William O. Johnson, Jr., *All That Glitters Is Not Gold: The Olympic Game* (New York: Putnams, 1972), p. 44. On the options available to the "new Negro" of the 1920s, see August Meier, *Negro Thought in America, 1880–1915: Racial Ideologies in the Age of Booker T. Washington* (Ann Arbor: University of Michigan Press, 1963), pp. 171–206.

26. Moro's interview with Owens.

27. Kusmer, *Ghetto Takes Shape*, pp. 204–5: Moro's interview with Owens; *Blackthink*, pp. 29, 91–92; *I Have Changed*, pp. 111–12; *Jesse*, p. 29.

28. Moro's interview with Owens; *Blackthink*, p. 91.

29. Moro's interview with Owens; *Jesse*, pp. 28–29.

30. Guichard Parris and Lester Brooks, *Blacks in the Cities: A*

History of the National Urban League (Boston: Little, Brown, 1971), p. 212; FBI Memo, October 2, 1956, no. 77–72778–22; Kusmer, *Ghetto Takes Shape*, p. 183.

31. Doherty, *Modern Track and Field*, p. 57; Charles H. L. Johnston, *Famous American Athletes of To-Day* (Boston: L.C. Page, 1934), p. 203; *Chicago Defender*, June 22, 1944; *New York Amsterdam News*, July 25, 1936; Vincent Matthews with Neil Amdur, *My Race Be Won* (New York: Charterhouse, 1974), p. 91.

32. FBI Memo, October 2, 1956, no. 77–72778–22; ARCO interview with David Albritton; Edwards, *The Struggle That Must Be*, p. 89.

33. Author's interview with Mel Walker; Moro's interview with Owens.

34. The *Cleveland Plain Dealer* is quoted in "The Saga of Jesse Owens," *The Crisis*, 43 (September 1936): 267; ARCO interview with David Albritton; Moro's interview with Owens; Cleveland *Gazette*, April 2, May 14, and May 28, 1932.

35. Sitkoff, *New Deal for Blacks*, pp. 330–31; Brawley, *Negro Builders and Heroes*, p. 257.

36. *Chicago Defender*, July 9, 1932; June 3, 1933; LeRoy Atkinson, *Famous American Athletes of Today*, 5th series (Boston: L.C. Page, 1937), p. 270; ARCO interview with David Albritton; Moro's interview with Owens; FBI Memo, October 2, 1956, no. 77–72778–24.

37. *Gazette*, August 27, 1932; Owens, *Track and Field*, p. 116; FBI Memo, October 2, 1956, no. 77–72778–8.

38. FBI Memo, October 2, 1956, nos. 77–72778–20, 22, 26; information by phone from Marriage License Bureau official, Erie, Pennsylvania, December 7, 1983.

39. *Blackthink*, p. 47; *I Have Changed*, pp. 52–54; *Jesse Owens Story*, p. 36; Moro's interview with Owens; Marriage License Bureau official, Erie.

40. Ray Leonard, "This Is My Championship," *Parade*, September 16, 1984, p. 7.

41. ARCO interview with David Albritton; *Chicago Defender*, May 5, 27, 1933; *Gazette*, May 6, 1933; Atkinson, *Famous American Athletes*, pp. 269, 275.

42. *Gazette*, April 1 and May 27, 1933.

43. *Chicago Defender*, June 10, 1933.

44. Atkinson, *Famous American Athletes*, pp. 266–67, 275; *Chicago Defender*, June 24, 1933.

45. "This Is Your Life, Jesse Owens"; *Chicago Defender*, June 24, 1933.

Chapter 3. College Pride and Prejudice (pp. 33–53)

1. Harvard Sitkoff, *A New Deal for Blacks: The Emergence of Civil Rights as a National Issue;* Vol. I, *The Depression Decade* (New York: Oxford University Press, 1978), pp. 329–330.

2. ARCO Interview with David Albritton.

3. Cleveland *Gazette,* June 10, 1933; author's interviews with LeRoy Walker, Mel Walker, and Eulace Peacock; Cleveland *Call and Post,* April 4, 1934; *Chicago Defender,* May 9, 1936.

4. Author's interview with Mel Walker; R. L. Quercetani, *A World History of Track and Field Athletics 1864–1964* (London: Oxford University Press, 1964), p. 16; *Chicago Defender,* August 5, 1933; "This Is Your Life, Jesse Owens," ARCO film; *Jesse Owens Story,* pp. 39–40; *Jesse,* p. 48; *Blackthink,* pp. 94–95; *New York Amsterdam News,* November 7, 1936.

5. James E. Pollard, *History of the Ohio State University: The Story of Its First Seventy-Five Years 1873–1948* (Columbus: The Ohio State University Press, 1952), p. 304; *Chicago Defender,* October 17, 1931.

6. *Gazette,* December 31, 1932, and January 14, February 4, and May 13, 1933; *Chicago Defender,* May 13, 1933; Pollard, *History of Ohio State,* p. 309.

7. *Chicago Defender,* August 5, 1933.

8. *Chicago Defender,* July 22 and August 12, 1933.

9. Author's interview with Harriet Bottorff; unidentified obituary clippings of Riley (1961) supplied by Harriet Bottorff; author's interview with William Heintz.

10. Letter from John L. Griffith to A. C. Callen, Clarence Updegraff, and W. J. Moenkhaus, September 3, 1935, and letter from Floyd A. Rowe to Ralph W. Aigler, October 28, 1935, both in the Ohio State University Archives; *Chicago Defender,* June 24, 1933.

11. Griffith and Rowe letters, Ohio State University Archives.

12. Griffith letter, Ohio State University Archives; *Blackthink,* p. 95; *Jesse,* p. 53.

13. ARCO interview with David Albritton; FBI Memo, October 2, 1956, no. 77–2778–22.

14. *Gazette,* August 26 and September 2, 1933; *Call and Post,* June 27, 1935.

15. *Cleveland Plain Dealer,* July 5, 1933; FBI Memo, October 2, 1956, no. 77–72778–22; Barbara Moro's interview with Jesse Owens; author's interviews with Gloria Hemphill.

16. *Chicago Defender*, September 9, 1953; *Gazette*, September 2, 9, and 23, 1933.

17. Pollard, *History of Ohio State*, p. 315; author's interviews with Charles Beetham and William Heintz.

18. Author's interviews with Charles Beetham, Mel Walker, and William Heintz; *Blackthink*, pp. 15–16; ARCO interview with David Albritton.

19. *Chicago Defender*, August 5, 1933; FBI Memo, October 4, 1956, no. 77–72778–21; author's interview with Mel Walker.

20. Moro's interview with Owens.

21. *Jesse Owens Story*, p. 44; Moro's Interview with Owens; "This Is Your Life, Jesse Owens"; *Call and Post*, January 16, 1934; Ohio State University Registrar's report in FBI Memo, October 4, 1956, no. 77–72778–21.

22. Pollard, *History of Ohio State*, pp. 302, 310, 312.

23. *Ibid.*, pp. 302, 305, 309, 322.

24. *Ibid.*, pp. 309, 316; Moro's interview with Owens.

25. Pollard, *History of Ohio State*, p. 313; author's interview with Charles Beetham.

26. Moro's interview with Owens.

27. *Blackthink*, pp. 13–14; Moro's interview with Owens.

28. Pollard, *History of Ohio State*, pp. 295, 307, 312.

29. Jack W. Berryman and Stephen H. Hardy, "The College Sports Scene," pp. 63–76 in William J. Baker and John M. Carroll, eds., *Sports in Modern America* (St. Louis: River City, 1981), esp. p. 66; Pollard, *History of Ohio State*, p. 295; *Call and Post*, February 10, 1934; *Gazette*, February 10, 1934.

30. Harold Eugene Ramsey, "A History of Track Athletics at the Ohio State University," unpublished M.A. thesis, Ohio State University, 1952, pp. 42–45; Larry Snyder, "My Boy Jesse," *Saturday Evening Post*, November 7, 1937, p. 14.

31. J. Kenneth Doherty, *Modern Track and Field: Promotion, History, Methods* (New York: Prentice-Hall, 1953), p. 69.

32. Larry Snyder, "World's Greatest Athlete: How He Trains," *Scholastic Coach*, March 1936, pp. 7, 32; Doherty, *Modern Track and Field*, pp. 52, 68; Larry Snyder, "Jumping Jesse," *Scholastic Coach*, March 1937, p. 16.

33. *Call and Post*, February 24, March 3, and March 24, 1934; *Gazette*, March 3, April 28, and May 12 and 19, 1934.

34. *Call and Post*, May 12, 1934; *Gazette*, May 12, 1934.

35. Author's interview with William Heintz; *Blackthink*, p. 133; ARCO interview with David Albritton; author's interview with Mel Walker.

36. *New York Times*, August 28, 1956, and August 7 and 13, 1936.

37. Dean Cromwell with Al Wesson, *Championship Techniques in Track and Field: A Book for Athletes, Coaches, and Spectators* (New York: McGraw-Hill, 1941), pp. 6, 30–31.

38. LeRoy Atkinson, *Famous American Athletes of Today* (Boston: L. C. Page, 1937), p. 272; ARCO interviews with David Albritton and Marty Glickman.

39. Snyder, "My Boy Jesse," p. 100.

40. Snyder, "World's Greatest Athlete," p. 7; *idem,* "My Boy Jesse," p. 100.

41. Author's interviews with Charles Beetham and Mel Walker; Snyder, "My Boy Jesse," p. 100.

42. *Gazette,* June 9, 16, and 23 and July 7, 1934; *Call and Post,* June 23 and July 7, 1934.

43. *Jesse,* p. 154; *Call and Post,* July 28, 1934.

44. *Gazette,* September 22 and November 10, 1934; *Call and Post,* April 27 and July 4, 1935.

45. Author's interview with Charles Beetham; ARCO interviews with Marty Glickman and David Albritton.

46. *Gazette,* March 3, 1934; Snyder, "My Boy Jesse," p. 15; author's interviews with Mel Walker and Eulace Peacock.

47. Atkinson, *Famous American Athletes,* p. 276; author's interview with Mel Walker; *Call and Post,* February 16 and 23 and March 3, 1935; *Chicago Defender,* March 2, 1935 and February 20, 1954; *Gazette,* February 16 and 23 and March 2, 1935.

48. *Call and Post,* February 16, 1935.

49. Author's interview with Eulace Peacock; Quercetani, *World History of Track and Field,* p. 19; Cromwell with Wesson, *Championship Techniques,* p. 42.

50. Author's interview with Eulace Peacock; *Chicago Defender,* May 4, 1935.

51. Atkinson, *Famous American Athletes,* p. 273; *Call and Post,* January 9, 1936; *Gazette,* May 11, 1935.

52. Quercetani, *World History of Track and Field,* p. 18; Doherty, *Modern Track and Field,* p. 142; *Call and Post,* May 30, 1935; *Gazette,* June 1, 1935.

53. *Jesse,* p. 27; *Jesse Owens Story,* pp. 47–48; Snyder, "My Boy Jesse," p. 14; author's interview with Roscoe C. Hildreth.

54. Author's interviews with Mel Walker and Charles Beetham; Moro's interview with Owens.

55. Doherty, *Modern Track and Field*, pp. 45, 389, 396; "This Is Your Life, Jesse Owens"; Snyder, "My Boy Jesse," p. 14.

56. Doherty, *Modern Track and Field*, pp. 55, 101; *Chicago Defender*, July 17, 1954.

57. *Chicago Defender*, June 13, 1953; author's interviews with Stan Saplin and Herbert Douglas.

58. Moro's interview with Owens; Snyder, "My Boy Jesse," p. 15; *Call and Post*, May 30, 1935.

59. Atkinson, *Famous American Athletes*, pp. 270–71; *Call and Post*, May 30, 1935.

60. *Call and Post*, May 30, 1935; *Gazette*, June 1 and 8, 1935.

61. *Call and Post*, June 27, 1935; typescript letter from Delbert Oberteuffer to L. W. St. John, August 20, 1936, Ohio State University Archives.

Chapter 4. Coping with Pressure (pp. 54–72)

1. Barbara Moro's interview with Jesse Owens.

2. *Ibid.;* author's interview with Charles Beetham.

3. Cleveland *Gazette*, June 1, 1935; *Los Angeles Times*, June 16, 23, and 28, 1935; LeRoy Atkinson, *Famous American Heroes of Today* (Boston: L. C. Page, 1937), p. 217.

4. *Los Angeles Times*, June 16, 21, 24, and 28, 1935; author's interviews with Eulace Peacock and Herb Douglas.

5. *Los Angeles Times*, June 16, 1935.

6. Moro's interview with Owens; author's interview with Charles Beetham.

7. Moro's interview with Owens; Cleveland *Call and Post*, June 27 and July 4, 1935.

8. Author's interviews with Eulace Peacock and Charles Beetham.

9. Letter from Floyd A. Rowe to Gustavus T. Kirby, December 9, 1935, Ohio State University Archives.

10. R. L. Quercetani, *A World History of Track and Field Athletes 1864–1964* (London: Oxford University Press, 1964), p. 19; *Los Angeles Times*, July 5 and 6, 1935; J. Kenneth Doherty, *Modern Track and Field: Promotion, History, Methods* (New York: Prentice-Hall, 1953), p. 67.

11. *Gazette*, July 13, 1935; Atkinson, *Famous American Athletes*, p.

274; FBI Memo, September 25, 1956, no. 77–72778–7; *Los Angeles Times,* July 6, 1935.

12. Moro's interview with Owens; Cleveland *Call and Post,* July 11, 1935.

13. *Cleveland Plain Dealer,* July 6, 1935; *Call and Post,* July 11, 1935; *Gazette,* July 13, 1935; FBI Memo, October 2, 1936, no. 77–72778–22.

14. *Los Angeles Times,* July 6, 1935.

15. *Los Angeles Times,* July 10, 1935; *Gazette,* July 27, 1935; *Call and Post,* February 16 and August 22, 1935.

16. *Call and Post,* August 22, 1935.

17. The details of this controversy are pieced together from letters in the Ohio State University Archives: John L. Griffin to A. C. Collen, Clarence Updegraff, and W. J. Moenkhaus, September 3, 1935; Ralph W. Aigler to Floyd A. Rowe, October 26, 1935; Rowe to Aigler, October 28, 1935; Rowe to Gustavus T. Kirby, December 9, 1935.

18. *Gazette,* June 8, 1935; *Cleveland Plain Dealer,* August 10, 1935.

19. *New York Times,* August 11, 1935.

20. Rowe to Aigler letter.

21. Moro's interview with Owens.

22. *New York Times,* August 13, 1935.

23. *Gazette,* August 17 and September 7, 1935; Rowe to Kirby letter; Atkinson, *Famous American Athletes,* p. 274: *New York Times,* September 1, 1935.

24. *Gazette,* August 17 and September 7, 1935; Rowe to Aigler letter.

25. *New York Times,* August 10, 1935.

26. *New York Times,* December 28, 1935.

27. Much of the following account of the American boycott movement is taken from Richard D. Mandell, *The Nazi Olympics* (New York: Macmillan, 1971), pp. 69–82.

28. For Brundage's role in the controversy, see Allen Guttmann, *The Games Must Go On: Avery Brundage and the Olympic Movement* (New York: Columbia University Press, 1984), pp. 66–78, 80–81.

29. *Gazette,* February 10 and 17 and November 17, 1934.

30. David K. Wiggins, "The 1936 Olympic Games in Berlin: The Response of America's Black Press," *Research Quarterly for Exercise and Sport,* 54, no. 3 (1983): 279–82.

31. *New York Amsterdam News,* August 23 and October 26, 1935; *Chicago Defender,* December 7, 1935; *Gazette,* December 7, 1935; *New York Times,* December 4 and 7, 1935.

32. *Call and Post,* November 14, 1935; unidentified newspaper clipping, November 10, 1935, in the Avery Brundage Collection, University of Illinois Archives.

33. *Call and Post,* January 9, 1936.

34. *Gazette,* December 14, 1936; *New York Times,* January 27, 1936; *Chicago Defender,* February 1, 1936.

35. *New York Herald-Tribune,* December 29, 1935; *Call and Post,* January 2, 1936; *Gazette,* January 4, 1936.

36. *Call and Post,* January 23 and March 12, 1936; FBI Memo, September 27, 1956, no. 77–72778–16.

37. ARCO interview with David Albritton; *Call and Post,* March 19, 1936; *Blackthink,* pp. 13–18.

38. *Call and Post,* March 25 and April 2, 1936.

39. *Chicago Defender,* March 14 and 28, 1936.

40. *Chicago Defender,* April 11, 1936.

41. *Call and Post,* January 2, 1936; *Chicago Defender,* April 25, 1936, and May 29, 1937.

42. *New York Amsterdam News,* May 2, 1936; *Chicago Defender,* May 2, 1936; *Call and Post,* April 23, 1936; author's interview with Eulace Peacock.

43. *New York Amsterdam News,* May 9, 16, 23, and 30, 1936; *Chicago Defender,* May 9 and 30, 1936; *Call and Post,* May 28, 1936.

44. *New York Amsterdam News,* May 9 and June 20, 1936; *Chicago Defender,* June 20, 1936.

45. *New York Amsterdam News,* June 20 and July 4, 1936; *New York Times,* June 27, 1936.

46. *Chicago Defender,* July 11, 1936.

47. "Trials and Tryouts," *Time,* July 20, 1936, pp. 50–54.

48. *Call and Post,* July 16, 1936; *Chicago Defender,* July 25, 1936.

49. *New York Amsterdam News,* July 18, 1936.

50. "Trials and Tryouts," p. 50; author's interviews with Mel Walker, William Heintz, Charles Beetham, and Eulace Peacock.

51. *I Have Changed,* p. 40.

Chapter 5. Bound for Glory (pp. 73–88)

1. On Louis, see Chris Mead, *Champion: Joe Louis, Black Hero in White America* (New York: Charles Scribner's Sons, 1985).

2. Cleveland *Call and Post,* May 31, 1934; "Joe Louis and Jesse Owens," *The Crisis,* 42 (August 1935): 241.

3. *Call and Post,* August 1, 1935.

4. *New York Amsterdam News,* June 27, 1936.

5. Letters from Avery Brundage to L. W. St. John, September 9, 1935, and from L. W. St. John to Joseph E. Raycroft, November 27, 1935, Ohio State University Archives.

6. Memo from John L. Griffith to NCAA Finance Committee District Chairmen, January 20, 1936; letter from Brundage to St. John, September 9, 1935; Memo from Frank G. McCormick to Big Ten Conference athletic directors, May 20, 1936, Ohio State Archives.

7. Letters from Frank G. McCormick to L. W. St. John, May 15, 1936, and June 19, 1936, Ohio State Archives.

8. Memo from John L. Griffith to Big Ten Conference athletic directors, June 24, 1936, Ohio State Archives.

9. Letters from L. W. St. John to Floyd A. Rowe, April 30, 1936; from Rowe to Edward Bang, May 1, 1936; and from Bang to St. John, May 2, 1936, Ohio State Archives.

10. Bang to St. John, May 2, 1936.

11. Author's interview with Francis L. Johnson; Jesse Owens manuscript diary, entry for July 15, 1936, Atlantic Richfield Company archives; *Blackthink,* p. 198.

12. Owens diary, July 15, 1936; author's interview with Francis L. Johnson; Alfred R. Masters, as told to Frank J. Taylor, "Olympic Pains," p. 12, from an unidentified magazine article xeroxed from the files of Stan Saplin.

13. Owens diary, July 16–22, 1936; *Amsterdam News,* July 25, 1936.

14. Allen Guttman, *The Games Must Go On: Avery Brundage and the Olympic Movement* (New York: Columbia University Press, 1984), p. 24; Owens diary, July 16, 1936; author's interview with Donald Ray Lash; ARCO interview with Marty Glickman.

15. Barbara Moro's interview with Jesse Owens; author's interview with Forrest Towns.

16. Author's interview with Francis L. Johnson; John Kieran, *The Story of the Olympic Games, 776* B.C.–*1936* A.D. (New York: Lippincott, 1936), pp. 258, 262.

17. For an extended account of the Eleanor Holm Jarrett case, see Richard D. Mandell, *The Nazi Olympics* (New York: Macmillan, 1971), pp. 242–48.

18. For contemporary coverage of these details, see *Newsweek,* August 1, 1936, p. 20, and *Time,* August 3, 1936, p. 21.

19. Jesse Owens with Paul Neimark, "My Greatest Olympic Prize,"

Reader's Digest, October 1960, p. 132; *Chicago Tribune*, October 10, 1978.

20. Mandell, *Nazi Olympics*, p. 225; Alexander M. Weyand, *The Olympic Pageant* (New York: Macmillan, 1952), p. 253; *Call and Post*, August 1, 1936.

21. Moro's interview with Owens; Larry Snyder, "My Boy Jesse," *Saturday Evening Post*, November 7, 1937, p. 92; *Call and Post*, August 1, 1936, *New York Times*, August 7, 1936.

22. Mandell, *Nazi Olympics*, pp. 141–43.

23. *New York Times*, August 16, 1936.

24. Kieran, *Olympic Games*, pp. 236–37; Mandell, *Nazi Olympics*, pp. 88–89; Owens diary, July 25, 1936; Moro's interview with Owens.

25. Owens diary, July 25–27, 1936.

26. Moro's interview with Owens; author's interview with William Heintz; ARCO interview with David Albritton.

27. Snyder, "My Boy Jesse," p. 97; *Call and Post*, August 1, 1936.

28. ARCO interviews with Bud Greenspan, Marty Glickman, and David Albritton; Snyder, "My Boy Jesse," p. 15.

29. Cleveland *Gazette*, August 1, 1936; *Chicago Tribune*, 1968 (date unidentified), from the xeroxed file of Stan Saplin.

30. Snyder, "My Boy Jesse," p. 15.

31. *New York Amsterdam News*, August 1, 8, 1936.

32. Mandell, *Nazi Olympics*, p. 147; Wayand, *Olympic Pageant*, p. 255.

33. Kieran, *Olympic Games*, p. 228; Mandell, *Nazi Olympics*, pp. 148–50.

34. *Die Olympischen Spiele 1936 in Berlin und Garmisch-Partenkirchen* (Hamburg: Cigaretten-Bilderdienst, 1936), pp. 14–15.

36. Mandell, *Nazi Olympics*, pp. 129–37, 151; Kieran, *Olympic Games*, p. 229; Weyand, *Olympic Pageant*, p. 256.

36. Glenn B. Infield, *Leni Riefenstahl: The Fallen Film Goddess* (New York: Crowell, 1976), pp. 113–43; Mandell, *Nazi Olympics*, pp. 250–74.

37. *New York Times*, August 6, 1936; *Die Olympischen Spiele 1936*, pp. 162–63.

38. For the clearest day-by-day sequence of events, see John Lucas, *The Modern Olympic Games* (New York: A. A. Barnes, 1980), pp. 124–30.

39. Mandell, *Nazi Olympics*, p. 145.

40. *Chicago Defender*, May 13–19, 1961.

Chapter 6. The Berlin Blitz (pp. 89–108)

1. John Kieran, *The Story of the Olympic Games, 776 B.C.–1936 A.D.* (New York: Lippincott, 1936), pp. 240–44; *New York Amsterdam News,* August 14, 1936; unidentified clipping, August 4, 1936, Avery Brundage Collection, University of Illinois Archives.

2. *New York Times,* August 3 and 4, 1936; *Call and Post,* August 9, 1936.

3. Grantland Rice, *The Tumult and the Shouting: My Life in Sport* (New York: Barnes, 1954), p. 253; ARCO interview with Bud Greenspan. For a few examples of the numerous uses Owens later made of the "snub" story, see *Chicago Defender,* April 1–7, 1961, and October 26–November 1, 1963, and *Jesse Owens Story,* p. 11.

4. *Die Olympischen Spiele 1936 in Berlin und Garmisch-Partenkirchen* (Hamburg: Cigaretten-Bilderdienst, 1936), pp. 26–27; *New York Times,* August 2, 3, and 5, 1936; *Chicago Defender,* August 8, 1936; *Gastonia* (N.C.) *Daily Gazette,* August 3, 1936.

5. *Chicago Daily News,* May 11, 1972; Larry Snyder, "My Boy Jesse," *Saturday Evening Post,* November 7, 1937, p. 97; *New York Times,* August 27, 1951.

6. *New York Times,* August 3, 1936.

7. Snyder, "My Boy Jesse," p. 15.

8. "Jesse Owens Returns to Berlin," TV documentary, ARCO archives; unidentified newspaper clipping from the Avery Brundage Collection, University of Illinois Archives; Owens's interview with David Condon, *Chicago Tribune,* 1968.

9. *Chicago Defender,* August 8, 1936.

10. Cleveland *Call and Post,* April 15, 1937; "Olympic Games," *Time,* August 17, 1936, p. 37; *New York Times,* January 27, 1950; Moro's interview with Owens.

11. Unidentified newspaper clipping, August 23, 1936, from the Avery Brundage Collection; *Chicago Defender,* August 8, 1936.

12. Dean Cromwell with Al Wesson, *Championship Techniques in Track and Field: A Book for Athletes, Coaches, and Spectators* (New York: McGraw-Hill, 1941), pp. 224–25; *Die Olympischen Spiele 1936,* p. 46; Jesse Owens with Paul Neimark, "My Greatest Olympic Prize," *Reader's Digest,"* October 1960, p. 132.

13. Owens, *Track and Field,* p. 106; Owens with Neimark, "My Greatest Olympic Prize," p. 132; *Blackthink,* pp. 185–86; *Jesse,* p. 63.

14. *New York Times,* August 5, 1936. For essentially the same report, see the *Chicago Defender,* August 8, 1936; Kieran, *Olympic Games,* pp. 246–47.

15. Owens with Neimark, "My Greatest Olympic Prize," pp. 132–35; *Blackthink,* pp. 184, 188–89; *Jesse,* pp. 62, 71–72; "Jesse Owens Returns to Berlin."

16. Rice, *Tumult and the Shouting,* p. 252; *New York Times,* August 5, 1936.

17. R. L. Quercetani, *A World History of Track and Field Athletics 1864–1964* (London: Oxford University Press, 1964), p. 252; Rice, *Tumult and the Shouting,* pp. 252–53.

18. Moro's interview with Owens; Jesse Owens, "Olympic Friendship," *Illinois History,* 14, no. 3 (December 1960): 65; *Blackthink,* p. 191; *New York Times,* August 5, 1936; unidentified clipping of August 5, 1936, in Avery Brundage Collection, University of Illinois Archives.

19. *Blackthink,* p. 191; *New York Times,* August 5, 1936.

20. Owens with Neimark, "My Greatest Olympic Prize," p. 134; *Blackthink,* p. 190; *Jesse,* pp. 72–73.

21. *New York Times,* August 7, 1936; *Blackthink,* p. 190.

22. Letter from Alice Grab (Tel Aviv) to the author, December 5, 1982; Kieran, *Olympic Games,* p. 253.

23. Richard S. Kennedy and Paschal Reeves, eds., *The Notebooks of Thomas Wolfe,* 2 vol. (Chapel Hill: University of North Carolina Press, 1970), II: 913–14.

24. Kieran, *Olympic Games,* p. 254.

25. Martha Dodd, *Through Embassy Eyes* (New York: Harcourt, Brace, 1939), p. 212; letter from Alice Grab to the author; Kieran, *Olympic Games,* pp. 25, 254.

26. Author's interview with Mack Robinson; *New York Times,* August 6, 1936.

27. Dodd, *Through Embassy Eyes,* p. 212; Andrew Turnbull, *Thomas Wolfe* (New York: Thomas Scribner's Sons, 1967), p. 234.

28. Kieran, *Olympic Games,* p. 255.

29. For the victors in the various events, see Lord Killanin and John Rodda, eds., *The Olympic Games: 80 Years of People, Events, and Records* (London: Barrie & Jenkins, 1976), pp. 230–35.

30. *New York Times,* August 6, 1936; Kieran, *Olympic Games,* pp. 257–62.

31. *New York Times,* August 9, 1936.

32. *New York Amsterdam News*, July 25, 1936; ARCO interview with Marty Glickman; author's interview with Mack Robinson.

33. William O. Johnson, Jr., *All That Glitters Is Not Gold: The Olympic Game* (New York: Putnam's, 1972), pp. 178, 182.

34. *New York Times*, August 8, 1936; Johnson, *All That Glitters*, p. 183.

35. Johnson, *All That Glitters*, pp. 178–79.

36. *Ibid.*, p. 179; ARCO interview with Marty Glickman.

37. Johnson, *All That Glitters*, pp. 181–82; ARCO interview with Marty Glickman. Both Owens and Dave Albritton agreed with Glickman, of course. Johnson, *All That Glitters*, p. 180; ARCO interview with Dave Albritton.

38. ARCO interview with Marty Glickman.

39. Allen Guttmann, *The Games Must Go On: Avery Brundage and the Olympic Movement* (New York: Columbia University Press, 1984), p. 79; Johnson, *All That Glitters*, p. 184; Kieran, *Olympic Games*, p. 267.

40. Kieran, *Olympic Games*, pp. 266–67; *New York Times*, August 10, 1936; author's interview with Forrest Towns.

41. Quercetani, *World History of Track and Field*, p. 326; *New York Times*, August 9 and 10, 1936; Johnson, *All That Glitters*, p. 181.

42. Paul Gallico, *A Farewell to Sport* (New York: Knopf, 1938), p. 309.

43. "Jesse Owens Returns to Berlin"; Gordon Lindsay, "Gold Digger of 1936," *Los Angeles*, June 1983, p. 269; Cleveland *Gazette*, August 15, 1936.

44. Kieran, *Olympic Games*, p. 270; Mandell, *Nazi Olympics*, pp. 200–201, 206.

45. Mandell, *Nazi Olympics*, pp. 206–7.

46. *Ibid.*, p. 277; Kieran, *Olympic Games*, p. 270.

47. *New York Times*, August 18, 1936.

48. On that brief "hiatus in German aggressiveness" after the 1936 Olympics, see Mandell, *Nazi Olympics*, pp. 282, 290.

Chapter 7. A Champion's Reward (pp. 109–128)

1. *Chicago Defender*, August 22 and 29, 1936.

2. Allen Guttmann, *The Games Must Go On: Avery Brundage and the Olympic Movement* (New York: Columbia University Press, 1984), p. 80.

3. Alexander M. Weyand, *The Olympic Pageant* (New York: Macmillan, 1952), p. 252; *New York Times,* August 19, 1936.

4. Author's interview with William G. Heintz; Larry Snyder, "My Boy Jesse," *Saturday Evening Post,* November 7, 1937, p. 97.

5. Snyder, "My Boy Jesse," p. 97.

6. Barbara Moro's interview with Jesse Owens; *Blackthink,* p. 198; *New York Times,* August 11, 1936; *Chicago Defender,* August 15, 1936.

7. Snyder, "My Boy Jesse," p. 98; *New York Times,* August 17 and 18, 1936.

8. *New York Times,* August 11, 1936; Snyder, "My Boy Jesse," p. 97; *Amsterdam News,* August 15, 1936.

9. Snyder, "My Boy Jesse," p. 97; *New York Times,* August 18, 1936; *New York Amsterdam News,* August 15, 1936.

10. Snyder, "My Boy Jesse," p. 98; *New York Times,* August 13, 1936.

11. *New York Times,* August 16, 1936; Snyder, "My Boy Jesse," p. 98.

12. Author's interview with John Woodruff.

13. *New York Times,* August 18, 1936; *Chicago Defender,* August 29, 1936.

14. *New York Times,* August 18, 1936; *Chicago Tribune,* August 18, 1936.

15. Guttmann, *Games Must Go On,* pp. 32–37.

16. *Chicago Defender,* August 22, 1936; *New York Times,* August 18, 1936.

17. Western Union cablegram, Larry Snyder to L. W. St. John, August 18, 1936, in Ohio State University Archives; Snyder, "My Boy Jesse," p. 98.

18. "Olympic Games," *Time,* August 24, 1936, p. 58; *Chicago Tribune,* August 18, 1936.

19. *New York Times,* August 16, 1936; *New York Amsterdam News,* August 22, 1936; R. L. Quercetani, *A World History of Track and Field Athletics 1864–1964* (London: Oxford University Press, 1964), p. 22.

20. Unidentified newspaper clipping, August 17, 1936, Avery Brundage Collection, University of Illinois Archives; Snyder, "My Boy Jesse," p. 98. The *New York Times,* August 18, 1936, erroneously reported that Brundage spoke to Owens rather than Snyder.

21. William O. Johnson, Jr., *All That Glitters Is Not Gold: The Olympic Game* (New York: Putnam's, 1972), pp. 123–24; Guttmann, *Games Must Go On,* p. 35.

22. Unidentified newspaper clipping, August 17, 1936, Brundage Collection; Snyder, "My Boy Jesse," p. 98; *New York Times*, August 18, 1936.

23. *New York Times*, August 18, 1936.

24. *Chicago Defender*, August 22, 1936; *New York Times*, August 17, 1936.

25. Cleveland *Call and Post*, August 20, 1936.

26. *New York Amsterdam News*, August 22, 1936; *New York Times*, August 14, 18, 1936.

27. *Chicago Defender*, August 15, 1936; *Call and Post*, August 20, 1936; *New York Amsterdam News*, August 22, 1936; "Olympic Games," p. 58; *New York Times*, August 16, 1936; Snyder, "My Boy Jesse," p. 100.

28. *Chicago Tribune*, August 18, 1936; unidentified newspaper clipping, Brundage Collection.

29. *Chicago Tribune*, August 20, 1936; *New York Amsterdam News*, August 22, 1936; unidentified newspaper clipping, August 18, 1936, Brundage Collection; *New York Times*, August 18, 1936.

30. *Boston Herald-American*, date unidentified, Brundage Collection; *Call and Post*, August 13, 1936; *New York Times*, August 18, 1936; *New York Amsterdam News*, August 15, December 5, 1936.

31. *Boston Herald-American*, date unidentified, Brundage Collection; *New York Amsterdam News*, August 15, 1936; *Call and Post*, August 20, 1936.

32. *New York Times*, August 18, 1936; letter from L. W. St. John to Roy Weed, August 17, 1936, Ohio State University Archives.

33. Letter from L. W. St. John to Larry Snyder, August 17, 1936, Ohio State University Archives.

34. Letter from Delbert Oberteuffer to L. W. St. John, August 20, 1936, Ohio State University Archives.

35. *New York Herald-Tribune*, August 25, 1936.

36. *Chicago Defender*, August 29, 1936.

37. "Olympic Games," p. 58; *Chicago Defender*, August 19, 1936.

38. *Chicago Defender*, August 19, 1936; *Call and Post*, August 27, 1936.

39. Unidentified newspaper clipping, August 14, 1936, Brundage Collection.

40. *New York Times*, August 25, 1936; *Chicago Defender*, August 19, 1936; *New York Amsterdam News*, August 29, 1936.

41. *Chicago Defender*, August 1, 1931; *New York Amsterdam News*, December 19, 1936.

42. *New York Herald-Tribune,* August 25, 1936; *Chicago Defender,* August 29, 1936; *New York Times,* August 25, 1936.

43. *Chicago Defender,* August 15, 1936; *Call and Post,* August 27, 1936; *New York Times,* August 26, 1936.

44. *Cleveland Plain Dealer,* August 26, 1936; *Chicago Defender,* August 29, 1936; *Call and Post,* August 27, 1936.

45. *New York Times,* August 29, 1936.

46. Moro's interview with Owens; *Chicago Defender,* September 12, 1936; *New York Times,* August 30, 1936.

47. *New York Times,* September 2, 1936; *New York Herald-Tribune,* September 2 and 13, 1936; *Chicago Defender,* September 12, 1936.

48. *New York Times,* August 19, 20, and 21 and September 3, 1936.

49. *New York Herald-Tribune,* September 4, 1936; *New York Times,* September 4, 1936.

50. *Chicago Defender,* September 12 and 19, 1936.

51. *Jesse,* p. 82; Johnson, *All That Glitters,* p. 49; "Jesse Owens Returns to Berlin."

52. *New York Times,* September 4, 1936; *New York Amsterdam News,* September 5, 1936; *Chicago Defender,* September 19, 1936.

Chapter 8. Tarnished Gold (pp. 129–145)

1. *Chicago Defender,* September 12, 1936; *New York Amsterdam News,* September 19, 1936.

2. Cleveland *Call and Post,* September 17, 1936; *New York Times,* November 22, 1964.

3. Larry Snyder, "My Boy Jesse," *Saturday Evening Post,* November 7, 1937, p. 100; *New York Herald-Tribune,* September 2, 1936; *New York Times,* September 2, 1936; *New York Amsterdam News,* September 5, 1936.

4. Author's interviews with Mel Walker and Eulace Peacock; *New York Times,* September 6 and 13, 1936.

5. *New York Herald-Tribune,* September 4, 1936; *New York Amsterdam News,* September 12, 1936.

6. *New York Times,* September 13, 1936.

7. *New York Times,* September 15, 1936.

8. *Call and Post,* September 17, 1936; *New York Times,* September 13, 15, and 16, 1936.

9. "Olympic Games," *Time,* August 17, 1936, p. 37; *Chicago Defender,* September 19, 1936.

10. "Jesse Owens Dashes to G.O.P. in Colored Vote Race," *Newsweek*, September 12, 1936, p. 18.

11. *New York Times*, August 22, 1936; *Chicago Defender*, August 29, 1936.

12. *Chicago Defender*, August 29, 1936.

13. *Chicago Defender*, August 29, 1936. Grant Ward's reference to "the Landon–Bricker club" pertained to John G. Bricker, Ohio's Republican gubernatorial candidate. *Call and Post*, October 8, 1936.

14. *New York Herald-Tribune*, August 22, 1936; *Chicago Defender*, August 29, 1936.

15. "Black Game," *Time*, August 17, 1936, pp. 10–11.

16. Harvard Sitkoff, *A New Deal for Blacks: The Emergence of Civil Rights as a National Issue*, Vol. I, *The Depression Decade* (New York: Oxford University Press, 1978), p. 42; "Jesse Owens Dashes to G.O.P.," p. 19; James Weldon Johnson, *Negro Americans, What Now?* (New York: Viking Press, 1934), p. 61.

17. Sitkoff, *New Deal for Blacks*, pp. 40–41, 90; Nancy J. Weiss, *Farewell to the Party of Lincoln: Black Politics in the Age of FDR* (Princeton, N.J.: Princeton University Press, 1983), pp. 34–119; *Chicago Defender*, May 9, 1936.

18. Sitkoff, *New Deal for Blacks*, pp. 43–52; *Baltimore Afro-American* quoted in *New York Amsterdam News*, October 24, 1936.

19. Donald R. McCoy, *Landon of Kansas* (Lincoln: University of Nebraska Press, 1966), p. 377; *New York Amsterdam News*, October 24, 1936.

20. *New York Times*, September 3, 1936; *New York Amsterdam News*, September 5, 1936; "Owens for Landon," *Time*, September 14, 1936, p. 15.

21. *Call and Post*, September 16, November 26, 1936; Arthur M. Johnson, *The Challenge of Change: The Sun Oil Company, 1945–1979* (Columbus: Ohio State University Press, 1983), pp. 10, 18; author's interview with Mel Walker.

22. "Owens for Landon," p. 16; *Call and Post*, September 17, 1936.

23. *Call and Post*, September 10 and 17, 1936; *Chicago Defender*, September 19, 1936; McCoy, *Landon of Kansas*, p. 297; *New York Times*, September 29, 1936.

24. "People," *Time*, September 28, 1936, p. 49; William O. Johnson, Jr., *All That Glitters Is Not Gold: The Olympic Game* (New York: Putnam's, 1972), p. 45.

25. *New York Amsterdam News*, October 31, 1936; *Chicago Defender*, October 17, 1936.

26. *Chicago Defender,* October 10, 17, 1936.

27. *Chicago Defender,* October 17, 1936; *New York Amsterdam News,* October 30, 1936.

28. Sitkoff, *New Deal for Blacks,* pp. 95–96; Weiss, *Farewell to the Party of Lincoln,* pp. 180–208; Johnson, *All That Glitters,* p. 45.

29. *Call and Post,* October 1, November 26, 1936, and October 6, 1938; Barbara Moro's interview with Jesse Owens; *New York Times,* November 21, 1936; *Chicago Defender,* October 15, 1938.

30. Emma S. Waytinsky, *Profile of the U.S. Economy: A Survey of Growth and Change* (New York: Praeger, 1967), p. 142; *Call and Post,* August 22, 1936.

31. *Cleveland Plain Dealer,* December 2, 1936; *Chicago Defender,* December 12, 1936; author's interview with Russell Brown; *New York Times,* December 2, 1936.

32. *Cleveland Plain Dealer,* December 25, 1936; *Chicago Defender,* December 26, 1936.

33. Johnson, *All That Glitters,* p. 49; manuscript letter from Charles Riley to Jesse Owens, undated, in the possession of Harriet Mae Bottorff; author's interview with Bottorff.

34. *New York Amsterdam News,* October 31, 1936; *Chicago Defender,* November 21, December 5, 1936; *Cleveland Plain Dealer,* December 2, 1936; *Call and Post,* November 26, 1936; author's interview with Harold Gast.

35. *Chicago Defender,* December 19, 1936; *New York Times,* December 15, 1936.

36. *Call and Post,* October 11, 1936.

37. Cleveland *Gazette,* November 21, 1936; *New York Amsterdam News,* January 2, 1937.

38. *New York Amsterdam News,* December 26, 1936.

39. *New York Times,* December 27, 1936; *Chicago Defender,* January 2, 1937; *New York Amsterdam News,* January 2, 1937.

40. Johnson, *All That Glitters,* p. 48; *Jesse,* p. 84; *Blackthink,* p. 49; *New York Times,* December 27, 1936; *Chicago Defender,* January 2, 1937.

41. *Jesse,* p. 94; *Blackthink,* p. 50; Johnson, *All That Glitters,* pp. 47–48.

42. *Blackthink,* p. 50; *Chicago Defender,* January 2, 1937; *New York Amsterdam News,* January 2, 1937.

43. *Jesse,* p. 94.

44. *New York Amsterdam News,* January 9, 1937; *New York Times,* December 31, 1936.

45. *Call and Post*, November 19, 1936; *New York Amsterdam News*, October 24, 1936.

46. *New York Times*, December 31, 1936; *New York Amsterdam News*, January 9, 1937.

Chapter 9.   Chasing Rainbows (pp. 146–162)

1. Quoted in *New York Amsterdam News*, January 9, 1937.

2. William O. Johnson, Jr., *All That Glitters Is Not Gold: The Olympic Game* (New York, Putnam, 1972), pp. 192–93; *New York Times*, August 26, 1936.

3. Paul Gallico, *A Farewell to Sport* (New York: Knopf, 1938), p. 299.

4. But see John Hope Franklin, *From Slavery to Freedom: A History of American Negroes* (New York: Knopf, 1947), pp. 489–511.

5. William Oscar Johnson, "A Star Was Born," *Sports Illustrated*, July 18, 1984, pp. 137–59.

6. Charles H. L. Johnston, *Famous American Athletes of To-Day* (Boston: L. C. Page, 1934), pp. 196–200: Cleveland *Gazette*, February 11 and April 12, 1933; Cleveland *Call and Post*, August 12, 1935; Johnson, *All That Glitters*, pp. 28, 182.

7. Gary Libman, "Pioneer Olympian Gold Medalist Helped Set Pace for Black Athletes," *Los Angeles Times*, July 15, 1984.

8. *Chicago Defender*, November 7, 1936, and September 9 and 26, 1939; ARCO interview with David Albritton; author's interview with John Woodruff.

9. *Blackthink*, p. 46.

10. *I Have Changed*, p. 56.

11. *Chicago Defender*, May 13, 1939.

12. FBI Memo, September 27, 1956, no. 77–72778–16, and October 1, 1956, no. 77–72778–18; *New York Amsterdam News*, February 20, 1936; *Call and Post*, February 4 and March 4, 1937.

13. *Chicago Defender*, March 6, 1937; Johnson, *All That Glitters*, pp. 47–48; *New York Amsterdam News*, February 20 and 27, 1937.

14. Johnson, *All That Glitters*, p. 48; *New York Amsterdam News*, March 20, 1937; *Call and Post*, April 22, 1937; *Chicago Defender*, April 24, 1937.

15. *Chicago Defender*, July 31, 1937; *New York Amsterdam News*, June 2, 1937.

16. "Mound Bayou," *Time*, July 26, 1937, p. 14; Janet Sharp Hermann, *The Pursuit of a Dream* (New York: Oxford University Press, 1981), pp. 219–45.

17. *Chicago Defender,* October 2, 1937; *Call and Post,* August 17 and October 14, 1937; ARCO interview with David Albritton.

18. *Call and Post,* November 11 and December 2, 1937; *Chicago Defender,* December 18, 1937, and January 8, 1938.

19. *Chicago Defender,* January 15, 1938.

20. *Chicago Defender,* January 15 and October 15, 1938; *Call and Post,* February 3, 1938.

21. *Call and Post,* January 20, February 10, and April 21, 1938; *Chicago Defender,* October 22, 1938.

22. *Call and Post,* April 21, May 5, and June 16, 1938; *Cleveland Plain Dealer,* April 28, 1938.

23. *Cleveland Plain Dealer,* June 23, 1938; FBI Memo, September 25, 1956, no. 77–72778–7; *I Have Changed,* p. 90; *Blackthink,* p. 48.

24. Rud Rennie, "Vander Meer Hurls Second No-Hitter in Row," in Bob Cooke, ed., *Wake Up the Echoes* (Garden City, N.Y.: Hanover House, 1956), p. 204; Joseph Durso, *Casey: The Life and Legend of Charles Dillon Stengel* (Englewood Cliffs, N.J.: Prentice-Hall, 1967), p. 102; *New York Times,* June 16, 1938.

25. *New York Times,* June 15, 1938; Harold Parrott, *The Lords of Baseball* (New York: Praeger, 1976), p. 104.

26. *Chicago Defender,* July 9, 1938.

27. *Cleveland Plain Dealer,* August 10, 1938; *Call and Post,* August 25 and September 1, 1938.

28. *Call and Post,* October 6, 1938; *Chicago Defender,* October 22, 1938.

29. *Call and Post,* October 6, 1938; *Chicago Defender,* October 15, 1938; FBI Memos, September 27, 1956, no. 77–72778–16, and October 1, 1956, no. 77–72778–18.

30. *Call and Post,* November 10 and 17, 1938; *Cleveland News,* November 4, 1938; FBI Memos, September 25, 1956, no. 77–72778–7, and October 1, 1956, no. 77–72778–18.

31. *Jesse,* pp. 95–98; *Blackthink,* pp. 71–73; FBI Memos, September 27, 1956, no. 77–72778–16, and October 2, 1956, no. 77–72778–22; *Call and Post,* May 11, 1939; *Chicago Defender,* May 13, 1939.

32. *Jesse,* pp. 105–14.

33. *Call and Post,* May 11 and June 15, 1939.

34. *Chicago Defender,* May 13–19, 1961; author's interview with LeRoy Walker.

35. William Heward, with Dimitri V. Gat, *Some Are Called Clowns* (New York: Crowell, 1974), p. 55; *Call and Post,* August 17 and September 7, 1939.

36. FBI Memo, October 2, 1956, no. 77–72778–22; *Call and Post,* February 15 and 17 and March 14, 1940.

37. FBI Memo, October 2, 1956, no. 77–72778–22.

38. *Call and Post,* March 14, 1940; *Jesse,* p. 123; FBI Memo, October 2, 1956, no. 77–72778–22.

39. *Call and Post,* June 15, 1940; *Chicago Defender,* June 15, July 13, 1940, and February 8, 1941.

40. R. L. Quercetani, *A World History of Track and Field Athletics 1864–1964* (London: Oxford University Press, 1964), p. 190; *Call and Post,* June 22, 1940; *Chicago Defender,* June 15, 1940.

41. FBI Memos, October 4, 1956, no. 77–72778–21, and September 2, 1956, no. 77–72778–6; Director of Athletics File, Ohio State University Archives, RG9/E.

42. James E. Pollard, *History of the Ohio State University: The Story of Its First Seventy-Five Years 1873–1948* (Columbus: Ohio State University Press, 1952), pp. 350–55.

43. *Jesse,* pp. 123–25; author's interview with Russell Brown; *New York Times,* November 1, 1940; FBI Memo, September 27, 1956, no. 77–72778–16; *Call and Post,* December 7, 1940.

44. Ohio State University Registrar's report in FBI Memo, September 25, 1956, no. 77–72778–8; FBI Memo, October 4, 1956, no. 77–72778–21.

Chapter 10. Patriotic Games (pp. 163–181)

1. Benjamin Quarles, *The Negro in the Making of America* (New York: Collier, 1969), pp. 215–28; Harvard Sitkoff, *The Struggle for Black Equality, 1954–1980* (New York: Hill & Wang, 1981), pp. 10–11.

2. Richard Dalfiume, "The 'Forgotten Years' of the Negro Revolution," *Journal of American History,* 55 (June 1969): 90–106.

3. *New York Times,* March 11, 1944.

4. *Jesse,* pp. 121–22; *New York Times,* January 11, 1942; *Chicago Defender,* January 17, 1942; FBI Memo, September 25, 1956, no. 77–72778–10; Barbara Moro's interview with Jesse Owens.

5. *Cleveland Plain Dealer,* February 20, 1942; FBI Memo, October 1, 1956, no. 77–72778–18; *Chicago Defender,* April 25 and May 23, 1942; Moro's interview with Owens.

6. Author's interview with Russell Brown.

7. Robert Shogan and Tom Craig, *The Detroit Race Riots: A Study in Violence* (Philadelphia: Chilton, 1964); Earl Brown, *Why Race Riots* (Detroit: Public Affairs Committee, 1944), p. 6.

8. Moro's interview with Owens; Shogan and Craig, *Detroit Race Riots*, pp. 22–26; author's interview with Russell Brown.

9. FBI Memo, October 2, 1956, no. 77–72778–22; James A. Geschwender, *Class, Race, and Worker Insurgency: The League of Revolutionary Black Workers* (Cambridge: Cambridge University Press, 1977), p. 37; Moro's interview with Owens.

10. Alfred McClung Lee and Norman Daymond Humphrey, *Race Riot* (New York: Dryden, 1943), pp. 81–87; Shogan and Craig, *Detroit Race Riots*, p. 89.

11. Moro's interview with Owens; author's interview with Russell Brown.

12. James Brough, *The Ford Dynasty: An American Story* (New York; Doubleday, 1977), pp. 237–39; Allan Nevins and Frank Ernest Hill, *Ford: Decline and Rebirth 1933–1962* (New York: Scribner's, 1963), p. 296; FBI Memo, March 30, 1953, no. 94–1–103G24; author's interviews with Al Gardiner and Russell Brown; *Chicago Defender*, October 20, 1945.

13. Author's interview with Russell Brown.

14. William J. Baker, *Sports in the Western World* (Totowa, N.J.: Rowman & Littlefield, 1982), pp. 287–88.

15. See Jules Tygiel, *Baseball's Great Experiment: Jackie Robinson and His Legacy* (New York: Oxford University Press, 1983).

16. Quarles, *Negro in the Making of America*, pp. 229–38; Sitkoff, *Struggle for Black Equality*, pp. 12–17.

17. See Gerald Aston, *"And a Credit to His Race": The Hard Life and Times of Joseph Louis Barrows* (New York: Saturday Review Press, 1974).

18. Author's interviews with Helen Stephens and Gloria Hemphill; *Cleveland Plain Dealer*, May 19 and September 15, 1946; *Chicago Defender*, February 8, 1947; Moro's interview with Owens.

19. Norman Katkov, "Jesse Owens, the Ebony Express," *Sport Magazine*, April 1954, p. 78; Barbara Moro's interview with Ruth Owens.

20. FBI Memos, March 30, 1953, no. 94–1–103G24; September 25, 1956, no. 77–72778–9; October 2, 1956, no. 77–72778–24; and October 4, 1956, no. 77–72778–21. *Chicago Defender*, May 21, 1949, February 4 and September 30, 1950 and January 19 and August 23, 1952; *Blackthink*, p. 44; author's interviews with Ted West and Mel Walker.

21. *Chicago Defender*, September 16, 1950, July 26, 1952, and June 13, 1953. In 1954 Owens erroneously recalled that the last time he ran "for real" was in Barcelona, Spain, in 1948. Katkov, "Jesse Owens, Ebony Express," p. 78.

22. See Ralph B. Levering, *The Public and American Foreign Policy, 1918–1978* (New York: William Morrow, 1978), pp. 92–105; Walter Lefever, *America, Russia, and the Cold War 1945–1980* (New York: John Wiley, 1980), pp. 97–99.

23. Ron A. Smith, "The Paul Robeson–Jackie Robinson Saga and a Political Collision," *Journal of Sport History*, 6 (Summer 1979): 5–27; Tygiel, *Great Experiment*, p. 334.

24. *New York Times*, January 17, 1950; *Chicago Defender*, February 4 and October 28, 1950.

25. *Chicago Tribune*, October 18, 1950; *Chicago Defender*, October 28, 1950.

26. Gunnar Myrdal, *An American Dilemma: The Negro Problem and Modern Democracy* (New York: Harper & Row, 1962), p. 1xi.

27. FBI Memo, October 2, 1956, no. 77–72778–24; printed program, "Jesse Owens Testimonial Dinner" in Chicago, 1950, in Avery Brundage Collection, University of Illinois Archives; *Chicago Defender*, January 20 and 27, April 21, and July 7, 1951.

28. Carl B. Wall, "The Solid Gold Champion," *Reader's Digest*, July 1958, pp. 97–100; *Chicago Defender*, April 5, 1980.

29. Katkov, "Jesse Owens, Ebony Express," p. 81.

30. *Ibid.*, p. 30. This remained a lifelong theme for Owens. He repeated it almost verbatim in an interview with the St. Louis sportswriter David Dore almost twenty years later.

31. Author's interview with William G. Stratton; Katkov, "Jesse Owens, Ebony Express," p. 78; *Chicago Defender*, Jaunary 24 and 31, 1953.

32. Enclosure in a letter from L. E. Osborne to Edward Pree, January 30, 1953, in the William G. Stratton Papers, Box 101, Illinois State Historical Library, Springfield; FBI Memo, September 26, 1956, no. 77–72778–13.

33. FBI Memo, October 2, 1956, no. 77–72778–22.

34. Katkov, "Jesse Owens, Ebony Express," pp. 29–30.

35. *Chicago Defender*, October 8, 1955; FBI Memos, September 26, 1956, no. 77–72778–13, and October 2, 1956, no. 77–72778–26 (WFO 77–57862).

36. For American interests in India, see "The Green Revolution: The United States and India in the Mid-Twentieth Century," in Morrell Heald and Lawrence S. Kaplan, *Culture and Diplomacy: The American Experience* (Westport, Conn.: Greenwood Press, 1977), pp. 267–88.

37. *New York Times*, October 4 and 5, 1955.

38. *New York Times*, October 5 and November 3, 1955; "A Famous

Athlete's Diplomatic Debut," *Life,* October 31, 1955, pp. 49–50.

39. *Chicago Defender,* January 7, 1956; FBI Memo, October 3, 1956, no. 77–72778–20; author's interview with William G. Stratton.

40. Author's interview with William G. Stratton; *Chicago Defender,* April 21, 1956 and July 23, 1957.

41. *Chicago Defender,* July 7, 1956; *New York Times,* August 28, 1956.

42. See Baker, *Sports in the Western World,* pp. 263–68.

43. *Chicago Defender,* January 7, 1956; George Orwell, *The Collected Essays, Journalism and Letters of George Orwell,* eds. Sonia Orwell and Ian Angus, 4 vols. (Harmondsworth, England: Penguin, 1970), IV: 63.

44. *Chicago Defender,* November 10, 1956

45. Letter from Dwight D. Eisenhower to Jesse Owens, October 15, 1956, Eisenhower Presidential Library, file no. 143–D, Abilene, Kansas; *New York Times,* November 17, 1956; Memorandum from Orray Taft, American Consul in Sydney, Australia, to the Department of State, Washington, D.C., December 21, 1956, file no. 143–D, Eisenhower Presidential Library.

46. Baker, *Sports in the Western World,* pp. 169–71.

47. Roberto L. Quercetani, *A World History of Track and Field, 1864–1964* (London: Oxford University Press, 1964), p. 328.

48. Letters from C. J. Delaney to Orray Taft, December 20, 1956, from K. F. Coles to Taft, December 5, 1956, and from Taft to the Department of State, December 21, 1956, Eisenhower Presidential Library, file no. 143–D.

49. Letter from Sherman Adams to Jesse Owens, February 5, 1957; membership list of Sports Committee of the People-to-People Program, Eisenhower Presidential Library, file no. 325–C.

Chapter 11.   The Back Side of Success (pp. 182–202)

1. *Chicago Defender,* January 2, 1960; *New York Times,* August 28, 1956.

2. FBI Memo, October 2, 1956, no. 77–72778–24 (CG 77–8864).

3. Norman Katkov, "Jesse Owens, the Ebony Express," *Sport Magazine,* April 1954, p. 29.

4. See Daniel J. Levinson with Charlotte N. Darrow, Edward B. Klein, Maria H. Levinson, and Braxton McKee, *The Seasons of a Man's Life* (New York: Ballantine Books, 1978), pp. 198–200. For

a popular rendering of the "midlife crisis," see Gail Sheehy, *Passages: Predictable Crises of Adult Life* (New York: E. P. Dutton, 1974), pp. 242–82.

5. *Blackthink*, p. 129.

6. Roberto L. Quercetani, *A World History of Track and Field, 1864–1964* (London: Oxford University Press, 1964), pp. 26–27; *Jesse*, pp. 137–38.

7. *Jesse*, p. 140; *Blackthink*, pp. 130–31.

8. Author's interview with Russell Brown.

9. Barbara Moro's interview with Jesse Owens; author's interviews with Eulace Peacock, Mel Walker, Marty Glickman, John Woodruff, Russell Brown, and Ted West.

10. On Ruth, see Robert W. Creamer, *Babe: The Legend Comes to Life* (New York: Penguin, 1983), pp. 320–23, 329–34; Moro's interview with Owens.

11. Barbara Moro's interview with Ruth Owens; author's interview with Gloria Hemphill, Marlene Rankin, and Beverly Prather.

12. Author's interview with Beverly Prather.

13. Moro's interview with Owens; author's interviews with Gloria Hemphill and Marlene Rankin.

14. Moro's interview with Ruth Owens; author's interview with Gloria Hemphill.

15. Moro's interview with Ruth Owens.

16. *Ibid.;* author's interview with Russell Brown.

17. Moro's interview with Ruth Owens.

18. FBI Memo, October 2, 1956, no. 77–72778–24 (CG 77–8864); author's interviews with Ted West and two of Owens's other acquaintances whose names are withheld by request.

19. Author's interview with Gloria Hemphill; *Chicago Defender*, December 26, 1953.

20. *I Have Changed*, p. 60; *Jesse*, p. 136; author's interview with Beverly Prather; Moro's interview with Ruth Owens.

21. Moro's interview with Ruth Owens; Betty Friedan, *The Feminine Mystique* (New York: Dell, 1963).

22. On Hoover, see Kenneth O'Reilly, *Hoover and the Un-Americans; The FBI, HUAC, and the Red Menace* (Philadelphia: Temple University Press, 1983).

23. J. Edgar Hoover, *Masters of Deceit: The Story of Communism in America and How to Fight It* (New York: Henry Holt, 1958), p. 246.

24. In broad outline, this episode is reported in *The Arizona*

Republic, January 19, 1985, in an article prepared by an investigative team headed by Jerry Seper and research assistant Ben Winton. I am grateful to Mark Harris for this reference.

25. FBI Memo, March 30, 1953, no. 94–1–103G24.

26. Letter from Scott McLeod to J. Edgar Hoover, September 13, 1956, in Owens's FBI file no. 77–72778–2.

27. FBI Memo, October 2, 1956, no. 77–72778–24 (CG 77–8864). From this source, the Chicago file, comes all the information for the next two paragraphs.

28. White House memo from Mary B. Keedick to Bud Barbra, October 10, 1956; letter from Dwight D. Eisenhower to Jesse Owens, October 15, 1956, in the Eisenhower Presidential Library.

29. "This Is Your Life," ARCO film; author's interview with Harriet Mae Bottorff; *Ohio State University Monthly,* November, 1960; *New York Times,* October 23 and December 9, 1960.

30. Quercetani, *World History of Track and Field,* pp. 254–55; *Jesse Owens Story,* pp. 89–90; *Cleveland Plain Dealer,* August 26, 1960.

31. Letters from Charles Riley to Jesse Owens, 1954 (unposted), and from Riley to a Miss Swain, postmarked July 21, 1960, in possession of Mrs. Harriet Mae Bottorff, Riley's daughter.

32. Letter from Riley to Miss Swain; *Cleveland Press,* August 25, 1960; *Cleveland Plain Dealer,* August 25, 1960; author's interview with Harriet Mae Bottorff.

33. *New York Times,* August 22, 1960; *Chicago Defender,* March 10, 1961; White House memo from Clyde Roberts, September 11, 1956, Eisenhower Presidential Library.

34. Author's interview with William G. Stratton.

35. *Chicago Daily News,* July 22, 1961.

36. Author's interviews with Herb Douglas, Mel Walker, and William G. Stratton; *Chicago Daily News,* July 22, 26, 1961.

37. *Blackthink,* p. 134; *Chicago Daily News,* July 26, 1961.

38. Author's interview with Ted West; *Chicago Defender,* December 30–January 5, 1962, September 29–October 4, October 12–18, October 26–November 1, and December 14–20 and 21–27, 1963, March 7–13, May 2–8, and October 3–9, 1964, and June 2–8, and 19–25, 1965; *New York Times,* November 22, 1964.

39. *Chicago Defender,* June 22–28, 1963; author's interviews with Herb Douglas and Ted West; Gordon Lindsay, "Gold Digger of 1936," Los Angeles, June, 1983, p. 264.

40. *New York Times,* February 11, 1965.

41. Joseph Durso, *Casey: The Life and Legend of Charles Dillon Stengel* (Englewood Cliffs, N.J.: Prentice-Hall, 1967), pp. 172–73.

42. *New York Times*, November 22, 1964.

43. *Blackthink*, pp. 141–44; *Jesse*, pp. 149–56; *I Have Changed*, p. 90.

44. *Jesse*, p. 158; author's interview with Ted West.

45. *Chicago Tribune*, November 20, 1965; William O. Johnson, Jr. *All That Glitters Is Not Gold: The Olympic Game* (New York: Putnam's, 1972), p. 51; *Blackthink*, p. 145; ARCO interview with Bud Greenspan.

46. *Chicago Defender*, April 8–14 and 22–28, 1961.

47. *Chicago Tribune*, November 20, 1965.

48. Transcript of Proceedings in the United States District Court, Northern District of Illinois, Eastern Division, December 21, 1965 (Clerk's file copy).

49. Transcript of Proceedings . . ., December 31, 1965; *Chicago Tribune*, December 31, 1965.

50. Author's interviews with Gloria Hemphill, Beverly Prather, Mel Walker, and Herb Douglas; *Blackthink*, pp. 145–48; *I Have Changed*, pp. 48–49; *New York Times*, February 2, 1966.

51. Transcript of Proceedings . . ., February 1, 1965; *Chicago Tribune*, February 2, 1966; *New York Times*, February 2, 1956; *Blackthink*, p. 148.

Chapter 12. An Athlete Growing Old (pp. 203–220)

1. *Blackthink*, p. 145; *I Have Changed*, pp. 47, 90; *Bangor Daily News*, May 15, 1967; *Chicago Defender*, May 13–19, 1967.

2. William J. Baker, *Sports in the Western World* (Totowa, N.J.: Rowman & Littlefield, 1982), pp. 290–92.

3. Transcript of Proceedings in the United States District Court, Northern District of Illinois, Eastern Division, February 1, 1966 (Clerk's file copy).

4. *I Have Changed*, pp. 148–50; author's interviews with Ted West and Gloria Hemphill.

5. *Chicago Defender*, March 25, 1961.

6. *Blackthink*, pp. 132–33; *Bangor Daily News*, May 16, 1967; author's interview with Gloria Hemphill; *I Have Changed*, pp. 55–64.

7. *I Have Changed*, p. 150; William O. Johnson, Jr., *All That Glitters Is Not Gold: The Olympic Game* (New York: Putnam's, 1972), p. 50.

8. Johnson, *All That Glitters,* p. 52; David Dore's interview with Jesse Owens.

9. Jon Hendershott, "Jesse Owens," *Track and Field News,* September 1974, p. 5; *Chicago Defender,* June 12 and 17, 1973.

10. Harry Edwards, *The Revolt of the Black Athlete* (New York: Free Press, 1969); cf. Baker, *Sports in the Western World,* pp. 290–93.

11. Transcript of Proceedings in the United States District Court ..., December 31, 1965; *Chicago Defender,* February 13 and May 7, 1960, and December 30–January 5, 1962.

12. *The Times* (London), November 11, 1967; *Chicago Defender,* December 2, 1967; Edwards, *Revolt of the Black Athlete,* pp. 60–61, 78–79.

13. Edwards, *Revolt of the Black Athlete,* p. 93.

14. *Chicago Defender,* February 10–16, 1968; letter from Avery Brundage to Jesse Owens, April 3, 1968, Avery Brundage Collection, University of Illinois Archives.

15. See Benjamin G. Rader, *In Its Own Image: How Television Transformed Sports* (New York: Free Press, 1984), pp. 111–13, 159–60.

16. ARCO interview with Bud Greenspan.

17. "An Olympian Returns," *Senior Scholastic,* March 14, 1968, p. 16; José M. Ferrer, "Tribute to an Old Olympian," *Life,* March 22, 1968, p. 11; *Chicago Defender,* August 27–29, 1968. I am grateful to ARCO for the opportunity to view its copy of "Jesse Owens Returns to Berlin."

18. *Chicago Defender,* May 11–17, 1968.

19. *Chicago Defender,* May 25–31, 1968.

20. *Chicago Defender,* June 29–July 5 and July 6–12, 1968; *Bangor Daily News,* July 3, 1968.

21. Jesse Owens, "The Olympics: A Preview," *TV Guide,* October 12–18, 1978, pp. 6–10.

22. *Chicago Defender,* October 19–25, 1968; *Blackthink,* pp. 76, 79; author's interview with Mel Walker.

23. See Christopher Brasher, *Mexico City 1968: A Dairy of the XIXth Olympiad* (London: Stanley Paul, 1968).

24. The details of this incident are reconstructed from Vincent Matthews with Neil Amdur, *My Race Be Won* (New York: Charterhouse, 1974), p. 191, and Owens's *Blackthink,* pp. 76–80.

25. *Blackthink,* p. 79; *Chicago Defender,* March 17, 1970.

26. Jesse Owens, "My Life as a Black Man," *Reader's Digest,* May 1970, pp. 126–31; *Blackthink,* pp. 50–51.

27. *Blackthink,* pp. 69–70, 77, 84.

28. *Blackthink,* pp. 44, 84.

29. *Chicago Defender,* July 19 and December 19–25, 1970; *Blackthink* p. 51; David Dore's interview with Jesse Owens: William O. Johnson, "Jesse Owens, Public Image," *Sports Illustrated,* July 17, 1972, p. 41.

30. *New York Times,* May 4, 1971; *I Have Changed,* pp. 99, 115–18.

31. *Chicago Defender,* May 11 and 18, 1971, and August 3 and 15, 1972; author's interview with Herb Douglas. I am grateful to Mr. Douglas for a copy of the film "The Black Athlete."

32. *I Have Changed,* pp. 9–13.

33. *Ibid.,* p. 141.

34. Hendershott, "Jesse Owens," p. 5.

35. *Chicago Daily News,* May 11, 1972; *Chicago Defender,* August 8, 1972; Baker, *Sports in the Western World,* pp. 278–79.

36. Matthews, *My Race Be Won,* pp. 335–36. To the best of my knowledge, Owens never commented publicly on this event. The following narrative is taken entirely from Matthews, pp. 336–61.

37. *Ibid.,* p. 192.

38. *Chicago Defender,* February 12, May 3, and August 8, 1972 and May 26 and August 26, 1976.

39. *Chicago Defender,* May 3, 1976; ARCO interview with Charlie Beetham; author's interviews with Charlie Beetham, Mack Robinson, Marty Glickman, and John Woodruff.

40. Hendershott, "Jesse Owens," p. 4; *New York Times,* November 22, 1964.

41. Johnson, "Jesse Owens, Public Image," p. 41.

42. *Chicago Defender,* January 10, 1974, and September 13, 1976; *Washington Post,* April 1, 1980; Ohio State–UCLA football program, October 4, 1980, pp. 23–26, Ohio State Univ. Archives.

43. *Chicago Defender,* March 9, 1976; *Decatur Daily,* July 16, 1983.

44. *Oakland Tribune,* February 5, 1975.

45. *Chicago Defender,* October 11, 1978; *I Have Changed,* pp. 145–46; author's interviews with Herb Douglas and Bud Leavitt.

46. *New York Times,* July 22, 1984.

47. Jesse Owens, "We're Too Athletic," *Today's Health,* January 1972, pp. 68–69.

48. Jesse Owens, *Track and Field,* ed. Dick O'Connor (New York: Atheneum, 1976).

49. A. E. Housman, "To An Athlete Dying Young," in Tom Dodge, ed., *A Literature of Sports* (Lexington, Mass.: D.C. Heath, 1980), pp. 518–19.

Chapter 13. A Legend Memorialized (pp. 221–231)

1. *I Have Changed*, pp. 83–84, 140.
2. Author's interviews with Charlie Beetham, John Woodruff, and Ted West; *Columbus Dispatch*, February 7, 1980; *Jesse.*
3. Author's interviews with Mel Walker, John Woodruff, Gloria Hemphill, and Beverly Prather; *I Have Changed*, pp. 151–52.
4. Author's interviews with Gloria Hemphill and Beverly Prather; *Chicago Tribune*, September 19, 1970.
5. *Chicago Tribune*, October 11, 1978; ARCO interview with David Albritton; author's interviews with Gloria Hemphill and Herb Douglas; *Columbus Citizen-Journal*, April 1, 1980.
6. *St. Louis Post-Dispatch*, March 31, 1980; ARCO and author's interviews with Herb Douglas.
7. ARCO interviews with David Albritton, Herb Douglas, and John Woodruff.
8. Author's interview with Mel Walker.
9. ARCO interview with Herb Douglas; author's interview with Gloria Hemphill.
10. Author's interview with Gloria Hemphill.
11. *Chicago Defender*, January 28, 30, 1980.
12. *Chicago Defender*, January 24, 1980.
13. *Columbus Dispatch*, February 7, 1980; *Los Angeles Times*, April 1, 1980; *Chicago Defender*, May 20, 1980.
14. *Chicago Defender*, March 5, 13, and 31, 1980; *Chicago Tribune*, March 30; *New York Times*, March 31 and April 1, 1980.
15. *Rocky Mountain News*, April 2, 1980; *Chicago Defender*, April 2 and 3, 1980.
16. ARCO interview with Marty Glickman; *Chicago Tribune*, April 5, 1980.
17. *Chicago Tribune*, April 5, 1980; *Washington Post*, April 5, 1980.
18. *Chicago Tribune*, April 5, 1980.
19. *Chicago Tribune*, April 5, 1980; *Chicago Defender*, May 20, 1980.
20. *Columbus Dispatch*, April 1 and 5, 1980; *Ohio State News* (press release), April 4, 1980, Ohio State University Archives; *Chicago Defender*, April 17, 1980.
21. *Columbus Dispatch*, June 5, 1980.
22. *Columbus Dispatch*, October 4, 1980; Cleveland *Call and Post*, October 25, 1980.
23. *Chicago Defender*, May 28, 1981.

24. International Amateur Athletic Association press release, 1984.

25. *Chicago Defender*, May 28, 1981: *Decatur Daily*, May 1, 1982; *Columbus Dispatch*, May 9, 1983.

26. *New York Times*, April 1, 1980; *The Tennessean* (Nashville), November 20, 1983; author's interview with Harold Gast.

27. *Ohio State Lantern*, February 7 and March 30, 1983; *Columbus Dispatch*, April 2, 1983.

28. "Sculptor's Statement" in *Jesse Owens: Celebration for a Champion* (Ohio State University publication, 1983); *Columbus Dispatch*, April 2, 1983.

29. "Preface" to *Jesse Owens: Celebration*.

30. *Decatur Daily*, June 30, 1983.

31. *Decatur Daily*, July 16, 1983; *Chattanooga Times*, September 19, 1983.

32. *USA Today*, August 30, 1983; *Chattanooga Times*, September 19, 1983.

33. *Atlanta Journal and Constitution*, September 11, 1983; *Columbus Dispatch*, September 10 and 14, 1983; *Chattanooga Times*, September 10, 1983.

34. *The Tennessean*, November 20, 1983.

Chapter 14. Durable Dreams (pp. 232–237)

1. *Los Angeles Times*, March 4, 1983.

2. Pete Axthelm, "Surprises of the Spirit," *Newsweek*, August 20, 1984, p. 15. For much of this information on Lewis, see Garry Smith, "I Do What I Want to Do," *Sports Illustrated*, July 18, 1984, pp. 22–39; Jane Gross, "The Quest for Olympic Greatness," *New York Times*, June 17, 1984; "No Limit to What He Can Do," *Time*, July 30, 1984, pp. 52–55.

3. Ira Berkow, "Carl Lewis Looks Back," *New York Times*, January 12, 1985.

4. Author's interview with Herb Douglas.

5. R. L. Quercetani, *A World History of Track and Field Athletics 1864–1964* (London: Oxford University Press, 1964), pp. 191–93.

6. Author's interview with Marvin Fitzgerald.

7. Harry Edwards, *The Revolt of the Black Athlete* (New York: Free Press, 1969), p. 78.

8. See Howard L. Nixon II, *Sport and the American Dream* (New York: Leisure Press, 1984).

9. Quoted in William J. Baker, *Sports in the Western World,* (Totowa, N.J.: Rowman & Littlefield, 1982), p. 303.

10. Nathaniel Clay, "The Meaning of Jesse Owens' Life," *Chicago Defender,* April 7, 1980.

11. *I Have Changed,* p. 17.

12. *Jesse Owens Story,* p. 9.

13. Marc Bloom, "Jesse Owens: The Legacy of an American Hero," *The Runner,* June 1980, p. 30.

Index